INDUSTRIAL SUBSIDIES

Also by Colin Wren

ECONOMIC DEVELOPMENT POLICIES: An Evaluative Study of the Newcastle Metropolitan Region (*with Fred Robinson and John Goddard*)

Industrial Subsidies

The UK Experience

Colin Wren
Department of Economics
University of Newcastle upon Tyne

First published in Great Britain 1996 by
MACMILLAN PRESS LTD
Houndmills, Basingstoke, Hampshire RG21 6XS
and London
Companies and representatives
throughout the world

A catalogue record for this book is available
from the British Library.

ISBN 0–333–65650–4

First published in the United States of America 1996 by
ST. MARTIN'S PRESS, INC.,
Scholarly and Reference Division,
175 Fifth Avenue,
New York, N.Y. 10010

ISBN 0–312–16016–X

Library of Congress Cataloging-in-Publication Data
Wren, Colin.
Industrial subsidies : the UK experience / Colin Wren.
p. cm.
Includes bibliographical references (p.) and index.
ISBN 0–312–16016–X
1. Subsidies—Great Britain. 2. Industrial policy—Great Britain.
I. Title.
HD3646.G7W74 1996
338.941'02—dc20 96–7682
CIP

---

10 9 8 7 6 5 4 3 2 1
05 04 03 02 01 00 99 98 97 96

Printed in Great Britain by
The Ipswich Book Company Ltd
Ipswich, Suffolk

To Shirley and George

Contents

List of Tables and Figures

Tables

Figures

List of Abbreviations

AMC	Agricultural Mortgage Corporation
ATP	Advanced Technology Programme
BES	Business Expansion Scheme
BIS	Business Improvement Scheme
BOTAC	Board of Trade Advisory Committee
BTAS	Business and Technical Advisory Service
BTG	British Technology Group
CADCAM	Computer Aided Design/Computer Aided Manufacture
CADMAT	Computer Aided Design/Computer Aided Manufacture and Test
CADTES	Computer Aided Design and Test Equipment Support
CAP	Common Agricultural Policy
CAT	City Action Team
CEP	Community Enterprise Programme
CoSIRA	Council for Small Industries in Rural Areas
CP	Community Programme
DA	Development Area
DATAC	Development Areas Treasury Advisory Committee
DEA	Department of Economic Affairs
DED	Department of Economic Development
DLG	Derelict Land Grant
DSIR	Department of Scientific and Industrial Research
DTI	Department of Trade and Industry
EAGGF	European Agricultural Guidance and Guarantee Fund
EAS	Enterprise Allowance Scheme
EC	European Community
ECGD	Export Credits Guarantee Department
ECSC	European Coal and Steel Community
EIB	European Investment Bank
EIE	English Industrial Estates
ERDF	European Regional Development Fund
ESF	European Social Fund
ESPRIT	European Strategic Programme for Research in Information Technology
EUREKA	European Research Co-operation Agency
FCI	Finance Corporation for Industry

FMS	Flexible Manufacturing Systems
GICP	General Industrial Collaborative Projects
IA	Intermediate Area
ICFC	Industrial and Commercial Finance Corporation
IDAB	Industrial Development Advisory Board
IDC	Industrial Development Certificate
IDE	Industrial Development Executive
IDOP	Integrated Development Operations Programme
IDU	Industrial Development Unit
ILIS	Innovation Linked Investment Scheme
IRC	Industrial Reorganisation Corporation
JCP	Job Creation Programme
JFIT	Joint Framework for support in Information Technology
JRS	Job Release Scheme
LDDC	London Docklands Development Corporation
MAP	Microprocessor Application Project
MISP	Microelectronics Industry Support Programme
MSC	Manpower Services Commission
NEB	National Enterprise Board
NEDC	National Economic Development Council
NCI	New Community Instrument
NPCI	National Programme of Community Interest
NRDC	National Research Development Corporation
NSA	National Selective Assistance
ODP	Office Development Permit
PPDS	Product and Process Development Scheme
RDA	Rural Development Area
RDG	Regional Development Grant
RDO	Regional Development Organisation
REG	Regional Enterprise Grant
REP	Regional Employment Premium
RIG	Regional Investment Grant
RIN	Regional Innovation Grant
RSA	Regional Selective Assistance
RSSL	Recruitment Subsidy for School-Leavers
SALAC	Special Areas Loans Advisory Committee
SARA	Special Areas Reconstruction Association
SDA	Scottish Development Agency
SDA	Special Development Area
SEFIS	Small Engineering Firms Investment Subsidy
SFES	Small Firm Employment Subsidy

SIB	Shipbuilding Industry Board
SIRGS	Service Industry Removal Grant Scheme
SMART	Small Firms Merit Award for Research and Technology
SMETAS	Small and Medium-sized Enterprises Technical Advisory Service
SPUR	Support for Products Under Research
STAR	Special Telecommunications Action for Regional Development
STEP	Special Temporary Employment Programme
STWCS	Short-Time Working Compensation Scheme
TES	Temporary Employment Subsidy
TOPS	Training Opportunities Programme Scheme
TSTWCS	Temporary Short-Time Working Compensation Scheme
UDC	Urban Development Corporation
UDG	Urban Development Grant
URG	Urban Regeneration Grant
WDA	Welsh Development Agency
WEP	Work Experience Programme
WEEP	Work Experience on Employers' Premises
YES	Youth Employment Subsidy
YOP	Youth Opportunities Programme
YTS	Youth Training Scheme
YWS	Young Workers Scheme

Preface

Like a good fashion, industrial subsidies have fallen out of use and few will admit to ever having liked them. In their heyday these subsidies extended to virtually every area of industrial and economic policy, but, as we know, they were cut back in the 1980s as the government sought to disengage from industrial intervention. The time is ripe for an appraisal, and in this book we review the United Kingdom experience of industrial subsidies. There are two main reasons for this. First, while there exist numerous accounts of industrial subsidies as practised in the UK context, there has been as yet no attempt to tackle the subject of industrial subsidies in the round. Studies focus on the application of the subsidies to different areas of policy – such as national economic growth objectives, stability purposes, support for ailing companies and national champions, spatial development, direct labour market interventions and sectoral adjustment – but almost treat these as distinct topics. Part of our purpose is to draw these disparate accounts together, since it is often the case that the application and expansion of subsidy in one area of policy can best be seen in the light of past and ongoing efforts in other areas, so that the different interventions often serve as complements or substitutes for one another.

As a second reason for writing this book it is equally clear that existing commentaries on industrial subsidies almost exclusively focus on the 1960s and 1970s, when the subsidies were applied most intensively. Part of our purpose is to examined the origins of this assistance, so that we trace the development of industrial intervention back to the First World War and before, and to consider the withdrawal from industrial support in the 1980s, which similarly has been something of a neglected area. Contrary to popular belief, small-scale subsidies continue to operate, and include financial assistance to particular firms, such as small firms; to certain industries, such as civil aviation; and for some technologies, such as information technology. It seems useful to have a single and wide-ranging account of the UK experience of industrial subsidies, but given the broad scope of the book we are unable to give full attention to all the related evaluative material, although the extent to which much of this subsidy was, and perhaps remains, unevaluated is remarkable. Nevertheless, if industrial subsidies should ever come back into fashion, then it is hoped that this book can provide a better appreciation of the UK experience of this policy instrument.

In preparing this book, acknowledgement must be made to many excellent texts on industrial subsidies, which are cited in the bibliography, and to the publication *British Business*, which was a good source for events over the 1980s, but which unfortunately is no longer published. I also gratefully acknowledge the comments received from an anonymous referee on a previous version of the manuscript, and from other referees on passages prepared from the body of the text. Finally, thanks must go to Linda Kelly for helping to track down many parliamentary papers and other such documents; to Keith Povey for his very careful copy-editing of the typescript; and to Giovanna Davitti and all those at Macmillan who helped with the production of the book.

C. WREN

1 Introduction

The use of industrial subsidies was little known in the eighteenth and nineteenth centuries, so that the rise and subsequent waning of this policy instrument has been an extraordinary phenomenon of the twentieth-century economy. Direct subsidy payments to private firms amounted to more than five per cent of national output at their peak in the late 1960s, and at different times have been an important means by which the government has sought to fine-tune and stabilize the economy; to correct for balance of payments difficulties; to redistribute activity between areas; to encourage enterprise, innovation and technology transfer; and to deal with the most serious of modern economic problems, that of unemployment. More recently, following sustained efforts by national and supranational bodies to eliminate these payments, industrial subsidies have found a more modest role as policymakers have come to understand the limits of these measures, and the pattern of spending has returned to that of an earlier period.

There exist many accounts of the UK experience of industrial subsidies focusing on some element of policy, such as regional or industry-specific interventions, but to date there exists no comprehensive account of these subsidies over a long period. This is no doubt a reflection of the many different forms and uses to which these subsidies have been put, and the frequency of changes to their operation. The purpose of this book is to describe the adoption, growth and subsequent relinquishment of industrial subsidies in the UK, tracing their development back to the early years of the twentieth century and following their extension to virtually every area of economic policy.

We describe the foothold gained for industrial subsidies in the run-up to and the aftermath of the First World War; the application of large-scale subsidies to agriculture in the Depression; the plans for an interventionist industrial strategy devised in the Second World War; and the gradual expansion of industrial subsidies from this time. This includes the various tax allowances, investment grants and the more managed selective interventions of the 1960s and 1970s, from which we demonstrate that subsidies extended in scope far beyond that envisaged even in the immediate post-war period. Further, we show that the failure of large-scale industrial subsidies to reverse long-term deteriorating economic conditions in fact led to the intensification of policy, and it was only with the monetary crises of the mid-1970s that a reappraisal was forced. This led to the withdrawal of industrial subsidies from this time, and in our study we devote considerable attention to this, describing the gradual reshaping of industrial subsidies in the early 1980s, and the near abandonment of these subsidies in the remainder of the decade.

Our account of industrial subsidies is often highly detailed, and the book partly serves as a vade-mecum, so important to our study are the circumstances, events and arguments that have at different times led to the adoption, intensification, modification and withdrawal of these subsidies. This, of course, means that there is insufficient space to discuss fully the related evaluative literature, which is worthy of a volume in its own right, but nevertheless we believe the account substantially improves on the understanding of industrial subsidies, as practised in the UK context. Throughout, we present figures for expenditure and, unless otherwise indicated, these are all in gross terms at current prices, so they take no account of the possible recoveries made by the Treasury, nor indeed of the subsidy element involved in different kinds of assistance payment. To aid presentation, these gross figures are given in a series of tables, but figures for the totality of expenditure over 1960–90 have been collated and are presented separately in Wren (1996a). In the concluding chapter, we pull these figures together and adjust them to give a series for grant equivalent expenditure on subsidies by UK central government over the post-war period at constant 1980 prices. These grant equivalents are an attempt to calculate the subsidy element of each assistance payment on comparable terms, and are reported in Wren (1996b). They enable a proper comparison of subsidy activity over time, and from time to time we make reference to these in the body of the text, making this clear in each case. We begin our discussion by considering the rationale for industrial assistance and what precisely is meant by an industrial subsidy.

THE RATIONALE FOR INDUSTRIAL SUBSIDIES

Shoup (1972) notes that industrial subsidies are the 'great fiscal unknown' in that the public finance literature invariably focuses on the tax and transfer functions of government activity, so that subsidies have received relatively little attention. Nevertheless, discussions of the rationale for government intervention inevitably concentrate on the circumstances in which the market economy fails to achieve an efficient allocation of resources. Sources of market failure are familiar and include such things as public goods, externalities, merit and demerit goods, increasing returns to scale, non-competitive pricing, common ownership, informational problems and differences in the private and social time preference rates. Each of these can essentially be viewed as a *microeconomic* argument for policy and, as we see, they give rise to a series of industrial interventions including competition, technology, small-firm and advisory-based policies. In addition, there are various *macroeconomic* reasons for industrial subsidies arising from Richard Musgrave's other rationales for government intervention. These are the stability and distributional arguments for industrial policy, which underlie the traditional fourfold goals for macroeconomic policy, concerning unemployment, economic growth, inflation and the balance of payments. These were central to the growth of industrial subsidies in the immediate post-war period, when the market failure arguments had not been fully developed, giving rise to various forms of tax incentive, regional policy instruments and lump-sum subsidies to ease adjustment in declining industries. Finally, from a public choice perspective, industrial subsidies may be seen as a means of generating electoral support (Peacock, 1977), and this can give rise to selective interventions.

The development of industrial subsidies has in some sense paralleled the development of economic ideas, and the associated greater post-war role assigned to the government in managing the economy. In the eighteenth and nineteenth centuries, government intervention was bound up with international trade issues, so that in Adam Smith's *Wealth of Nations* much of the discussion of subsidies focused on the efficiency and possibly inflationary consequences of trade subsidies on the exportation of corn. Adam Smith drew a distinction between *bounties* on production – which were viewed favourably when compared with export subsidies, but given a very limited role so that 'bounties ought to be given to those branches of trade only which cannot be carried on without them' – and *premiums* to manufacturers which excelled in their occupations. Premiums were strongly favoured by Smith because of their efficiency consequences, so that 'their tendency is not to overturn the natural balance of employments, but to render the work which is done in each as perfect and complete as possible'. Throughout this period, production subsidies were little used, although an exception to this were the white-herring and whale-fisheries bounties. The role of these was to augment the number of sailors and shipping for reasons of national defence, giving a further rationale for subsidies. As we shall see, strategic reasons were an important motivation for the subsidies introduced prior to and during the First World War.

In the modern economy, the growth of industrial subsidies has much to do with the acceptance of Keynesian ideas. These overturned the Classical economic doctrines, with the implication that the government had a role in demand management through monetary and fiscal policies, including investment incentives. However, it would be wrong to suggest that industrial assistance commenced with J. M. Keynes' *General Theory*, since support schemes had existed in pre-war Britain, and massive subsidy had been extended to the agricultural sector from the time of the Depression onwards. Rather, the contribution of Keynes was to suggest the possibility of large-scale subsidies to the industrial sector, and through successive post-war recessions this principle became firmly established. While Keynes gave a role to the government in stabilizing the economy, the application of policy was rarely weakened in the upswing of the trade cycle, and as economic conditions worsened from cycle to cycle so the subsidies were applied with increasing intensity. However, the policy failed to reverse the trend of rising unemployment, and in time industrial subsidies became more focused; first in the case of regional and urban policies, and then in the form of direct labour market interventions in the context of high inflation and mass unemployment.

The turning-point in post-war economic policy occasioned by the sterling crises of the mid-1970s led to the reappraisal of industrial subsidies and to their gradual withdrawal, except in a more narrowly-defined allocative role. Demand management policies had evidently failed to yield economic stability and, with the conditions of stagflation, policymakers sought new explanations. The implication of the new monetarist theories was that governments could not permanently reduce unemployment below its natural level without inducing accelerating inflation, so policy became concentrated on the supply-side and industrial subsidies were used in a microeconomic context to improve industrial efficiency to affect the long-run levels of output and employment. Further, these ideas became wedded to New Classical economics which viewed markets as adjusting instantaneously, so that even in the short run the scope for policy was extremely limited, while the rational expectations hypothesis argued that agents would assimilate past policy changes into their expectations and behaviour, further lessening the impact of policy. At the same time, decelerative selective interventions aimed at easing adjustment were heavily criticized for engendering permanent levels of subsidy, while accelerative industrial policies aimed at stimulating new activity were criticized for the fallacy of 'picking winners' (Burton, 1983). Others pointed to the bureaucratic costs of intervention (Rowley, 1982), while arguments based on asymmetric information in a principal–agent setting between the public sector and firm served to undermine selective programmes (Peacock, 1990). It is these ideas which continue to hold sway at the time of writing, but while the macroeconomic role for industrial subsidies has fallen into abeyance, the microeconomic role continues to exist, based largely on the argument of allocative inefficiency.

DEFINING AN INDUSTRIAL SUBSIDY

Industrial intervention can take many different forms – and recently the debate has centred on the appropriate amount of public ownership of industry, coupled with arguments over regulation – so that industrial subsidies form just one instrument of government policy. For our purposes, we may consider just what is meant by an industrial subsidy. This is not straightforward since, as Prest (1976) observes, there can be 'no neat and tidy single all-purpose definition' of a producer subsidy, although he puts forward what he considers to be the least unsatisfactory definition as those 'payments which directly affect relative prices in the commercial sector, broadly defined' (p. 65). A more pragmatic approach is taken by Wiseman (1977), who remarks that such definitions are only a matter of convenience, to be broadened or narrowed as we find them operationally useful. Nevertheless, we take a rather more precise definition of an industrial subsidy which is used by Lehner *et al.* (1991) in their study of European Community state aid, and by examining this we are able to set out our own definition. Lehner *et al.* define a producer subsidy as any government intervention satisfying each of five criteria, which we may consider in turn.

First, the intervention provides a transfer from the government sector which directly or indirectly benefits enterprises and which entails a direct budgetary cost either in terms of expenditure or revenue foregone. Thus, as such, a subsidy is defined only when it imposes a cost to the public sector. Here, we broaden this to include certain arrangements which benefit the firm, but which in principle may involve no budgetary consequences for the Exchequer, and which perhaps helps distinguish industrial assistance from an industrial subsidy. These comprise some of the earliest government interventions, including loans made at commercial rates, loan guarantees, levy schemes, venture capital and industrial insurance schemes. The second criterion of Lehner *et al.* is that the recipient must be outside the administrative sector. This highlights that assistance can be given to enterprises in the private and public sectors alike, but like Feinstein (1972), we rule out those government transfers and grants to local authorities, non-profit-making organisations, overseas governments and other such bodies. This also includes payments to nationalized industries, although the distinction is sometimes blurred, such as when government intervention involves taking an ailing enterprise into public ownership, or payments are made to nationalised firms prior to privatization.

Third, the government must receive no equivalent compensation in return for the transfer. This draws the distinction between government-funded transfers and the public procurement of goods and services, by which the government may purchase goods at above market prices or, conversely, may offer services at below cost. Public procurement has been used for the purpose of conferring benefits on particular firms, but provided the transaction is carried out at market rates, then the equivalent compensation exists in the form of the goods and services, and such transactions can be ruled out as a subsidy. Fourth, the intervention is used for the purpose of affecting a given or expected outcome of the market process by changing relative prices so as to encourage or discourage certain economic behaviour. Under this, Lehner *et al.* argue that the assistance must change relative prices in some way, and this finds support in an earlier study by Shoup (1973). However, like Feinstein (1972), we broaden this to include 'unrequited payments to a producer or trader with the objective of reducing the selling price below the factor cost of production' (p. 80). Thus we include lump-sum payments which may have no factor substitution effects, and bring within our scope the various bail-outs of ailing companies which have been a feature of UK industrial subsidy policy.

In this latter respect, Grove (1962) distinguishes between *incentives*, which encourage the firm to engage in some new activity it would not otherwise undertake, and *profitability supports*, which enable the firm to carry on some existing activity it presumably would not otherwise do. Short of cash-flow constraints, a change in relative prices must be made to encourage the firm to engage in some new activity, while if the firm is making a loss then a temporary lump-sum subsidy is sufficient to sustain economic activity for some period provided the firm is compelled to put the funds to productive use. In this respect a similar distinction can be made between the accelerative and decelerative industrial policies mentioned above, and between *premiums* and *bounties*.

Finally, Lehner *et al.* argue that the intervention must contain an element of specificity, so that it is destined for a specific group of economic agents or for the producers of a particular product, service or factor of production. This last condition requires that the assistance provides a relative advantage to some subgroup of firms, which are defined by sector, region or size, or through the use of some common assisted factor or technology. This partly reflects the view of the European Commission of those interventions that are prejudicial to competition, but it is also an attempt to rule out the general spending and taxing functions of the public sector. Such a distinction is not always clear, and has been a constant source of difficulty in the discussion of industrial subsidies. Prest (1976), for example, cites the case of a two-tier expenditure tax and questions whether it is right to think of the higher rate as an extra tax or the lower rate as a subsidy. Similarly, Adam Smith argues that many of the bounties in the eighteenth-century economy were no more than drawbacks of domestic duties on exports, while Ricketts (1985) sees the notion of an industrial subsidy as a purely normative concept. This problem is always present since identical firms in different local government jurisdictions may be treated differently according to the taxing and spending functions of the government. Finally, it is often wrong to view a subsidy as simply a negative tax, since while optimal taxation seeks to minimize the efficiency loss of taxation for the purpose of funding expenditure, subject to equity considerations, Wolfson (1990) notes that the use of subsidies usually presumes a second-best position, so that there may be difficulties in defining the counter-factual position for efficiency purposes.

In our discussion of industrial subsidies we include tax incentives in the form of accelerated depreciation allowances above the current conventions laid down by the Inland Revenue for capital depreciation purposes. We also include investment allowances, which give a total annual depreciation allowance above the initial asset value, and the refund on Selective Employment Tax which was made to alter the composition of industry. Premiums in the form of the Selective and the Regional Employment Premium are included, since these were payable to manufacturing and in certain geographical areas, and we also include the spending under the special employment measures where training was not the primary intention. As a general rule, we exclude those activities which may be considered the normal activity of government, such as support for defence-related projects, and that relating directly to trade and infrastructure provision. Nevertheless, our study extends to consider measures such as agricultural support, factory construction under regional policy, support for commercial property development under urban policy, and the loans and grants policies of local authorities, although we do not necessarily attempt to provide figures for expenditure on all of these.

THE BOOK'S STRUCTURE

The discussion is organized on a chronological basis, and while more concerned with policy than politics, the book chapters tend to be arranged around electoral periods, reflecting the structural shifts in industrial policy which have sometimes been coincident with changes of government. We use subheadings extensively, so that readers who are interested in a particular topic, such as spatial development policy, special employment measures or even the European Union dimension, can skip from chapter to chapter to follow these through. Chapter 2 covers the pre-war period stretching back to the strategic interventions before the First World War. Chapter 3 considers the legislative basis for industrial subsidies in the immediate post-war period and the emergence of subsidies as economic conditions deteriorated in the late 1950s and early 1960s. Chapter 4 details the expansion of industrial assistance in the late 1960s, and Chapter 5 describes the attempt to withdraw from these subsidies in the early 1970s and the subsequent reinvigoration of these measures. Chapter 6 examines the period of the mid-1970s and describes the turning-point for assistance, and Chapters 7 and 8 describe in some detail the attempts first to limit and then to eliminate large-scale subsidies in the 1980s. Conclusions are drawn in Chapter 9 and, as noted above, this provides figures for expenditure since the Second World War in grant equivalent terms, enabling a comparison of spending over time. This chapter also reports the results of an analysis of these figures, and helps quantify some of the effects described in this book.

2 Industrial Assistance in Pre-War Britain

EARLY FORMS OF INTERVENTION

The potentially adverse effect of imports on domestic wealth and employment had been recognized as early as the fifteenth century, and early forms of state intervention in industrial affairs took the form of trade protection to both restrict imports and to secure for English goods a favourable position in export markets (Skuse, 1972). Measures included the 1651 and 1660 Navigation Acts, which gave English ships a monopoly of imperial trade; the 1663 Staple Act, which required all European goods destined for the colonies to pass through England; and the 1660 Restoration Subsidy Act, which taxed Irish woollens. By 1721, the import of manufactures was officially discouraged, while raw materials could be imported free of tariff, and virtually all the export duties on English goods had been eliminated. This system of trade protection was in place for much of the eighteenth century, but was gradually eliminated in the nineteenth century with the rise of *laissez-faire* free market economics. The last of the Navigation Acts was withdrawn in 1849, and other protectionist measures such as the Corn Laws, which had limited competition in agriculture, were repealed in 1846.

The freeing of trade promoted strong economic growth, and by 1870 the volume of UK external trade was greater than that of France, Germany and Italy combined, and more than three times that of the United States (Pollard and Crossley, 1968). However, the economic boom peaked in 1873 and the period known as the Great Depression followed, in which economic growth continued, but at a much reduced rate. This lower growth rate may have resulted from a slow-down in technological advance, but both Germany and the United States achieved markedly higher growth rates in the forty years up to the First World War, which perhaps reflected some 'catching up' phenomenon rather than any underlying weakness in the domestic economy (Floud, 1981).[1] The decline of agriculture continued in the period before the First World War, but such was the pace of industrialization that employment expanded by over 50 per cent between 1871 and 1911 (see Table 2.1). However, even this was

Table 2.1 Population and employment, 1851–1911

Industry Grouping (1958 SIC)	*1851* (*000s*)	*1871* (*000s*)	*1891* (*000s*)	*1911* (*000s*)	*1851–1911 change* (*000s*)	(*%*)
Population	**20 817**	**26 072**	**33 029**	**40 831**	**20 014**	**96.1**
Employment						
Agriculture	2 017	1 769	1 502	1 553	−464	−23.0
Mining	394	528	758	1 210	816	207.1
Metal manufacture	572	915	1 210	1 923	1 351	236.2
Textiles and clothing	2 205	2 294	2 556	2 766	561	25.4
Other manufacturing	835	1 129	1 604	2 343	1 508	180.6
Construction	497	716	902	1 145	648	130.4
Services	2 260	3 388	4 780	6 426	4 166	184.3
Other	520	1 096	1 136	925	405	77.9
Total	**9 300**	**11 835**	**14 448**	**18 291**	**8 991**	**96.7**

Notes: Figures are for Great Britain and for males and females.
Source: Mitchell and Deane (1962).

not sufficient to meet the increase in labour supply from population growth, and with increased urbanization and cycles in economic activity, unemployment became an increasingly serious problem in the late nineteenth century.

A Royal Commission on the Depression of Trade and Industry (Cd 4896, 1896) was established in 1885. This recognized deficiencies in industry, but while new taxes meant that government income trebled in real terms between 1870 and 1914, and expenditure increased fivefold in nominal terms, much of this was used to fund new social policy measures such as secondary education, state pensions and national insurance. Industry was undergoing transformation at this time, and was becoming increasingly concentrated as the corporate enterprise gradually replaced the owner-managed firm, so that by the outbreak of war the staple industries of coal, cotton and textiles, iron and steel, and shipbuilding accounted for more than half of British exports.[2] However, despite the relatively poor performance of industry and the narrowing of the industrial base, government intervention in economic affairs was extremely limited in the early twentieth century, so that where the government did intervene it was generally for reasons of strategic importance.

INTERVENTION FOR STRATEGIC PURPOSES

Early examples of state intervention in industry resulted from growing Anglo-German rivalry, arising either from the superior German economic performance or as a strategic measure in the run-up to the outbreak of the First World War. One of the earliest cases of selective financial intervention was the £2.6 million loan granted to the Cunard Company over the period 1905–8 to help finance the construction of the sister ships *Mauretania* and *Lusitania*. The loan, which was made under the 1904 Cunard Agreement (Money) Act and repaid in annual instalments of £130 000 up to 1928, was made for reasons of national prestige, with the *Mauretania* taking the Blue Riband trophy from Germany and holding it for a further twenty-two years.[3] Early strategic interventions include the purchase of a controlling interest in the Anglo-Persian Oil Company in 1913 to secure the supply of oil to the Navy in the event of war, and the establishment of the National Physical Laboratory in 1900 to combat technological superiority gained by Germany. The National Physical Laboratory was later to become part of the Department of Scientific and Industrial Research (DSIR), which was established in 1916 to provide government support for scientific research in independent institutions with possible industrial applications. The DSIR was superseded by the government Research Councils and the Ministry of Technology in the early 1960s.

The growing role of the state in welfare matters led it to acknowledge the role it could play in economic matters, so that the 1909 Development Act recognized for the first time that wise expenditure by the State could add to the national wealth even though it never showed a visible profit; and that, by careful timing, expenditure on public works could help to mitigate the recurring crises of trade depression and unemployment. For this purpose, the 1909 Act, together with the 1910 Road Improvements Fund Act, established a Development Fund to be used to finance development projects carried out by public bodies and companies not trading for a profit. Under Part I of the 1909 Act, the Treasury could make free grants and loans for the purpose of aiding and developing forestry, agriculture and rural industries, the reclamation and drainage of land, the improvement of rural transport (other than roads), the construction and improvement of harbours and canals and the development and improvement of fisheries, and for any other purpose calculated to promote the economic development of the United Kingdom.[4]

The 1909 Act constituted a body of Development Commissioners to consider and report to the Treasury on applications made to them for support from the Fund and to frame schemes for financing. Finance was voted annually, usually at around £500 000 per annum, which was used mainly to fund agricultural research at universities and other institutions, but the scope of the Fund was gradually reduced over time as functions such as forestry, the construction and improvement of fishery harbours, and fisheries research were all made the responsibility of other bodies. The Act required the Commissioners to have regard for the state of employment when examining schemes, but the Development Fund was never a source of funds for unemployment relief, and its grants for rural business were usually of a few hundred pounds. However, the approach was later (in the 1930s) extended to the Depressed Areas, when further Commissioners were appointed to report and undertake work in these areas. The Development Commissioners themselves operated until 1984, when they were replaced by the Development Commission, which mainly assisted small firms in rural areas.

Of course, the outbreak of war in 1914 provided a strong reason for government intervention in the economy, but initially the belief was that the market economy could respond to the imperatives of war, and the slogan 'business as usual' was coined. Control was taken of the railways and the government made efforts to secure food and other necessary supplies, such as optical equipment and dyestuffs which prior to the war came almost exclusively from Germany, but generally such measures were kept to a minimum. In the case of dyestuffs, the government supplied half the share capital to establish a new company, British Dyes Ltd, which at the end of the war was amalgamated with the only substantial private firm to become British Dyestuffs Corporation. This merged with three other companies in 1926 to form Imperial Chemical Industries. Legislation gave the government the power to control sectors of industry, but this was only invoked as the economy strained to meet the war effort, with the 'Great Shell Scandal' just one example. Thus, from December 1916, the Lloyd George War Cabinet took control of large areas of the productive economy, through a mixture management takeovers, requisitioning of output, licensing, import and export restrictions, price fixing, controls over distribution and rationing (Morgan, 1952).

By the end of the war, the government had direct charge of shipping, railway and canal transport; it purchased about 90 per cent of all imports; and it marketed over 80 per cent of the food consumed at home. However, this system of control was largely abandoned at the end of the war, along with plans to improve business organization and industrial efficiency through the Ministry of Reconstruction, since evidently the defeat of the principal economic competitor, plus the conditions for peace, made these controls and plans appear largely irrelevant. Nevertheless, quite apart from the wartime destruction, the war had dislocated the economy in a number of important respects. First, it had provided a precedent for large-scale intervention, and public expenditure in the inter-war period was never less than twice that of pre-war years (Peacock and Wiseman, 1967). Second, the government policy of encouraging mergers over many sectors of the engineering industry was an important progenitor of the rationalisation movement in the late 1920s (Kirby and Rose, 1991). Third, the war severely disrupted the pre-war pattern of trade, and Britain's narrow export base was particularly susceptible to these shifts. The European market, which had received around a third of exports, was in ruins, and here, as elsewhere, protectionism was in the ascendancy, partly reflecting the passing of imperial power. India, for example, had received 13 per cent of UK exports, mainly in the form of cotton, before the war, but after the war tariffs on these imports were doubled to protect the growing indigenous industry, while export duties were abolished.

ECONOMIC CRISES IN THE INTER-WAR PERIOD

The period after the First World War was characterized by acute economic instability. A short-lived post-war boom was followed by deflation and a slump in 1920–2, and then, after a period of unsteady growth, by Depression between 1929 and 1932, and then by further economic growth. If anything, the economic cycle was more accentuated in the UK than elsewhere (Rostas, 1943), and the rising protectionism and the eventual abandonment of free trade were mirrored in the UK by a series of protectionist measures, culminating in the 1932 Import Duties Act, which placed a general 10 per cent tariff on most imported goods (except basic foodstuffs and raw materials), later increased to 20 and 30 per cent on some luxury goods. Further factors having an impact on the UK position were the return to the gold standard at the pre-war parity, which is generally thought to have over-valued sterling by up to 10 per cent, and by as much as 25 per cent in later times (Redmond, 1980), and the over-reliance on exports from the staple industries, which were not only affected by the tariffs abroad, but also by the development of industry elsewhere. Moreover, much of the UK's industry was organized in small-scale production units and was becoming increasingly uncompetitive in the face of the larger and more efficient plants being constructed elsewhere.[5]

Newer industries, such as motor vehicles and electrical engineering, were coming on stream, but these mainly served domestic markets and were unable to capture the export markets vacated by the older industries, while industries based on new technologies, such as the lighter new consumer goods industries, were not yet sufficiently developed to compensate for the loss of employment. Thus, despite an average annual growth of 1.9 per cent for GDP and 2.8 per cent for manufacturing output over 1920–9, and 1.8 and 3.3 per cent respectively over the 1930s (Pollard, 1992), unemployment was a serious problem throughout the inter-war period, running at an average rate of 14 per cent of insured workers and almost always above 10 per cent (see Figure 2.1). This can be contrasted with the period 1850–1914, when unemployment was thought never to have reached 10 per cent.[6] In the worst years, unemployment reached 18 per cent in 1921 and nearly 23 per cent in 1932, and it was chiefly in response to these high rates of unemployment in each of these periods that industrial subsidies gained a foothold in economic policy.

Figure 2.1 Unemployment in the staple industries, 1923–38

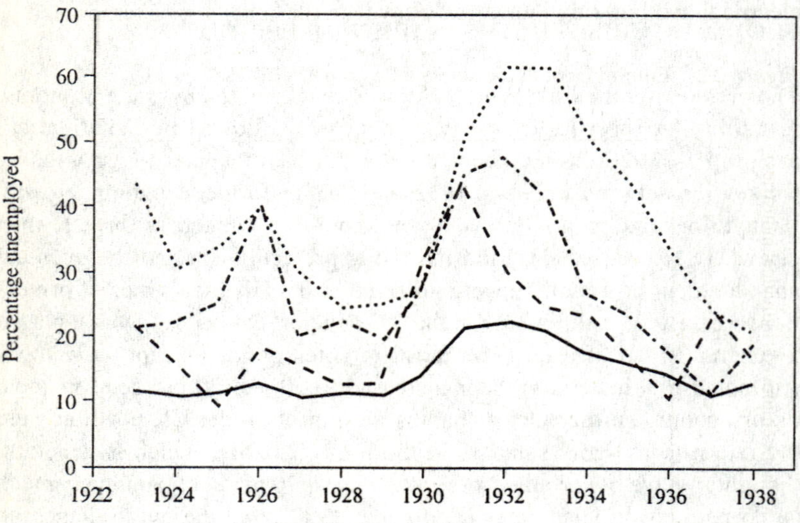

Notes: Unemployment rates refer to insured employees only.

Key: All industries ——— Shipbuilding and repair ·······

Cotton textiles – – – Iron and steel –·–·–·

Source: Mitchell and Deane (1962).

GOVERNMENT INTERVENTIONS IN THE EARLY 1920S

Employment fell by 2.4 million between 1920 and 1922, and the staple industries of textiles, mining, shipbuilding, engineering and iron and steel were badly affected, losing 1.1 million jobs over this period (see Figure 2.2). The 1919–22 coalition government of Lloyd George enacted a number of measures which were designed to both afford trade protection and relieve unemployment, and these formed some of the earliest efforts to assist industrial activity systematically.[7] As a general measure, the Export Credits Guarantee Department (ECGD) of the Board of Trade was established in 1919 to provide export guarantees up to a maximum of 85–95 per cent of the export amount in return for a premium, but operating on a non-profit-making basis. Later, the 1921 Trade Facilities Act extended the cover provided by the ECGD to private loans made to capital development schemes for 'purposes calculated to promote employment'. With a fund of £25 million, the Act gave the Treasury the power to guarantee private loans, mainly helping firms in iron and steel, engineering, and the electrical and building industries. However, the scheme was terminated in

Figure 2.2 Employment in the staple industries, 1920–38

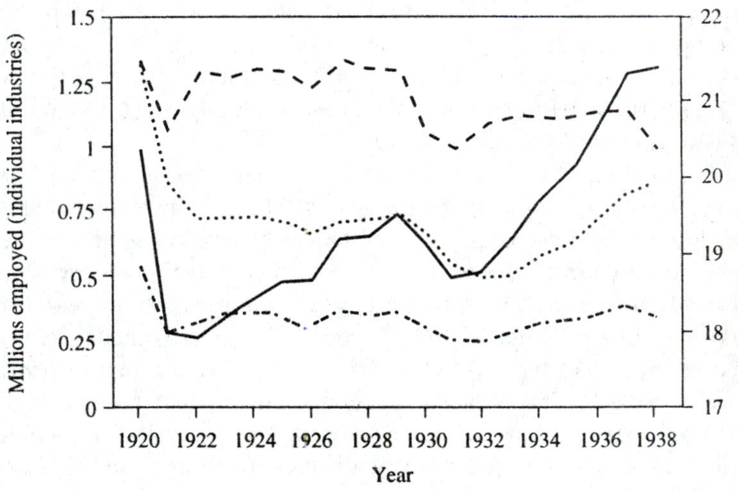

Key: All industries (right scale) ——— Engineering and shipbuilding ·······

Textiles – – – Iron and steel –·–·–·

Source: Feinstein (1972), table 59.

the mid-1920s by the Conservative government because it interfered with the normal business of the commercial banks (Grove, 1962). Further measures included tariffs in respect of certain strategic industries under the 1921 Safeguarding of Industries Act, and protection for the government-sponsored dyestuffs industry under the 1920 Dyestuffs Industry Act.

To tackle unemployment, the Road Fund, which had been in abeyance during the war years, was restarted with increased funds to lay out a new road network as a form of public works. A new Unemployment Grants Committee was also established in December 1920 'for the purpose of assisting Local Authorities in the United Kingdom in carrying out approved schemes of useful work other than works on roads and on housing schemes'. This was extended in 1921 to Statutory Boards not trading for a profit, and to public utilities from 1923. Initially, the terms of reference of the Committee was somewhat limited in that total expenditure was not to exceed £3m, but by the time the Committee was wound up in 1932 it had provided £24m, and was anticipating further Exchequer calls of £59m in respect of a total capital outlay of £191m (Cmd 4354, 1933). Conditions for funding were that works would only be approved in areas experiencing serious unemployment, which were certified as such by the Ministry of Labour; that preference would be given to ex-Service men; and that the grant should not exceed 30 per cent of the wages bill of additional men taken on. The types of public works funded by the Committee included sewage schemes (£46.5m in total project costs), unclassified roads and footpaths (£39.3m), electricity supply (£24.5m), dock and harbour improvements (£20.8m), water supply (£20.4m), and parks and recreation grounds (£12.6m).

The original intention of the Unemployment Grants Committee was to provide temporary relief up to the spring of 1921 in localities where unemployment was severe, arising from the failure of industry to absorb men demobilized from the Services. In the event, the scheme was renewed for successive winters, and the grant rate against wage costs increased to 75 per cent. In the winter of 1920/1 alone, 73 000 individuals were on funded schemes (Howson, 1981), but by 1925 it was apparent that local authorities were finding difficulty in submitting suitable schemes which would not otherwise have been carried out, and it seemed that public funding was serving only to bring work forward through time (Hicks, 1938). From this time, funding became more focused on the high unemployment areas, and the government would only provide grants for work not ordinarily undertaken within a period of five years (known as the acceleration condition), which in effect put the scheme into abeyance. The grants were reactivated in November 1928 to give support to the work of the Industrial Transference Board (see below), when the government authorized the Committee to make grants to local authorities in the more prosperous areas who were willing to undertake works of public utility and to employ not less than 50 per cent of the men required for the works from the depressed areas (Cmd. 4354, 1933). For these 'transfer' projects the acceleration condition was relaxed and a higher grant rate was available. Table 2.2 gives figures for spending on the Unemployment Grants Committee, as well as on the Road and Development Fund. This shows the considerable funds devoted to the Unemployment Grants Committee, but also that this was dwarfed by the spending under the Road Fund which was, at least in part, a form of public works.

Other interventions in the immediate post-war period were made on an *ad hoc* basis for strategic purposes. The Forestry Commission, which was founded in 1919, took over several functions of the Development Commissioners, and was provided with public funds to buy or lease land for afforestation (Wiles, 1952). Similarly, the wartime shortage of sugar encouraged the government to subsidize sugar beet production under the 1926 British Sugar (Subsidy) Act. This was intended to be a temporary subsidy declining over a ten-year period, but with the collapse of commodity prices in the Depression the subsidy was renewed under the 1936 Sugar Industry (Reorganisation) Act and maintained throughout the 1930s. Payments of assistance were also made to the infant civil aviation industry in 1921 and 1922 to enable it to compete with subsidized industry on the Continent. This aid proved unsuccessful, and after the Hambling Committee (Cmd 1811, 1923) had reported, the government amalgamated existing private firms to form the Imperial Air Transport Company, later known as Imperial Airways. Concerns over the monopoly position of this firm led the establishment in 1935 of a competitor, British Airways, but these two firms were later merged to form the British Overseas Airways Corporation.

STRUCTURAL INTERVENTIONS AND THE BANK OF ENGLAND

The Baldwin Government from 1924 to 1929 was generally far less enthusiastic about industrial intervention than its immediate predecessors had been. The loan guarantees under the 1921 Trade Facilities Act were cut, and as high unemployment proved to be a permanent rather than a temporary phenomenon, public works under the Unemployment Grants Committee effectively went into abeyance from December 1925. A temporary profitability support that had been afforded to the coal industry was

Table 2.2 Spending on public works, 1910–38 (£000s, current prices)

	1910/11	*1911/12*	*1912/13*	*1913/14*	*1914/15*	*1915/16*	*1916/17*	*1917/18*	*1918/19*	*1919/20*	*1920/1*	*1921/2*	*1922/3*	*1923/4*
Development fund	–	432	294[1]	767	433[1]	433[1]	433[1]	192	318	825	636	368	511	480
Road fund	863	1 210	1 172	1 395	1 528	694	–	–	–	–	8 937	10 795	11 772	14 090
Unemployment grants committee[2]	–	–	–	–	–	–	–	–	–	–	3 386	2 023	3 086	2 630

	1924/5	*1925/6*	*1926/7*	*1927/8*	*1928/9*	*1929/30*	*1930/1*	*1931/2*	*1932/3*	*1933/4*	*1934/5*	*1935/6*	*1936/7*	*1937/8*
Development fund	513	558	403	384	395	722	667	473	417	344	491	641	724	740
Road fund	15 563	17 455	17 373	19 666	21 131	21 882	22 866	22 519	22 910	25 512	26 438	25 775	27 427	–
Unemployment grants committee[2]	2 238	101	41	788	212	5 323	4 511	4 170	4 450	4 463	4 421	4 334	3 954	3 672

Notes: 1. Apportioned to financial years based on figures for cumulative spend.
2. Total Exchequer spending over 1920/1–1931/2 amounted to £24.4m and this has been apportioned to financial years according to known figures for total project costs. Figures for years after 1931/2 are estimates of Exchequer liability based on schemes approved up to this time.

Sources: *Annual Reports of the Development Commissioners* (London: HMSO); *Statistical Abstract of the United Kingdom* (London: HMSO); Cmd 4354 (1933).

also cut around this time. After wartime control, the coal industry had been returned to private owners in 1921, and on condition that it agreed a national wage negotiating procedure, it had received a temporary subsidy to support wages, amounting to around £15 million in 1920/1. However, faced with continued falls in demand, the agreement broke down in 1925, when employers sought to worsen the terms of employment and adopt regional wage determination. In response, the government established the Samuel Commission (Cmd 2600, 1925), and in the meantime provided a further subsidy to maintain existing conditions. The Commission recommended the reorganization of the coal industry to achieve greater efficiency, but also came out strongly against the subsidy, arguing that it would induce similar strikes in other industries. The withdrawal of the subsidy in 1926 was a precursor to the General Strike, by which time the total subsidy to the coal industry had amounted to some £26 million.

While cutting back on direct industrial assistance, the government was still keen to provide trade protection to industry, and new measures consisted of an extension in 1926 of tariffs under the 1921 Safeguarding of Industries Act to selected non-strategic industries (the Act initially covered strategic industries only) and the continuation of the wartime McKenna Duties on certain luxury goods, which had briefly been in abeyance in 1924. A general subsidy was given to industry through de-rating under the 1929 Local Government Act, which (after some delay) was designed to offset the effect on exports of the higher exchange rate after 1925 by providing relief to firms against three-quarters of industrial property rates, with central government reimbursing local authorities through block grant arrangements.[8] The central constraint on government expenditure in this period was the Treasury's insistence on a balanced budget to maintain overseas confidence in the pound, to keep the fixed value of sterling against gold. Thus, as the decade progressed, government interventions became much more structural in nature, as it sought to encourage the rationalization of surplus capacity, especially in cotton and iron and steel, and to reorganize industry elsewhere. The general view was that lost overseas markets should be regained via increased efficiency through reaping scale economies, and that subsidies should be limited to those which lowered production costs (Howson, 1981; Peden, 1985). However, rather than intervene directly to reorganize and rationalize industry, much of the work was left to the privately-owned Bank of England, whose Governor regarded this as the most effective contribution to the revival of industry and to the reduction of unemployment (Sayers, 1976).[9]

The first case in which the Bank of England became directly involved was the restructuring of the armaments manufacturer Armstrong

Whitworth, whose attempts to diversify after the war through the acquisition of a Canadian paper mill had gone badly wrong. The Bank had a clear interest, since the firm was by far its biggest customer at its Newcastle branch, but the Bank soon moved outside its traditional role, providing a £1m guarantee to the firm in 1927 to enable its armaments capacity to be merged with that of Vickers, and becoming a shareholder in the remaining interests which it only disengaged from in 1944 at some cost. Shortly afterwards, the Bank became more actively involved in reorganizing and rationalizing other parts of industry, including a plan for Lancashire Steel Corporation and the rescue of a Glasgow armaments manufacturer. In 1929 it played a key role in forming the Lancashire Cotton Corporation (later taken over by Courtaulds in the early 1960s), which sought drastic reductions in capacity and the reorganization of parts of the cotton industry, and in 1930 the National Shipbuilders Security Ltd was formed, which sought to purchase and dismantle redundant shipyards through a 1 per cent levy on the sales of participating firms. By 1937, twenty-eight firms had been dismantled under the National Shipbuilders Security Ltd, accounting for around 30 per cent of total capacity, of which the most notable case was Palmer's shipyard at Jarrow. When this closed in 1934 unemployment in the area rose to around 70 per cent, prompting the Jarrow March.

A change of government in June 1929, and a minority Labour government, made little difference to industrial policy, with the emphasis remaining on the rationalization and reorganization of industry. The Bank of England sought to bring other financial institutions in on its efforts to reorganize industry, and in 1930 a co-operative, the Bankers' Industrial Development Company, was formed, which gave the Bank a formal mechanism through which to intervene in industry. The Bank subscribed a quarter of the nominal capital of £6m, and an open invitation was issued to industry for schemes of reorganization, but as the world economy slumped, attention shifted elsewhere, and the facility appears to have been little used before it was wound up in 1945. The new government took office pledging to deal with the unemployment problem. A Committee on Trade and Industry (the Macmillan Committee) (Cmd 3897, 1931) was established, and an Economic Advisory Council set up in 1930 to both investigate and give an airing to the policy options (see Howson and Winch, 1977). However, it was soon faced with a rapid rise in unemployment, and its response was to intensify existing measures, while resisting proposals for a massive expansion of public works (see Peden, 1984). The central commitment remained the gold standard, but as the tensions posed by worsening economic conditions increased, the abandonment of the gold standard was forced in September 1931. The new national government, which had been formed in August 1931, introduced a range of protectionist measures on manufactures and agricultural products, but within the context of a balanced budget, industrial policy remained largely unchanged.

THE BEGINNINGS OF REGIONAL POLICY

In the slump of the early 1920s, the Lloyd George Government had introduced public works programmes, but the Baldwin Government was sceptical about these, arguing that public works would crowd out private investment and in the words of the Chancellor of the Exchequer in 1929, create, 'very little additional employment and no permanent employment'.[10] Thus, as unemployment again increased, a different approach was tried, which involved relocating individuals away from the areas of high unemployment to more prosperous parts. Initially, the work was carried on through the employment exchange machinery of the Ministry of Labour, which from 1927 transferred miners between coalfields and from mining to other industries, but was given formal effect by the establishment of the Industrial Transference Board in 1928 to encourage occupational and geographical mobility and facilitate relocation. The Board could provide retraining through training centres, and loans and grants to assist with the relocation of individuals, and it was supported in its work by the Unemployment Grants Committee. At first, the Board focused on unemployed miners, but its work was quickly extended to include other occupations, and on average 22 500 adults a year were transferred under the scheme over the period 1929–38 (Pitfield, 1978). However, the scheme made little sense in the Depression, when unemployment was high across the country, and most of the transferees were under 35 years of age, which left an ageing population in areas often experiencing high unemployment. Moreover, after the first few years, the quality of unemployed workers offering themselves for transfer deteriorated, such that fewer retained their new jobs, and around a quarter of transferees returned subsequently (Odber, 1965).

After the change in government in June 1929, one of the earliest measures to receive Royal Assent was the 1929 Development (Loan Guarantees and Grants) Act, which placed the Unemployment Grants Committee on a statutory basis, enabling the Ministry of Labour to make grants, with the approval of the Treasury and on the recommendation of the Committee, to local authorities and statutory bodies not trading for profits for the funding of public works. The Act also allowed loan guarantees and grants to be made to public utilities for the same purpose. In order to encourage the maximum number of projects, the conditions which had been introduced in December 1925 were relaxed, so that grants for 'transfer' projects would be made if the proportion of transferred labour did not reach 50 per cent, while the period of acceleration was reduced from five to three years. The definition of areas experiencing exceptional unemployment was also relaxed, so that these were defined as localities with an average unemployment rate of not less than 10 per cent in the previous twelve months, whereas previously it had been 15 per cent. This substantially increased the number of eligible local authorities, including those that before had been unable to obtain grant aid on both the transfer and non-transfer basis, and in the year to June 1930 around 1850 schemes were approved involving capital spending of about £37 million. Nevertheless, the response was seen as inadequate, and from July 1930 all local authorities were assisted at the maximum rate, which had previously been available to 'transfer' projects only, and the employment of men from the depressed areas was no longer made a condition of grant. In the following six months, 2344 schemes were submitted, involving spending of £32.5m. At its peak in March 1931, 59 000 men were employed on schemes but at this time the adult male unemployment rate had reached 23.6 per cent (or around three million) against 17.7 per cent just eight months earlier. Further changes were made to the scheme, but a national financial crisis overtook events and no further projects were approved after August 1932 when the Act, which had a life of three years, lapsed.

The impact of the Depression on the staple industries was severe, not least because the fall in commodity prices in developing countries had considerably reduced the effective demand for UK exports. The efforts to rationalize industry in this sector further exacerbated the unemployment problem over the short term, and employment in the staple industries declined relative to total employment throughout the 1930s (see Figure 2.2). The rise in unemployment in these industries was dramatic, and in the worst years of the Depression unemployment (as a percentage of insured workers) stood at 34.5 per cent in coal mining, 47.9 per cent in iron and steel, 62.0 per cent in shipbuilding and repair, 43.2 per cent in cotton textiles and around 34 per cent in other textile industries (see Figure 2.1). Much of this industry was concentrated in the peripheral regions, and in some areas unemployment was extraordinarily high, averaging 25 to 35 per cent across whole regions. Moreover, the efforts of the Bank of England and the work of the Unemployment Grants Committee and Industrial Transference Board had only a limited impact, so that increasingly the government was led to the view that improvements in economic efficiency and public works were insufficient to cure unemployment, and that further interventions were necessary to promote employment in the worst affected areas.

A series of reports into conditions in areas with very high unemployment was commissioned by the government, but these recommended the extension of industrial transference, the encouragement of work by voluntary organisations to provide employment, and public works in infrastructure provision (Cmd 4728, 1933). Following this, the 1934 Special Areas (Development and Improvement) Act led to the appointment of two Commissioners who were to act in four designated Special Areas comprising South Wales, North East England, West Cumberland and Clydeside/North Lanarkshire, excluding the major towns (see Figure A.1 in the Appendix, p. 215). Like the Unemployment Grants Committee, the Commissioners were unable to provide funds for profit-making enterprises and projects receiving a government grant from other sources, but like the Development Commissioners which operated in rural areas, the funding of the initiative was very small at just £2 million, or around 0.05 per cent of gross domestic product (GDP). This was supposed to be an initial sum and was used almost entirely for sewerage schemes and for the settlement of labour on land, but it fell well short of what was required (McCrone, 1969).

Faced with criticism, the Bank of England, with government backing, established the Special Areas Reconstruction Association (SARA) in 1936 with funds of £1 million to provide loans of up to £10 000 to small firms in the Special Areas which could not otherwise obtain finance. These loans were guaranteed by the Treasury, which also met the administration expenses, and were in line with the recommendations of the Macmillan Committee which had earlier pointed to the difficulty of small firms in obtaining finance. The measure represented the first scheme of direct financial assistance to industry from public funds, but again was limited in scale. However, the assistance was supplemented in December 1936 by direct private action when Lord Nuffield established the Nuffield Trust for the Special Areas, which made available limited funds 'for the initiation or support of measures likely to give employment to those living in the area as well as measures designed for social betterment'. In total, £1.2 million in loans and £1.1m in equity finance was disbursed under the Trust by 1954, mainly in the period 1937–9.

By the mid-1930s unemployment was falling across the country, but remained at high levels in many areas, and with a recession in 1937–8 began to rise again in those regions not affected by rearmament.[11] Faced with continued criticism, not least from one of its own Commissioners, the government shifted ground in 1937 and the Special Areas Amendment Act gaves powers to the Treasury to make loans to firms in the Special Areas. Total loans of £2 million were available and were made on the advice of a Special Areas Loans Advisory Committee (SALAC). Attracted by the apparent success of private trading estates, the Commissioners had earlier established non-profit making bodies to lay out industrial trading estates and construct factories in the Special Areas, of which the first was at Team Valley, Gateshead in 1936. These moves were now encouraged by the government, and the powers of the Commissioners extended so that they were able to induce occupation of these factories by contributing to a firm's rents, rates or income tax for a period not exceeding five years (McCrone, 1969). By 1939, ten estates with over three hundred factories had been established, employing 12 000 people (Grove, 1962).

These early regional policy measures showed considerable innovation in industrial and employment policy, although as yet there was no explicit policy to encourage industrial relocation.[12] Expenditure on financial assistance was small, and by the outbreak of war stood at £0.75m on loans under SARA and £1.1m under SALAC, but this was less than the £2m in loans and equity which had been disbursed by the Nuffield Trust by this time. Further, the government had little enthusiasm or faith in the effect of these measures, so that in November 1936 Prime Minister Neville Chamberlain commented that 'the Commissioner has made certain proposals and politically it might be helpful to try. If they failed, as I think they would, we should have done little harm, but we should have met the reproach that we neither accept others' suggestions nor produce any of our own'. In addition to these spatial measures, the government provided a loan and special insurance facilities to the Cunard Line in 1934 to complete the construction of the *Queen Mary*, on which work was at a standstill, and to build the *Queen Elizabeth*. Unlike the previous assistance given to Cunard, the major reason cited by the government this time was for the promotion of employment in shipbuilding.

THE ORIGINS OF ASSISTANCE TO AGRICULTURE

During the 1920–2 slump agricultural prices had fallen sharply – from an index number of 292 in 1920 to 169 in 1922 following a sharp rise from a base year in 1913 – but at that time the government had refused to provide long-term subsidies. Instead, it provided temporary support to offset some losses and essentially left the running of agriculture to the market (Venn, 1933).[13] However, continuing depressed prices in agriculture meant that state intervention remained a contentious issue throughout the 1920s. A White Paper (Cmd 2581, 1926) argued that the only means of securing increased agricultural production at world prices was through the introduction of subsidies or trade protection, but the governing Conservative Party was split between protectionists and free traders, while the incoming Labour government of 1929 favoured free trade to keep prices low, advocating subsidies to support farmers' incomes, but only if the industry was taken out of private hands (Smith, 1990). In the event, the government decided to establish Marketing Boards to increase the bargaining power of farmers and raise incomes. This was given effect by the 1931 Marketing Act which enabled any group of producers of an agricultural product to submit a scheme that could involve the control of all sales of the product (either by regulation or purchase), the negotiation of prices with distributors, and the specification of the terms of resale. These were subject to parliamentary approval, but only partly resolved the problem because farmers could still be undercut by overseas suppliers (McCrone, 1962; Self and Storing, 1962).

Measures were also taken to meet a shortage of long-term finance for the acquisition of farms and general agricultural working capital, and again involved the Bank of England, which, with the commercial banks, provided the initial share capital. In England and Wales secured loans were made through the Agricultural Mortgage Corporation (AMC) set up in 1928, and in Scotland through the Scottish Agricultural Securities Corporation, established a year later. However, the interest rates charged by these Corporations were at commercial rates and resulted in a poor take-up, leading a government inquiry to conclude that the AMC had been only moderately successful (Cmnd 827 (1959) Radcliffe Report, para. 911). As the plight of agriculture continued to worsen in the Depression, it was the formation of the national government which led to a change in policy. Within months this established an Agricultural Policy Committee, which highlighted the need to raise prices and reduce costs, and recommended immediate special assistance in the case of wheat, and for protection for some other parts of agriculture. The 1932 Wheat Act guaranteed the wheat price at a fixed standard price up to maximum level of domestic output, but then at a declining price thereafter. The scheme was funded by a levy on non-imperial imported wheat, and led to a 47 per cent increase in domestically produced wheat between 1931 and 1937. The national government viewed wheat as being strategically important, even if it was uneconomic in Britain, and while the primary purpose of the subsidy was to support, not expand, production, it recognised that the subsidy could lead to overproduction.

Once these principles had been established, further measures were added through the 1930s. These included a general tariff on goods under the 1932 Import Duties Act, and duties on some agricultural imports, including vegetables, fruit and flowers. The powers of the Marketing Boards were extended under the 1933 Marketing Act, which enabled these Boards to control imported supplies in some circumstances, and to limit home supplies in accordance with previous output. Temporary subsidies were given to livestock producers in 1934 and 1936, and these were made permanent by the 1937 Livestock Industry Act; and to reflect the reduced acreage of oats and barley following the Wheat Act, subsidies were made to these cereals in 1937, which were paid by means of a standard price. Subsidies were also given to the fishing industry through minimum prices for herring and white fish amounting to around £2.25m annually, and such was the extensiveness of this support, that by the outbreak of the Second War only the potato industry was not receiving direct assistance (Wiles, 1952). Towards the end of this period, measures were introduced to improve efficiency and output, and while these were to be of greater significance after the war, they indicated the later shift towards support for productivity. These included grants towards lime and slag to improve soil fertility under the 1937 Land Fertility Scheme, and grants from 1939 towards the ploughing-up of grassland for agricultural use.

INDUSTRIAL SUBSIDIES IN PRE-WAR BRITAIN

In his *Wealth of Nations*, Adam Smith saw advantages in production subsidies over export subsidies in that they would be more immediate in their effect and would tend to lower the price in the domestic economy, thereby at least repaying to consumers part of the tax contribution. As such, Adam Smith attributed the rarity of industrial subsidies in the eighteenth century to the prejudices established by the commercial system, which argued that production subsidies were more liable to fraud than were trade subsidies and that national wealth arose more immediately through exportation than from production. Thus, prior to the First World War industrial intervention was very limited and made mainly for strategic purposes. The Great Depression of the late nineteenth century and its aftermath led to some economic development measures through the Development and Road Funds, and while substantial controls were taken over industry during the First World War these were later relinquished when it was anticipated that the economy would return to the pre-war position.

The slump of the early 1920s affected employment badly, particularly in the staple industries, and for a short time during the term of the Lloyd George Coalition Government subsidies gained a strong foothold in policy. In addition to public works programmes in the areas receiving transferred men from the depressed areas, measures included Treasury loan guarantees for capital development projects for the purpose of employment creation, and *ad hoc* subsidies to industry, most notably to the coal and infant civil aviation industry. However, the Baldwin Government of the late 1920s withdrew from this direct industrial support, and instead backed the efforts of the Bank of England to restructure and rationalise industry to make it more competitive. Agriculture was also struggling to compete at world prices, and while debate centred on the relative merits of trade protection and production subsidies, the initial measures consisted of the provision of long-term finance and Marketing Boards to increase market power. Subsidies were only adopted in the Depression, and then for the protection of wheat for strategic purposes. However, more general subsidies for agriculture followed and by the outbreak of war virtually the whole of agriculture was receiving assistance.

In this pre-war period, governments generally disliked direct industrial intervention, and so efforts to tackle unemployment involved encouraging occupational and geographical mobility both through training and public works in the recipient areas. However, these had only a very limited impact, and the Special Areas were designated in high unemployment areas, in which Commissioners were appointed to carry out public works. This involved only a very small amount of funds and, when pressured into taking further action, the government acted indirectly through the Bank of England to establish the first formal loan scheme. This had £1 million in funds, and provided finance mainly to small firms in line with the recommendations of the Macmillan Committee which had reported a few years earlier. However, the government had little faith in such measures, but were keen to be seen to be doing something, and in the face of a further downturn in demand in the late 1930s it made further loan finance available directly from the Treasury. An important precedent for this was the availability of funds for employment measures under the privately-sponsored Nuffield Trust for the Special Areas.

Outside agriculture, industrial assistance in the pre-war period was far less prevalent than is perhaps sometimes supposed. Measures consisted of a few of *ad hoc* payments to industries in difficulty, and small-scale schemes to support small firms in the depressed areas sometimes disbursed at arm's length by the Bank of England and its agents. By the outbreak of war the Nuffield Trust for the Special Areas had disbursed only £2m in loans and equity finance, but this exceeded the combined amounts provided by the Bank of England and the Treasury in the same assisted areas. Moreover, this assistance consisted almost exclusively of loans available at commercial rates, so that the actual subsidy amount was very small. Further, much of the aid was disbursed in the period 1937–9 when, as Figure 2.1 on p. 14 shows, unemployment in the staple industries had returned to the level of the late 1920s. Nevertheless, the principle of state finance for industry had been established, and coupled with the large-scale subsidies to agriculture and the gradual acceptance of Keynesian ideas it signalled the increased role to be played by industrial subsidies in the post-war period.

3 The Legislative Basis for Industrial Intervention (1940–63)

WARTIME PLANNING

The lessons from the First World War had been learnt, and with the outbreak of war in 1939 controls were introduced immediately on imports, foreign exchange and materials, and quickly extended to give a level of comprehensiveness far greater than that which existed in the earlier period. Controls were exercised over investment, the allocation of raw materials, industrial action and over the movement of individuals between industries, so that by the end of the war it is estimated that as many as 80 per cent of manufacturing employees were working either directly or indirectly for the state (Skuse, 1972). Consumer demand was rationed, prices were fixed and the government pursued a policy of industrial concentration whereby production was restricted to a limited number of firms, which paid compensation to those firms put out of business. Taxes, which had been used almost continuously from 1915 to discourage the consumption of luxuries, were extended, with Purchase Tax placed on a wide range of goods.

Unemployment stood at 75 000 in April 1944, but the coalition government was nevertheless keen to avoid the dramatic inflation and deflation that had followed the First World War, and so planned to remove the controls on production and consumption only gradually after the war. By this time the ideas of Keynes were in the ascendant and as the view of the government's role in the economy changed, so it sought to avoid the persistent high levels of unemployment that had characterized the inter-war years. It set out its ideas in the 1944 White Paper *Employment Policy* (Cmd 6527, 1944), which made it clear that the next government would be far more interventionist, whichever party came to power.[1] To tackle unemployment, the White Paper proposed to set 'domestic expenditure at a high level' (para. 24), to secure overseas markets and promote efficiency in the basic industries. But rather than rationalization and reorganization, which occurred at a rapid pace in the 1930s and through wartime measures, efficiency would be achieved through a tax policy designed to encourage industrial research and the modernization of plant, machinery and buildings. However, it was recognized that the effect of these policies would be at best long-term, and that it would be inadequate to solve locally high unemployment levels, so that three specific measures were proposed to address this (para. 25):

(a) removing obstacles to the transfer of workers from one area to another and from one occupation to another;
(b) providing training facilities to fit workers from declining industries for jobs in expanding industries; and
(c) influencing the location of new enterprises so as to diversify the industrial composition of areas which are particularly vulnerable to unemployment.

The proposals under (a) and (b) had already been pursued under the 1928 Industrial Transference Act and other measures, but the proposal under (c) was new. Proposals to deter industrial development had been recommended by the 1940 Report of the Royal Commission on the Distribution of the Industrial Population (Cmd 6153, (1940) Barlow Report), but for the purpose of limiting population growth in those areas already well developed.[2] The White Paper now proposed that all new industrial development, comprising new factories, relocations and extensions to existing factories, all above some specified size, should be notified to the government in order that it could both deter industry from locating in some areas and encourage it to locate in others. To facilitate relocation, the government undertook to construct factories and provide rented premises for smaller firms, and to disburse financial assistance to firms to secure their location in designated areas. Financial assistance would be available in the form of loans and share capital to firms with good commercial prospects. Other measures were also proposed to favour some firms in designated areas through public procurement and the treatment of munitions factories.

The war left the economy in a parlous state, since as well as the substantial wartime destruction, debts of £3 billion had been run up and a further £1 billion of overseas assets had been realized. In addition, there existed a considerable imbalance in trade as exports slumped, and this resulted in severe difficulties in obtaining sufficient US dollars to acquire basic commodities from abroad. However, the incoming government of 1945 also inherited substantial economic powers, and unlike after the First World War many of these controls were retained to deal with specific economic problems and to ease the transition to the peacetime economy.[3]

Controls over imports and foreign exchange, for example, helped to deal with the dollar shortage, while rationing and controls on consumer credit helped keep consumer demand in check. Gradually, as the economy got back to normal and exports began to boom, these controls were relinquished, and by 1950 very few remained (Pollard, 1992). At the same time, the government's commitment to economic planning led it to nationalize whole industries and in the five years after the war, civil aviation, coal, railways, ports, canals, long-distance road services, electricity, gas, steel and the Bank of England had all been taken into public ownership.[4]

RELOCATING INDUSTRY

One control the government did not give up was its power over investment, and the 1945 Distribution of Industry Act put into effect many of the proposals in the 1944 White Paper regarding the depressed areas. The Act replaced the pre-war legislation relating to the Special Areas, and redefined and renamed these areas as Development Areas, a term first introduced in the White Paper. The areas were essentially the same as the pre-war areas, but re-drawn to include major towns, with later additions to include parts of north-east Scotland, Lancashire and Merseyside. The Board of Trade was assigned to take over the role of the Commissioners, and the Factory Control – which was responsible from 1940 for allocating scarce factory space for war production, and had in fact located much of this in the Special Areas, so that after the war 13 million square feet of surplus ordnance factory space was available in the assisted areas – now became the Board of Trade Distribution of Industry and Regional Division to administer this (McCallum, 1979). To assist the growth of new industry in the Development Areas, the Board of Trade was empowered to undertake the following actions in these areas:

(a) build factories and purchase land, if necessary by compulsory purchase order;
(b) with Treasury consent, make loans to industrial estate companies to provide industrial premises;
(c) provide those basic public services upon which industrial development depends; and
(d) reclaim derelict land and improve amenities.

The provisions of the 1934 Special Areas Act regarding subsidies towards rent, rates and income tax were withdrawn, but instead the

Treasury could now give loans and grants to assist manufacturing undertakings already located or proposing to establish in the Development Areas. Payments were made on the advice of a Development Areas Treasury Advisory Committee (DATAC), which superseded the Special Areas Reconstruction Association and the Special Area Loans Advisory Committee (McCrone, 1969). The Act required that assisted undertakings should have good prospects of being 'carried on successfully without further assistance' and that the undertaking 'cannot for the time being, without assistance, obtain the capital required on the requisite terms'. Later, the 1950 Distribution of Industry Act widened the availability of the financial assistance to the actual relocation of firms and personnel to the Development Areas, which were not covered under the 1945 Act, although these mobile firms could claim assistance *in situ*. In addition to these formal inducements, firms moving to the Development Areas were given preference in capital issue queues, and priority in both defence contracts and the allocation of scarce raw materials, and these may have been of as much importance in attracting mobile industry (Grove, 1962).[5]

The disbursement of financial assistance was kept firmly under Treasury control throughout this early period of regional policy, but the subsidies were used in only limited measure. By the end of 1954 only seventy cases of financial assistance had been approved, and all these were in the form of loans, involving total advances of £5.9 million. Two-thirds of applications for loan assistance had been turned down, while only two applications for grant assistance had been received. In its review of the Distribution of Industry Acts, the Select Committee on Estimates (HC 139, 1955) were concerned that only four approvals for assistance had been made in 1954, but took evidence from the managers of the Nuffield Trust to the effect that firms could now obtain sufficient funds from sources not available before the war. As such, they recommended that financial assistance measures be put in abeyance, and that, if reactivated, a risk premium should be introduced to recompense for loan defaults. The DATAC itself felt entitled to 'take a greater degree of risk than is customarily taken by commercial institutions', and of the twenty-seven closed cases at this time, around 17 per cent of the amount advanced had been written off as bad debts.

In addition to the formal inducements under the Distribution of Industry Acts, the government put into effect measures to discourage industrial development outside the Development Areas.[6] The control of new development through building licences was retained after the war, and the Board of Trade let it be known that firms would get a licence quickly, and possibly automatically, if they located in a Development Area (Grove,

1962). These licences remained in usage up to 1950, and were abolished in 1954, but they had been effectively superseded at the beginning of 1948 by Industrial Development Certificates (IDCs) under the 1947 Town and Country Planning Act. These were a prerequisite for planning permission on new factory buildings and extensions of 5000 square feet or more, and were granted by the Board of Trade on condition that the development was consistent with the 'proper location of industry', although the exact terms were left vague. The IDCs sought to discourage development in certain areas, rather than to promote active industrial relocation to the Development Areas, and this, coupled with the gradual relinquishment of emergency wartime measures, meant that the Development Area share of new industrial development became much smaller after 1948, falling from 35 per cent in 1945–8 to 16 per cent in 1948–51.[7]

THE ENCOURAGEMENT OF INVESTMENT

Aside from measures of a spatial nature, the government took action in 1945 to promote national reconstruction through efforts to channel funds to investment. Existing tax allowances on capital depreciation, which were assessed on an historical cost basis, were thought insufficient for capital replacement at post-war prices, and in 1945 accelerated depreciation in the form of initial allowances was introduced for the first time. This gave an additional 20 per cent allowance for plant and machinery, and 10 per cent for building works in the first year, and acted as an interest-free loan to firms in that the subsequent allowance on the same capital equipment was correspondingly reduced.[8] With tax rates at around 50 per cent, the effective loan amount was about half the allowance, or equivalent to about an 0.5 per cent reduction in the interest rate (Dow, 1970). While the basis for introducing the allowances was to reflect a change in underlying economic conditions, once introduced they became an important instrument by which the government sought to fine-tune the level of economic activity, although the frequent changes to the system meant it was difficult to take them into account in investment appraisal.

In 1946/7, as Table 3.1 shows, the initial allowances had a total value of around £129m, but given that they led to subsequent reduction in the annual writing-down allowance, then under the reasonable conditions they had a present value grant equivalent of around £25m. The allowance provided only a temporary advantage to firms, because once introduced it meant that company tax payments would be correspondingly higher in future years. To give a further boost to investment in 1949 the initial

Table 3.1 Subsidies to agriculture, investment and local employment, 1946–59 (£m, current prices)

	1946/7	*1947/8*	*1948/9*	*1949/50*	*1950/1*	*1951/2*	*1952/3*	*1953/4*	*1954/5*	*1955/6*	*1956/7*	*1957/8*	*1958/9*
Assistance to agriculture													
	301	374	447	413	378	358	302	275	295	197	227	276	236
Depreciation allowances													
Gross amount	129	158	142	233	272	243	127	154	244	244	271	326	413
Grant equivalent	(25)	(32)	(27)	(41)	(49)	(45)	(25)	(54)	(180)	(133)	(151)	(196)	(277)
Assistance to local employment													
	5.9	12.8	11.5	7.1	5.8	5.8	4.0	4.2	6.2	6.3	5.2	2.8	3.6
Levies to the civil aircraft industry													
	24.2	0.3	1.4	1.3	2.7	8.2	0.0	0.0	0.1	1.0	4.2	5.7	6.6

Notes: The depreciation allowance figures include both initial and investment allowances, and represent the gross amount paid, even though the subsequent writing-down allowance would have been reduced in the case of initial allowances. For this reason we also report the grant equivalent figures for these. The data for levies relate to the year of contract and the gross amount only is reported. Subsequent recoveries on these levies was relatively small, amounting to £25.04m out of £88.37m by 1960. In the case of the depreciation allowances, levies and agriculture for years 1946/7–1954/5, calendar year figures have been apportioned to financial years.

Sources: *National Income and Expenditure* (London: HMSO); McCrone (1962, 1969); Cmnd 2853, (1965) (London: HMSO), Appendix G.

allowance on plant and machinery was doubled to 40 per cent. However, the allowances were cut in April 1952, before being reinstated the following year at 20 per cent to help with the urgent need for more investment (see Dow, 1970, ch. 7). The April 1954 Budget introduced investment allowances for the first time, at a rate of 20 per cent on plant and machinery and 10 per cent on buildings. These differed from initial allowances in that they gave a total depreciation allowance of 120 per cent on plant and machinery and 110 per cent on buildings, so that after an increased allowance of 20 and 10 per cent respectively in the first year there was no subsequent reduction in the annual writing-down allowance. Table 3.2 shows that these initial or investment allowances were available in one form or another and against plant and machinery or buildings throughout much of the post-war period, and were only abandoned in the mid-1980s.

Investment grew strongly in the immediate post-war period, rising by 45 per cent between 1946 and 1951 as resources were diverted away from consumption, but the exact link between the allowances and investment was somewhat vague, and they were probably ineffective in expansionary periods when firms could draw much more on internal funds. Moreover, they were available automatically to firms, so that the government had no direct control over the type and timing of the investment being undertaken. Table 3.2 shows that there were frequent changes to the system of incentives, and by the late 1950s gross expenditure reached around £400m per annum (or nearly £300m in grant equivalent terms) when the investment allowances were operating. As such, the tax allowances represented by far the greater part of state subsidy to industry, exceeding the support for agriculture by the 1960s (Table 3.1). However, in the case of plant and machinery, the tax allowances were abandoned in the mid-1960s in favour of investment grants, which were thought to be quicker and more certain in their effect (Morris and Stout, 1985).

As well as the depreciation allowances, the wartime coalition government sought to promote two loan finance companies to plug certain gaps in the supply of long-term funds to firms (Ward-Perkins, 1952). The Macmillan Committee had stressed the problems faced by small and medium-sized businesses in raising long-term finance, and the Industrial and Commercial Finance Corporation (ICFC) was established with funds from the Bank of England and commercial banks to provide loans to these firms of between £5000 and £200 000. The Bank of England also contributed share capital to the new Finance Corporation for Industry (FCI), which provided funds to larger firms in new and expanding industries. The FCI obtained its working capital by borrowing from a consortium of clearing banks, and played a major role in establishing the Steel Company of

Table 3.2 Rates of assistance to capital, 1945–72

Date of announcement	Date effective	Plant and machinery			Industrial buildings		
		Allowances		Grants	Allowances		Grants
		Initial	Investment		Initial	Investment	
1945	April 1946	20	–	–	10	–	–
1949, April	Immediate	40	–	–	10	–	–
1951, April	April 1952	–	–	–	–	–	–
1953, April	Immediate	20	–	–	10	–	–
1954, April	Immediate	–	20[1]	–	–	10	–
1956, February	Immediate	20[2]	–	–	10	–	–
1958, April/July	April 1958	30[2]	–	–	15	–	–
1959, April	Immediate	10[3]	20	–	5	10	–
1960, March	Immediate	10[3]	20	–	5	10	(17)[4]
1963, April	November 1962	10[3]	30	–	5	15	(17)
	April 1963	10/(100)[3]	30	(10)	5	15	(25)
1966, August	January 1966[6]	–	–	20/(40)	15	–	(25–35)[5]
1966, December	January 1967	–	–	25/(45)	15	–	(25–35)
	January 1969	–	–	20/(40)	15	–	(25–35)
1970, October	Immediate	60/(100)[8]	–	–	30/(40)[7]	–	(25–45)
1971, July	Immediate	80/(100)[8]	–	–	30/(40)	–	(25–45)
1972, March	Immediate	100[8]	–	–	40	–	–
1972, August	March 1972	100[8]	–	(20–22)	40	–	(20–22)

Table 3.2 (*Continued*)

Notes: The table gives the nationally available rate of assistance which applied to the manufacturing sector. Where a different rate applied in the scheduled areas this is given in parentheses. Dashes indicate a zero rate. Different rates have applied to the agricultural, mining and construction sectors.

1. If the investment allowance did not apply, then an initial allowance was available at a rate of 20 per cent.
2. Between February 1956 and April 1959 the investment allowance was available for certain types of expenditure, in which case the initial allowance did not apply.
3. Where the investment allowance did not apply from April 1959 to January 1966, then an initial allowance was available at 30 per cent. Similarly if the investment grant did not apply from January 1966 to October 1970, then an investment allowance at 30 per cent was available.
4. Building grants were variable, but averaged 17 per cent.
5. Building grants were available at the standard rate of 25 per cent, but an extra 10 per cent was available at Board of Trade discretion, and as of right in Special Development Areas, from 1967.
6. Legislation was retrospective in the case of plant and machinery grants only.
7. Initial allowances on buildings were introduced from April 1970.
8. These are first-year writing-down allowances, so that unlike the other initial allowances in the table they were not available in addition to the usual annual writing-down allowance.

Sources: Dow (1970); HC 1 (1973) Annex B; *Annual Report on the 1972 Industry Act* (London: HMSO).

Wales in the early 1950s, providing over half of the initial £65m investment. Neither the ICFC nor the FCI received any public subsidy, both having been established as private limited companies. In 1959 the ICFC went public, enabling it to raise funds on the money markets, and in 1973 it merged with FCI to form Finance for Industry, later renamed Investors in Industry. Other finance companies were set up about this time, including the National Film Finance Corporation in 1948 (initially known as the National Film Finance Company), which was provided with working capital through Exchequer loans and borrowings from commercial banks under Treasury guarantee, but its lending was generally unsuccessful and large losses were later written off. The general principle was copied elsewhere, and in 1951 the privately-funded Ship Finance Company was established to assist with the financing of new ships.

PRICE GUARANTEES FOR AGRICULTURAL PRODUCTS

After the war the government sought to boost agricultural production, partly to save on foreign exchange, but also as a response to a world food shortage and to ease food rationing. Subsidies played a role here: the pre-war lime and ploughing grants were either extended or available on more favourable terms; payments were made to rehabilitate hill farming land and for hill sheep and cattle under the 1946 Hill Farming Act in order to bring marginal land into production; and subsidies for fertilizers were introduced in 1950. The 1947 Agriculture Act consolidated much of the pre-war legislation, and sought to achieve greater stability and efficiency in agricultural output through guaranteed prices and assured markets in line with planned production targets, so that price guarantees continued to account for the bulk of the assistance to agriculture. The guarantees covered cereal, milk, egg, potato, fatstock, wool and sugar beet prices, but were differentiated to alter the pattern of food supplies (Britton, 1952). As Table 3.1 shows, the amount expended on agricultural support was substantial, totalling around £450m in 1948/9, but this was heavily criticized and in 1951 the price guarantees were replaced by a system of deficiency payments similar in nature to those introduced under the 1932 Wheat Act.

The new system of support was complex; for example in the case of cereals (wheat, barley and oats) and fatstock (cattle, sheep and pigs), where there was intense competition from imports, farmers sold their output at the best market price and the government made good the difference between the average market price and a guaranteed price agreed by an Annual Review. Milk and potatoes were included under this from 1954 and eggs from 1957, but here the government paid the relevant Marketing Boards sufficient subsidy to cover the guaranteed prices which again were agreed at the Annual Review. The system as a whole was designed to give the consumer the benefit of lower world food prices while encouraging efficiency in farming by allowing the farmer to decide on the level of production in the light of expected costs, prices and subsidy (Self and Storing, 1962). At the time, price guarantees may have been the most effective means of support, because while the UK was one of the most protected markets in Western Europe, Commonwealth Preference meant that zero or very low duties were charged on trade with Commonwealth countries and as a consequence food was generally imported duty-free (Morgan, 1978).

Price guarantees cost £133.6m in 1955/6 and a further £58.1m was spent on the various production and improvement grants noted above (McCrone, 1962). The new arrangements enabled the government to reduce successfully the amount of support going to agriculture to just over £200m in 1957/8, and around to £150m in 1960/1. However, spending on the other agricultural assistance measures increased steadily to stand at £75m in 1957/8 and £105m by 1960/1, so that these took an increasing share of the budget. Details of total spending on agricultural support over the period 1946–59 are given in Table 3.1, and this shows that expenditure on agriculture was greater than the effective subsidy (in grant equivalents) on the depreciation allowances through much of the 1950s, and that it dominated that on local employment measures under the Distribution of Industry Acts. Indeed, assistance to agriculture amounted to £236m in 1958/9, when the Treasury reported *total* expenditure on private sector subsidies (excluding tax allowances) to be only a little higher at £262m.[9]

INDUSTRIAL SUBSIDIES IN ABEYANCE

In the immediate aftermath of war, economic management was a haphazard and somewhat uncertain affair, but apart from occasional crises, the macroeconomic outcome was generally successful. The dollar shortage was overcome both through Marshall Aid and through efforts to hold down domestic consumption to promote exports, while investment was carried out at a high rate, encouraged by the policies of low interest rates and accelerated depreciation allowances. Inflation was kept in check, partly through food subsidies and later through fiscal policy as controls on consumer demand were relaxed. The system of stable exchange rates agreed at the 1944 Bretton Woods Conference also served to counter inflation, although this agreement was effectively violated in September

1949 when a run on the pound led to a devaluation of sterling against the dollar (Pollard, 1992). The conditions for sustained economic growth had evidently been put in place, and coupled with a high level of technical progress and application, economic growth averaged 2.8 per cent per annum between 1948 and 1960, compared with 1.3 per cent in the inter-war years.[10] The adoption of demand management policies in the UK and elsewhere undoubtedly played an important role, and while technical advance brought forward strong increases in productivity, such was the growth in demand that employment increased by 1.75 million between 1948 and 1960, despite a reduction of over 400 000 in the armed services.

Table 3.3 shows that this growth in employment was spread across many sectors of the economy, being felt most strongly in manufacturing and distribution, and in financial, professional and scientific services. However, some industries declined in employment, including agriculture, coal and transport. The newly nationalized coal industry lost jobs sharply, both as a result of reorganization and as the economy began to switch to oil from coal, while public transport declined as the private motor-car and civilian aircraft took an increasing share of passenger traffic, causing

Table 3.3 Employment by industry, 1948–60

Industry grouping (1958 SIC)	*1948 (000s)*	*1952 (000s)*	*1956 (000s)*	*1960 (000s)*	*1948–60 (000s)*	*(%)*
Agriculture, forestry and fishing	1 203	1 130	1 062	1 015	–188	–15.6
Mining and quarrying	885	883	866	774	–111	–12.5
Manufacturing	7 791	8 196	8 754	9 004	1 213	15.6
Construction	1 489	1 482	1 603	1 636	147	9.9
Public utilities	327	379	383	380	53	16.2
Transport and communication	1 837	1 808	1 771	1 721	–116	–6.3
Distributive trades	2 733	2 904	3 196	3 389	656	24.0
Financial services	445	462	498	566	121	27.2
Professional and scientific services	1 564	1 782	1 986	2 204	640	40.9
Government	1 352	1 312	1 279	1 293	–59	–4.4
Armed Forces	940	878	775	515	–425	–45.2
Misc. services	2 498	2 339	2 338	2 326	–172	–6.9
Total employment	**23 064**	**23 555**	**24 511**	**24 823**	**1 759**	**7.6**

Source: Feinstein (1972), table 129.

railway employment to fall by 200 000 between 1951 and 1966 (Cairncross, 1981). Within manufacturing, employment growth was not just restricted to the newer industries, but extended to the traditional industries of iron and steel, mechanical engineering and shipbuilding. Combined, these heavy industries had already increased numbers in employment by 500 000 between 1938 and 1948, partly because much capacity had been destroyed elsewhere, and a further 250 000 employees were to be added by 1960 (Feinstein, 1972). However, these older industries were once again to lose their competitive edge as more efficient plants were constructed elsewhere and as the advantage provided by the world dollar shortage eased, but this relative decline was not to become apparent until the 1960s, and in the meantime employment was maintained.

The Conservative government of 1951 continued its predecessor's commitment to demand management and, using monetary and fiscal policies, was generally able to fulfil the threefold macroeconomic objectives of full employment, low inflation and balanced trade. Unemployment was kept to around 300 000 (although fluctuations in employment were much greater because of the greater involvement of women in the labour market, who tended not to register as unemployed when out of work (Cairncross, 1981)) and the buoyancy of the iron and steel and heavy engineering industries produced regional unemployment rates which would have been considered desirable for the national economy in wartime planning, so that the economies of Wales and Northern Ireland actually grew faster than the national rate. As such, regional policy measures fell largely into abeyance, and expenditure under the Distribution of Industry Acts amounted to less than £40 million between 1951 and 1958 (see Table 3.1). Advance factory construction had ceased in 1947 in the wake of balance of payments difficulties, and from that time the pressure on firms to locate in the Development Areas had weakened, so that by 1951 IDCs were generally readily obtained in the South-East and Midlands (Odber, 1965).[11] Thus by the mid-1950s it became evident that the government viewed regional policy as a social measure to tackle locally high unemployment, rather than as the economic policy envisaged by some wartime reports.

The government continued to use changes in tax policy to stimulate and discourage investment, and in 1954 it replaced initial allowances with investment allowances available on plant, machinery, and industrial and agricultural buildings. However, strong economic growth and balance of payments difficulties in 1955 led to the withdrawal of investment allowances in February 1956 and to the restoration of the pre-existing initial allowances (Dow, 1970; Denton, 1976). Nevertheless, the principle of investment allowances had been established, and they were reintroduced in the late 1950s in a period of recession (see Table 3.2). Elsewhere, the government sought to ease control, and while most of the nationalized industries were retained in public ownership, the iron and steel industry was sold back to private industry under the 1953 Iron and Steel Act. Denationalization proceeded slowly, so that by 1957, 14 per cent of the shares were unsold, and by the time industry was renationalized in 1967 the firm of Richard Thomas and Baldwin had never been privatized. However, as the physical planning of the 1940s gave way to the fiscal and monetary policies of the 1950s, the nationalized industries were generally unable to fulfil the role given to them at the time of nationalization, and far from acting as the instrument to control the rest of industry, as Pollard (1992) notes, they were increasingly directed to become its servants.

THE END OF THE BOOM

Outside agriculture, industrial subsidies had largely fallen into disuse by the mid-1950s. Some profitability supports did remain, most notably coal prices, which were kept below market rates as a general subsidy to industry; the publicly-owned aviation industry, which continued to receive protection; and the defence and aircraft construction industries, which received indirect support through wartime equipment and government-built factories let at favourable rates. Civil aircraft and engine development projects also received support through the levies described below. Nevertheless, the considerable powers to disburse financial assistance which had been enacted in the immediate post-war period, and designed partly to offset any repetition of the economic instability that had characterized the aftermath of the First World War, were little used after 1948. Further, where measures were taken to promote the availability of finance to industry, these were usually provided in loan form and on a commercial basis. No doubt, the taking into public ownership of around one-fifth of industry had obviated the need for intervention in many cases, and while the government had equipped itself to influence industrial decision-making to a much greater extent, economic conditions dictated otherwise. The pre-war malaise did not return, and output and employment grew strongly after 1948, so that unemployment was generally kept below 2 per cent of the working population.

It was in the late 1950s that economic growth faltered, as the government deflated the economy to ease a balance of payments problem, and a recession followed, from 1957 to 1959. Prior to this time, the economy had absorbed job releases from the armed services, but with recession this was no longer the case. Unemployment increased by 197 000 (from 256 000) between 1956 and 1958, but the size of the working population contracted by 92 000 as women left the labour market, so that total employment shrank by 289 000 jobs. Of these, 162 000 were net job losses from the armed services and a further 123 000 net jobs were lost in textiles and clothing, although elsewhere employment remained relatively stable (see Table 3.3).[12] The policy response in 1958 was to raise twice the initial allowances to 30 per cent on plant and machinery and to 15 per cent on industrial buildings, and then in April 1959 to replace two-thirds of this assistance with investment allowances (see Table 3.2), so that the value of initial and investment allowances rose to £413m in 1958/9 (see Table 3.1). Industrial subsidies also emerged in this period, first to deal with specific industrial and agricultural problems, but later to tackle disparities in local unemployment as the national unemployment rate increased from 1.1 per cent in 1956 to 1.9 per cent in 1958.

SECTORAL INTERVENTIONS

Measures in 1957 included loans to cover the operating deficits of the railways, a compulsory levy on cinema projections for distribution to makers of British films (the Eady levy) and an extension of the life of the National Film Finance Corporation for a further ten years to aid film-making. However, it was the loss of jobs in cotton which promoted one of the first schemes of sectoral assistance. Falling demand and duty-free imports from the Commonwealth meant that the cotton industry had been in decline through the 1950s, and as in the 1920s the response of the government was to rationalize capacity.[13] Under the 1959 Cotton Industry Act it agreed to pay two-thirds of the cost of scrapping obsolete plant, conditional on a minimum level of rationalization being achieved, with the remainder being met by a compulsory levy on firms. The scheme also provided re-equipment grants of 25 per cent for a period of five years towards the cost of modernizing existing machinery, and buying and installing new equipment. Rationalization was achieved quickly, at a cost to the government of £10.6m by April 1962, but the take-up of re-equipment grants was slow, amounting to only £1.9m by this time against an estimated £9.3m. This was attributed to the reluctance of firms to invest during uncertain economic conditions (HC 191, 1962), but by April 1967 the industry had been reorganized into six major firms, and final expenditure on the re-equipment grants amounted to £13.4m.

More one-off interventions followed, for which further details can be found in Grove (1962) and Henderson (1962). In shipbuilding, the Cunard Company had been an early recipient of state aid, and then, as now, national prestige figured in the calculation to provide assistance, this time for the construction of a replacement for the *Queen Mary*. Partly to counter subsidies being paid to its competitors on the North Atlantic route, and amid considerable controversy, the government agreed in 1959 to provide £18m to Cunard in the form of a grant and a cheap loan out of a total cost of £30m.[14] A Bill was introduced and tenders for the new liner invited, but the affair ended in fiasco in 1961 when the Cunard Company postponed the scheme in the face of falling demand on its North Atlantic route, but in any case was found to be holding negotiations over the possibility of an air service. In many ways the Cunard project was reminiscent of pre-war efforts where assistance was given either for reasons of national prestige or to rationalize capacity, but other decisions to assist projects in iron and steel and the motor vehicle industry in the early 1960s represented a departure from this. In both cases, the aid was given to encourage firms to locate in the Development Areas, and while such powers had existed since the 1950 Distribution of Industry Act, these represented the first major use of this policy measure.

In the iron and steel industry, the need for a fourth continuous-strip mill had been recognized since the mid-1950s, but the decision to build two smaller strip mills again raised considerable controversy, and was bound up with the October 1959 general election. The decision was reached in 1958, and involved a £70m loan to the publicly-owned firm of Richard Thomas and Baldwin for a plant at Llanwern in South Wales and a £50m loan to the privately-owned firm of Colvilles for the Ravenscraig plant in Scotland; the latter on the grounds that no private company could otherwise obtain the requisite finance. The loans were made under the 1960 Iron and Steel (Financial Provisions) Act, and were broadly on the terms under which the nationalized industries were able to borrow from the Exchequer. In bringing the decision forward, no formal analysis was undertaken of the consequences of splitting the project into two smaller plants, and after much difficulty the Ravenscraig plant was wound down and eventually closed in 1992. The other case was the announcement in 1960 of assistance for the five largest motor vehicle manufacturers to help them undertake existing expansion plans in scheduled localities (Ford, Vauxhall and Standard-Triumph on Merseyside; BMC and the Rootes Group in Scotland). The exact details were not published, although £36m in loans and grants was offered to the motor industry by April 1961.[15] While the subsidy was important, Parsons (1988) notes that the government let it be known that it was prepared to forgo the expansions altogether if need be through the use of its development controls.

A major recipient of state assistance in the immediate post-war period was the civil aircraft industry, arising chiefly from the government funding of civil aviation and engine research and development work. Of those projects started between 1945 and 1951, the government committed £71m, and a further £17m on projects started by 1958 (see Table 3.1). The amount of funding was based on the estimated project costs, and while the government sought to recoup its contribution through a levy on sales, only £25m had been recovered by the mid-1960s (Cmnd 2853, 1965, Appendix G). Indirect support was also provided through public procurement and other means noted above, and this was probably of as much significance. Denton (1976) notes that between 1950 and 1964 payments to the aircraft industry from the government for defence equipment, for civil aircraft through state-owned airlines, and for research and development accounted for some 70 per cent of the total output of this sector.

Rising costs in aircraft development and construction prompted rationalization of the civil aviation sector in the late 1950s, and through mergers the number of producers fell from twenty-two in 1958 to nine in 1960 (Hartley, 1965). To reduce the cost advantages of American competitors, the Ministry of Aviation announced in early 1960 that Launching Aid would be given, whereby the government agreed to contribute up to fifty per cent of the estimated launching or pre-production costs of British civil aircraft and engine projects, which would be recouped through a levy on sales. Where the pre-production costs were shared equally between government and firm, the levy was 25 per cent of the difference between production costs and the selling price of the aircraft, but once the firm had recouped its pre-production costs the levy was raised to 75 per cent until the government's costs were covered (Hartley, 1974). Expenditure under Launching Aid was substantial, amounting to £747m up to the mid-1970s, of which £340m was in respect of aircraft and £407m for aero-engines, including £234m and £147m respectively for the Concorde and RB211 projects (Gardner, 1976). However, of the £747m, only £61m had been recovered by April 1974.

UNEMPLOYMENT AND THE DEVELOPMENT OF REGIONAL POLICY

As unemployment increased, the areas of locally high unemployment did not match the existing Development Areas neatly. Under the 1958

Distribution of Industry (Industrial Finance) Act, the scope of industrial assistance was widened, enabling loans and grants to be made to firms outside the designated Development Areas, to firms outside manufacturing, and for purposes not necessarily consistent with a proper distribution of industry, but which would reduce unemployment in areas where this was high. Thus, the Development Areas effectively became redundant in July 1958, when the first list of areas qualifying for assistance was announced (localities with at least 4 per cent of their working population 'persistently unemployed'). At this time, the Board of Trade also stated that a tighter policy would be followed in the granting of IDCs, and areas outside London and Birmingham with a low level of unemployment were effectively made subject to control. Coinciding with this, the construction of advance factories recommenced, and it was announced that rent relief was available on government-funded factories, and that local authorities in the scheduled areas could apply for grants towards derelict land clearance (Henderson, 1962).

Unemployment fell back by nearly 100 000 in 1959/60, but it was clear that local unemployment would remain a problem, and existing legislation, which had developed piecemeal, was consolidated under the 1960 Local Employment Act. Under this new legislation, the 1945 and 1950 Distribution of Industry Acts, parts of the 1947 and 1954 Town and Country Planning Acts, and the 1958 Distribution of Industry (Industrial Finance) Act were repealed, and while many of their provisions were retained, a number of important changes were made to policy (Thirlwall, 1966). First, Development Areas, which had become redundant, were replaced by Development Districts. These were defined as local Employment Exchange areas with actual or expected unemployment persistently at or above 4.5 per cent, and the President of the Board of Trade was given the power to vary or 'stop-list' these areas. An initial list of 166 Development Districts was announced in March 1960, which extended assistance to small parts of South East England and East Anglia (Townsend, 1977).

Second, building grants became available towards the cost of factory construction, enabling firms to construct a factory according to their own specifications. A problem for firms in the depressed areas was that the market value of industrial premises was generally below the construction cost, partly because of public provision, and so the building grant met 85 per cent of the difference between the construction cost and the estimated market value at the time of application. In practice, the subsidy varied between 12 and 28 per cent of construction costs, averaging 17 per cent across Development Districts, but because of its uncertain nature it was replaced by a standard building grant in 1963. This met 25 per cent of construction costs, including essential services and facilities (McCrone, 1969).

A third development under the 1960 Local Employment Act was that direct control over the provision of loans and grants was effectively taken away from the Treasury and given to the Board of Trade, although the Board still had to obtain Treasury approval for its broad financial activity and also for some assistance cases (see below). Financial assistance was made in consultation with an independent committee made up of part-time members, known as the Board of Trade Advisory Committee (BOTAC), which replaced the Treasury committee DATAC, formed under the 1934 Special Areas Act. Assistance was discretionary, and in addition to building grants, the powers under the 1945 and 1950 Acts to make loans and grants to encourage industrial development in scheduled areas and for the transfer of employees were essentially retained, although grants were generally only available to firms moving to the Development Districts, to cover the additional costs involved.[16] However, the conditions for assistance were weakened, so that an undertaking (be it a manufacturing firm, shop, commercial house or hotel) was required only to show that the project had good prospects of success. Previously, it was also necessary to show that the project did not have access to alternative sources of capital on reasonable terms, which, as Odber (1965, p. 341) notes, 'made the sieve of rather a fine mesh'.

Fourth, the effectiveness of assistance spending became a concern for the first time. As well as having regard for the proper diversification of industry in the local area, section 1 of the 1960 Act stated that the Board of Trade should pay attention to 'the relationship between the expenditure involved and the employment likely to be provided'. It was at this time that employment cost-effectiveness first gained usage, and it became an important intermediate objective in the disbursement of assistance. The Board of Trade sought a gross Exchequer cost-per-job (created or transferred) of less than £1500, with up to £2500 reasonable only in exceptional circumstances, and would pass cases to the BOTAC for consideration only if this initial test was passed. However, the Treasury considered £1000 for each job as being more normal, so that cases above this level had to be passed to the Treasury for approval. In the two years after the Act, expenditure averaged around £970 gross for each job, although substantial geographical variations existed.[17] By April 1962, expenditure under the Act amounted to £24.75m on loans, £1.14m on building grants and £0.73m on other grants, with a further £17.95m on the provision of land and buildings, so that loans continued to form the bulk of financial assistance expenditure. However, apart from a waiver of initial interest in some cases, the subsidy on these loans continued to be small, and was criticized by the House of Commons Estimates Committee as being 'somewhat limited' (HC 229 (1963) para. 29).

The 1960 Local Employment Act tightened the operation of Industrial Development Certificates in order to control industrial development outside the scheduled areas. The redrawing of the Assisted Area map also necessitated a reorganization of the industrial estate companies, since some estates were no longer in the scheduled areas. Three Industrial Estate Management Corporations were formed, one each for England, Scotland and Wales, to replace the five that had existed previously, in each of the major Development Areas. These Management Corporations continued to act as agents for the Board of Trade in the construction, letting and sale of factories, but their powers were heavily circumscribed, so that they undertook no role in advertising factory space, and the setting of rents was undertaken by the Valuation Office of the Board of the Inland Revenue through their local offices. Rents were charged at market rates, but this involved some subsidy because, as already noted, market rents did not provide an adequate return on construction costs. Some of the powers introduced under the 1945 Distribution of Industry Act were retained by the 1960 Act, so that, with Treasury consent, grants could be made to local authorities towards the cost of clearing derelict land (the grant rate was 50 per cent, but increased to 85–90 per cent in the 1963 Budget), and loans and grants could be made to various bodies to improve basic services. Also, support for the relocation of personnel under the 1950 Distribution of Industry Act was continued, so that the government would meet the removal and lodging expenses of key workers transferred to a new development in the Development Districts, and around five hundred people a year were assisted through this over the 1960s.

ASSISTANCE SPENDING IN THE 1950s

The plans for a more interventionist economic policy which had been set out during the war embraced Keynesian prescriptions, and involved an active fiscal policy to moderate demand, tax incentives to encourage investment, and an industrial transference programme to bolster and diversify industry in the areas vulnerable to unemployment. The intention was to avoid the economic instability that had followed the First World War, and while some effort was made to influence investment through initial allowances and the location of industry through development controls, the macroeconomic outcome was generally favourable, so that industrial subsidies were used in limited measure, and only seventy cases of assistance were made under regional policy before the policy was effectively put into abeyance in the mid-1950s. As in the pre-war period, all the cases of financial assistance were in the form of loans, although possibly available to more risky projects, and the initial allowances were not intended as a subsidy to firms, but rather to compensate them for the effect of inflation on the existing tax allowances of capital depreciation, which were assessed on an historical cost basis.

Once introduced, the initial allowances became a readily available means by which the government could give a boost to investment. The rate on these was doubled in 1949 in the case of plant and machinery, and in 1954 they were replaced by investment allowances which represented a more generous subsidy. However, in expenditure terms, by far the most important subsidy over this period was that afforded to agriculture. A new system of deficiency payments from 1952 had relieved the government of some economic planning, since the burden was now placed on farmers to obtain the best market price, with the guaranteed price determined only retrospectively. But this led to overproduction and the concern that the guarantees were supporting the more prosperous farmers, so that attention shifted away from encouraging production and towards efficiency and the support of more marginal farmers. The 1957 Agriculture Act introduced the Farm Improvement Scheme (which paid one-third of the cost of approved capital works to farm buildings, and encouraged the amalgamation of farms into viable units) and the 1959 Small Farmer Scheme (which paid grants to small farms and towards the cost of additional livestock, machinery, the ploughing-up of grassland and so on).

It was the recession from 1957 that first promoted the extensive use of subsidies to industry. The war and nationalization provided the precedent for large-scale intervention in industry, and the tax incentives and agricultural support provided precedents for large-scale subsidies to private industry, and these were now applied to the manufacturing sector. As in the 1920s and 1930s, attention turned to industrial rationalization, but now this involved grant and levy schemes, and one-off payments were made for the purpose of industrial expansion and employment. The near doubling of national unemployment and the re-emergence of disparities in local unemployment prompted the first major piece of legislation – the 1958 Distribution of Industry (Industrial Finance) Act – which enabled loans and grants to be given for purposes not necessarily consistent with the proper distribution of industry. This was extended in 1960 by the introduction of building grants, by the removal of direct control over loans and grants from the Treasury, and by the introduction of explicit grant-per-job targets.

In Table 3.4 we present figures for gross expenditure on industrial subsidies over this period of transition. Again, this shows that agriculture was

Table 3.4 The origins of post-war financial assistance, 1958–62 (£m, current prices)

Purpose of assistance	*1958/9*	*1959/60*	*1960/1*	*1961/2*
Agriculture				
Price guarantees	154.7	154.7	151.2	225.5
Lime and fertilizers	35.0	40.4	40.9	41.8
Ploughing grants	9.2	9.4	10.9	11.5
Calves	14.3	16.5	17.6	17.8
Farm improvements	3.3	6.6	7.8	9.2
Small farmers	0	1.1	5.9	7.1
Other	19.1	17.0	21.4	20.1
(Sub-total)	(235.6)	(277.8)	(255.7)	(333.0)
Horticulture	0	0	0.1	0.5
Fisheries	8.4	11.5	11.5	9.8
Forestry	0.7	1.1	1.2	1.3
Tax allowances	413	484	565	621
Local employment	3.6	8.4	11.7	32.8
Cotton industry	0	0.9	8.4	3.1
Civil aircraft	6.6	3.8	6.9	8.8
Shipping	0.3	0.3	0.3	0.3
Fuel conversion loans	0.6	0.3	0.07	0.02
Loans to Colvilles	0	0	15.0	20.0
Loans to building societies	0	13.1	34.3	44.8
Total assistance	**667**	**767**	**900**	**1 074**

Notes: The table gives details of gross expenditure on loans, grants and tax allowances. 'Other' agriculture assistance comprises assistance towards marginal production, tuberculosis eradication, field drainage, hill cattle and sheep, live-stock-rearing land, and water supply. The tax allowances include initial and investment allowances, and represent the gross amount paid, even though the subsequent writing-down allowance would have been reduced in the case of initial allowances. These calendar year figures have been apportioned to financial years. Grant equivalent expenditure for these tax allowances in each year are £277m, £336m, £404m and £452m respectively. Local employment assistance includes the cost of work to land and buildings, amounting to £1.5m, £5.5m, £7m and £11m for the respective years. The loans to building societies under the 1960 Building Societies Act were to enable the lending of money for the purchase of older houses.

Sources: HC 142 (1962); Cmnd 1965 (1963); Cmnd 2738 (1965); *National Income and Expenditure* (London: HMSO); HC 229 (1963).

the major recipient of state support, and further that the price guarantees continued to dominate, so that spending on the lime, fertilizer, ploughing-up grants and other efficiency measures was relatively small.[18] The other major element was the tax allowances, and spending on these increased over the period with the reintroduction of investment allowances in 1959. However, the table also shows that expenditure on the other measures increased steadily, from £19m in 1958 to nearly £120m in 1961. This includes the local employment measures referred to above, the loan to Colvilles for the Ravenscraig steel plant, assistance for the rationalization of the cotton industry, and the Launching Aid to the civil aviation industry, which was potentially recoverable through a levy on sales. Evidently, industrial assistance had become established as an instrument of industrial policy in this period of economic turbulence, and with further economic crises in the 1960s it was to spread to virtually every area of economic policy.

4 The Expansion of Industrial Assistance (1960s)

THE ECONOMIC CONTEXT

Economic growth resumed in 1959, but after heady growth and a trade imbalance in 1960, a credit squeeze followed from July 1961, and UK unemployment rose sharply, from around 300 000 in June 1961 to just over 515 000 in June 1963. The rise in unemployment was felt across all sectors of the economy, but was most severe in the engineering and metal industries, and in coal-mining, where supply had caught up with demand and pits were closed, particularly in North East England and Scotland (Table 4.1). Pockets of high unemployment once again appeared, and the hope expressed by the Treasury that spending on local employment measures would soon cease was dashed.[1] The measures taken in April 1963, both through the Budget and through legislation to extend the provisions of the 1960 Local Employment Act, were significant in two respects. First, they represented the beginnings of large-scale industrial assistance, separate from the depreciation allowances and the support afforded to agriculture. Second, spatially-based employment policy was to become as much concerned with inducements as with controls, so that the balance of policy shifted away from the 'stick' and towards the 'carrot'. Prior to 1963, local employment policy had operated largely through the mechanisms of Industrial Development Certificates to restrict development outside scheduled areas, and through various physical planning measures to ease the location of firms into these areas, and while financial assistance was available, this was relatively small in scale. Grants amounted to no more than £5m by April 1963, and were mainly used to reimburse the costs involved in transfer and to compensate for differences in factory construction costs above market value, while loans and rents on government-built factories carried very little actual subsidy (McCrone, 1969).[2]

TOWARDS A REGIONAL POLICY

The 1963 Budget increased the nationally available investment allowances to 30 per cent on plant and machinery, and to 15 per cent on buildings, and

Table 4.1 UK unemployment by industrial sector and region, 1957–69 (000s)

	1957	*1959*	*1961*	*1963*	*1965*	*1967*	*1969*
Sector							
Agriculture	14	22	13	17	12	15	17
Mining and quarrying	3	9	5	10	6	9	26
Manufacturing	108	197	94	176	85	190	161
Construction	39	64	40	76	46	94	105
Services	108	181	113	187	125	191	203
Not classified	25	45	34	50	31	40	48
Region							
South East and East Anglia	65	104	62	102	64	128	130
South West	15	25	13	20	16	27	34
Midlands	40	54	29	56	29	74	68
Yorkshire and Humberside	14	35	15	37	20	40	49
North West	42	88	41	84	43	69	69
North	18	42	26	57	28	49	62
Scotland	49	95	60	95	56	77	75
Wales	20	37	20	29	22	36	37
Northern Ireland	32	38	33	36	29	39	37
Total	**297**	**518**	**299**	**516**	**305**	**539**	**560**

Notes: The figures are for mid-year and include all unemployed persons on the registers of Employment Exchanges. Prior to 1963 the Yorkshire and Humberside figures relate to the East and West Ridings.
Source: *Ministry of Labour Gazette* (London: HMSO).

introduced geographically differentiated tax allowances for the first time, in the form of free depreciation on plant and machinery for firms located in Development Districts. Firms in these areas were allowed to write-off capital expenditure against tax at any rate they wished, which amounted to an interest-free loan. Under the 1963 Local Employment Act, a 10 per cent grant was also made available to firms in Development Districts towards the cost of plant and machinery, and the variable rate building grant was fixed at 25 per cent (see Table 3.2 on pages 36–7). This assistance was substantially more generous than that which had previously existed, and was available automatically to all firms in the designated areas. However, the employment link in the form of the 'grant-per-job' rule was retained, and the Board of Trade Advisory Committee (BOTAC) had to be satisfied that the project had good prospects of success. Selective assistance in the form of loans and grants under the 1960 legislation was also retained, and in making this the BOTAC had to take into account the fixed rate of assistance available for plant, machinery and buildings. It was this basic structure for regional assistance, of fixed-rate capital grants plus discretionary assistance, which was to form the basis for regional policy interventions for the next twenty years.

In the early 1960s, high levels of unemployment were perceived as being a local rather than a regional problem, and policy was focused on the Development Districts, rather than the Development Areas that had characterized earlier efforts. However, as well as the shift in policy from physical measures and controls to more active intervention through industrial subsidies, the nature of the unemployment problem was also undergoing revision at this time. A privately sponsored report on the Scottish economy synthesized much of the existing literature on regional development (Scottish Council, 1961), but also brought the issue of regional planning into the national economic debate at a time when the government had already demonstrated an increased willingness to become involved in the affairs of industry (Parsons, 1988). The thrust of the report's recommendations was that the government should concentrate policy on those areas with the potential for economic growth, rather than on localities with long-running problems of high unemployment, and as the recession intensified and areas of high unemployment again appeared, local unemployment came to be seen as a *regional* problem.

Lord Hailsham was appointed as Minister for North East England in 1962, and economic plans for this region and for Scotland were published in November 1963. These proposed the setting-up of 'growth zones' as points of focus for new economic activity, supported by a programme of infrastructure provision, but as McCrone (1969) notes, the implementation of these plans proved to be an odd compromise between the old and new policies, with the availability of assistance to these areas still dependent on the unemployment criterion. Further, the notion of a growth zone was never followed through, so that it was not until the extension of assistance in 1966 that the government became firmly committed to the idea of regional development. Nevertheless, some of the ideas were taken on board, and in the last year of the Conservative Party's term of office, a commitment was made to New Towns, the process of decentralizing government departments was started, and a Regional Development Division was established to produce economic plans for each region (Parsons, 1988).

THE INSTITUTIONAL FRAMEWORK

Output grew strongly in 1963, but government attention was drawn to the substantial loss of export markets, which had underlain repeated balance of payments crises and led to a 'stop–go' cycle and comparatively poor economic growth.[3] An initial recognition of this was the formation of the National Economic Development Council (NEDC) in 1961 as a forum for management, labour and the government to co-ordinate, monitor and seek methods of improving economic performance (Bailey, 1968). The NEDC lacked executive power, but the Labour government of October 1964 was more committed to economic planning, and in the same month as coming to power it established the Department of Economic Affairs (DEA). This produced a National Plan in September 1965, consistent with a 25 per cent growth in output over six years, which placed the emphasis on increased investment, to be achieved by encouraging nationalized industries to organise on the basis of the planned rate of growth; by switching government assistance from investment allowances to investment grants; and by encouraging new foreign investment in the UK (Cmnd 2764, 1965). While some of these ideas were later taken up, the DEA fell victim to further balance of payments difficulties and to Treasury resistance, and the Plan itself was effectively shelved in July 1966 (Opie, 1972).

A key element of the Labour government's economic policy was the promotion of science and technology, and several measures were taken to advance basic research and its application to industry. Initially, an Industrial Research and Development Authority was proposed, but in the event a Ministry of Technology ('Mintech') was set-up in October 1964, and the Department of Scientific and Industrial Research, which had been established in 1916, was replaced by Research Councils in science, medicine, agriculture and the natural environment to fund basic science and research. Mintech sought to redress perceived scientific and technological deficiencies in industry, focusing its efforts on four industries with the potential for growth: machine tools; computers; electronics; and communications. It took over several research stations from the Department of Scientific and Industrial Research, and played an increasingly prominent role in policy, acquiring functions relating to aircraft design and production from the Ministry of Aviation and various functions from the Ministry of Power. It also provided a general technical support to industry and financial assistance in limited measure to promote industrial research.

Mintech was supported by the National Research Development Corporation (NRDC), which was established in 1948 both to supervise the commercial exploitation of patents derived from government-sponsored research and to support promising research unable to attract private funding. NRDC was essentially self-financing, but had access to government loans and to interest relief on private funds, and the financial provision for its activities were increased from £10m to £25m in 1965, and to £50m in 1968. The Research Councils were created by the 1965 Science and Technology Act, under which the government was also able to provide support for projects by procurement and by purchasing preproduction models which could then be loaned free of charge to potential buyers (Denton, 1976). The Act was important in the government's support for more basic research and development, and was later much used to help fund the commercial exploitation of research work. Various measures under this Act were brought together in 1977 under the Product and Process Development Scheme, which proved to be a forerunner of the many technology-based investment schemes devised in the late 1970s and early 1980s. In some cases, the 1965 Act continued to provide the enabling legislation.

A measure which was to be of significance after the Labour government was returned in March 1966 was the announcement at the end of 1965 of an Industrial Reorganization Corporation (IRC). This came into being in December 1966, and was the latest manifestation of government attempts to reorganize and rationalize industry to achieve greater efficiency and international competitiveness. The IRC was made up of industrialists and overseen by the DEA, and its role was to promote rationalization and modernization schemes yielding benefits to the national economy in the form of increased exports, reduced imports and more rapid technological advance. It could draw on funds up to £150m, and under section 2 of the 1966 Industrial Reorganization Corporation Act was given powers to: acquire, hold and dispose of securities; form corporate bodies; make loans and provide guarantees; and acquire and place at the disposal of others premises, plant, machinery and other equipment.

The IRC was wound up in May 1971 and its assets transferred to the Secretary of State for the new Department of Trade and Industry, by which time it had involved itself in 76 projects, of which 53 were concerned with mergers and rationalization. Notable merger cases involved those between English Electric and Elliott Automation in 1967 (for which a loan of £15m was made); between Leyland Motor Corporation and British Motor Holdings in 1967–8 (which received a £25m loan); and the formation of Rank Hoffman Pollard in 1969. Financial assistance was later given to technically advanced companies, and in June 1970 a £10m loan was made to British Leyland to help modernize and expand production. In total, £120m in loans was disbursed by the IRC over its life, mainly to the motor vehicle, computer and shipbuilding industries, and it also took share capital, sometimes to assist with mergers. The balance of payments was an underlying motivation for many of the IRC's interventions, although in merger cases it often cited the maintenance of a significant British interest as a rationale.[4] However, its interventions occurred at a time when merger activity was already intense, and by receiving IRC approval firms could guard against an investigation by the Monopolies Commission, so it is difficult to assess its precise contribution (Mottershead, 1978; Young and Lowe, 1974).

Dissatisfaction with the performance of the IRC in its early years led the government to give general powers to itself through the 1968 Industrial Expansion Act. Under section 2 of this Act, loans, grants, guarantees and equity finance could each be made towards industrial investment schemes which: improved the efficiency and profitability of industry; or created, expanded or sustained productive capacity; or promoted or supported technological improvements in products or processes. These powers were sweeping, but a change of IRC management in 1967 and a more pro-active approach, meant that they were in fact used only twice, both times in 1968. The first case involved loans of £33m to Rio Tinto-Zinc and £30m to British Aluminium, to establish domestic aluminium smelting capacity at Anglesey and Invergordon. Loans were on fixed terms (7 per cent interest) over a long period, and in addition the firms claimed investment and building grants under regional policy. The second case involved a merger to form International Computers Ltd (ICL), representing a significant British presence in the computer industry. Over a five-year period, the government agreed £13.5m in grants for research and development and £3.5m in shares. In addition, a public procurement progamme accounted for around 10 per cent of ICL's output up to 1971.

INTERVENTIONS IN THE AIRCRAFT AND SHIPBUILDING INDUSTRIES

The civil aircraft industry received assistance in one form or another since the Second World War including Launching Aid from 1960 (see above), but following a number of cancellations of UK projects in favour of American alternatives, the 1964 Labour government established a Committee of Inquiry on the aircraft industry (Cmnd 2853 (1965) Plowden Report). This reported in December 1965, and recommended government intervention to secure a UK presence in both the civil and military aircraft industries. While the government favoured collaborative projects, it also made interventions to support particular companies in difficulty, including £22.5m in loans and grants to the Belfast company of Short Bros and Harland (later Short Brothers) from the Westminster and Stormont governments over 1961–7, and a convertible loan of £10m made through the IRC to Rolls-Royce in 1970 in respect of the troubled RB211 engine project. In total, this project was subsequently to receive government support totalling nearly £200m (see Table 4.2). Employment was an important consideration in the support for Short Bros and Harland, and this was also the case in the taking into public ownership of the subsequently failed Beagle light aircraft company in 1968 at a cost of £8m, but elsewhere the maintenance of a significant national interest and the relaxation of the balance of payments constraint were the main motivation.

The *Concorde* supersonic airliner collaborative project with France, which had been agreed in November 1962, was given the go-ahead in January 1965. The Plowden Report on the aircraft industry argued that the funding required and the risks involved were so great that private concerns were unwilling to contribute towards the development costs of this project, so that it was publicly-funded with arrangements made for a levy on sales of the production aircraft and spares (Cmnd 2853 (1965) Appendix G). Development over-runs on the project were substantial, amounting to around £760m against initial estimates of between £200m and £225m (all at 1970 prices), and the production costs could not even be covered. As Table 4.2 makes clear, support for the *Concorde* project exceeded that for the rest of civil aviation put together.

Table 4.2 Gross expenditure on aircraft assistance, 1962–71 (£m, current prices)

	1962/3	*1963/4*	*1964/5*	*1965/6*	*1966/7*	*1967/8*	*1968/9*	*1969/70*	*1970/1*
Concorde	–	–	–	19.2	34.1	44.5	55.7	50.9	64.5
RB211	–	–	–	–	–	0.5	10.2	28.2	15.2
Other	13.0	15.9	14.4	3.6	2.7	11.3	9.2	6.9	5.3
Total	**13.0**	**15.9**	**14.4**	**22.8**	**36.8**	**56.3**	**75.1**	**86.0**	**85.0**

Notes: The table shows gross expenditure and takes no account of recoveries by the Exchequer.
Sources: *Civil Estimates and Estimates for Revenue Departments*, Memorandum by the Financial Secretary to the Treasury, 14 April 1961, House of Commons Session 1961/2, and years thereafter up to 1964/5; Mottershead (1978), table 10.6.

The other industry that was to receive substantial injections of public money was shipbuilding. Increased international competition meant that the UK share of total merchant tonnage launched had fallen from 38 to 8 per cent between 1950 and 1966, and in 1959 the UK had become a net importer of ships. Reports commissioned by the government pointed to the more favourable credit terms offered by competitors, and in the early 1960s the policy response involved the commercial banks making loans available for orders from overseas, with Bank of England support. However, rising unemployment and the more interventionist stance of the government, meant that this was extended under the 1964 Shipbuilding Credit Act, which made £30m available in low-interest-rate loans under the Shipbuilding Credit Scheme, providing loans for up to 80 per cent of the cost of ships for British shipowners ordering from domestic yards. The limit on this was soon raised to £60m, and after Cunard negotiated a £17.6m loan under the scheme, the limit was raised to £75m, but closed for applications soon after.

The 1964 Labour government established a Committee of Inquiry to investigate the problems of shipbuilding (Cmnd 2937 (1966) Geddes Report), and this recommended the reorganization of the industry into four or five regionally based groups, with the provision of financial assistance as a temporary measure to help facilitate this. The Shipbuilding Industry Board (SIB) was established in May 1966 to give effect to these proposals, and under the 1967 Shipbuilding Industry Act it was enpowered to make assistance to shipbuilding and marine engineering firms as: grants towards consultancy advice on regrouping, up to a total of £150 000; grants to meet expenses incurred during reorganization, up to £5m (later increased to £20m by the 1968 Industrial Expansion Act); and loans and equity finance to assist with investment during amalgamation, up to a combined total of £32.5m. The equity finance could only be made with ministerial approval, and was politically contentious, but the government sought SIB representation in companies where substantial public funds were involved.

In reference to the earlier efforts to ease credit terms, the 1967 Shipbuilding Industry Act also provided guarantees on private loans for UK purchasers of domestically produced ships, where yards were re-organizing with a view to increasing efficiency. The guarantees were available on up to 80 per cent of the contract value of ships, totalling £200m (against the £30m suggested by the Geddes Report), but this limit was later raised to £400m and then to £700m, and under the 1972 Industry Act it was further raised to £1000m with the provision for an extension to £1400m. The Chairman of the SIB considered this to be the most beneficial measure in enabling shipbuilding to effect some recovery

(Hogwood, 1979). A recommendation of the Geddes Committee for indirect tax relief on domestic shipbuilding orders, amounting to 2 per cent of the gross value of completed ships, was given effect by the 1966 Finance Act, and known as Shipbuilders' Relief. Details of gross expenditure on the various shipbuilding measures is given in Table 4.3, showing that the major element of support were the loan guarantees, but that otherwise direct assistance was relatively modest.

By 1969, the SIB-sponsored merger had succeeded in combining the twenty-one of the twenty-seven shipbuilding undertakings covered by the Geddes Report into seven groups. One grouping was Upper Clyde Shipbuilders, which had been formed in August 1967. This faced substantial losses on contracts and difficulty in attracting new orders, and after further restructuring in 1969, it received £14m in assistance from the SIB, including £3m in equity (the SIB's only such payment). However, this was not sufficient to overcome financial difficulty, and after a further approach to the SIB for assistance was refused on the commercial grounds required by the Act, the government became directly involved in December 1969, providing £7m in loans 'in view of the wider economic, regional and Scottish considerations'. Other shipbuilding groups faced difficulties. In the case of Cammell Laird on Merseyside, the IRC became involved when this threatened the company's engineering activities, and it provided £5m of the £6.5m in early 1970 to hive-off and support the shipbuilding business. Harland and Wolff of Belfast was initially ineligible for SIB assistance because it was not involved in a regrouping scheme, but the 1968 Industrial Expansion Act lifted this requirement, and the company was saved from liquidation in 1970 by a £3.5m loan from the Northern Ireland government and £15m in assistance from the SIB. Other major recipients of SIB assistance were Swan Hunter, which received £5.8m for merger and entry into new markets; Scott Lithgow, with £5.2m for reorganization and new capital; and Yarrow, which received £1.6m (Booz-Allen, 1973).

The SIB was dissolved at the end of 1971, by which time £19.2m had been provided in grants, £18.6m in loans and £3m in share capital (see Table 4.3). Loans were made mainly for working capital and for capital equipment, while around £5m in grants was for entry into new markets, £4m for modernization and reorganization, and £9m to support Upper Clyde Shipbuilders and Harland and Wolff (HC 1365, 1972). However, the objective of the SIB to create a competitive shipbuilding industry through reorganization seems to have been largely unsuccessful, since the shipbuilding industry continued to receive substantial amounts of state aid in the early 1970s. The problem was that while economic conditions had

Table 4.3 Gross expenditure on shipbuilding assistance, 1962–71 (£m, current prices)

	1962/3	*1963/4*	*1964/5*	*1965/6*	*1966/7*	*1967/8*	*1968/9*	*1969/70*	*1970/1*
Shipbuilding Credit Scheme (R)	–	–	21.0	30.4	4.8	–	14.1	3.5	–
SIB grants	–	–	–	–	–	–	5.3	5.7	5.6
SIB loans and equity (R)	–	–	–	–	–	3.5	5.9	3.6	2.6
Guarantees (R)	–	–	–	–	–	92.0	198.4	227.2	235.2
Shipbuilders' Relief	–	–	–	–	0.4	3.5	3.6	3.7	4.7
Other	–	–	–	1.5	–	–	–	7.2	5.6
Total recoverable (R)	**0.0**	**0.0**	**21.0**	**30.4**	**4.8**	**95.5**	**218.4**	**234.3**	**237.8**
Total non-recoverable	**0.0**	**0.0**	**0.0**	**1.5**	**0.4**	**3.5**	**8.9**	**16.6**	**15.9**

Notes: The table shows gross expenditure, and in the case of the guarantees under the 1967 Shipbuilding Industry Act shows the guaranteed loan amount. The figures for guarantees are based on 80 per cent of the contract value of ships insured under the scheme, but this may overestimate the true position since not all of the guarantees may have been taken up. SIB = Shipbuilding Industry Board.

Sources: *Annual Abstact of Statistics* (London: HMSO); *Annual Reports and Accounts on the Shipbuilding Industry Act* (London: HMSO); Mottershead (1978), table 10.9.

brought about a sharp increase in orders after devaluation in 1967, subsequent inflation rendered many of these fixed-price contracts unprofitable.

INVESTMENT INCENTIVES

The aim of the National Plan to encourage capital investment was given effect by the August 1966 Industrial Development Act. This legislation also completed the transformation of regional policy that had begun in 1963. The government set out its intentions in the January 1966 White Paper *Investment Incentives* (Cmnd 2874, 1966), which gave a key role to manufacturing investment in achieving industrial expansion, faster modernization, greater output, and the strengthening of the balance of payments. Paragraph 2 of the White Paper stated that 'it is not simply a matter of building more factories and thereby creating more work places in total. The vital task is to accelerate the process of modernization, by which new equipment incorporating new techniques of production and making new products is introduced into the economy'. As a means of achieving this, free depreciation was ruled out on the grounds of cost, while investment allowances, which had been available since 1959, were ruled out for five reasons. First, it was argued that investment allowances were available on some items of equipment (for example, office furniture and carpets) with little or no relationship to productive investment. Second, that the initial effect of allowances was not felt until about eighteen months after the expenditure had been incurred. Third, that the benefit of an allowance accrued over a relatively long time period, and was uncertain in that it depended on future tax rates. Fourth, that investment allowances did not provide assistance to those firms which are not paying tax; and fifth, that the effect of an investment allowance had been reduced by the introduction of Corporation Tax at 40 per cent in April 1965, against the old 56 per cent Income plus Profits Tax (see Black, Cuthbert and Simpson, 1967).

Investment grants were thought to not suffer from any of these defects and were seen as the most direct means of stimulating investment. Under the 1966 Act they were introduced towards plant and machinery at a rate of 20 per cent, but at a higher rate of 40 per cent in newly designated Development Areas to 'give more powerful encouragement to a better geographical distribution of industrial growth'. For a while, the emphasis of regional policy shifted away from the amelioration of local unemployment, which had characterized the previous 'blackspot' approach, to the development of whole regions, and the replacement of Development Districts with Development Areas was a reflection of this.[5] These

Development Areas covered some 40 per cent of the land mass of Great Britain, comprising virtually all of Scotland, Wales and the Northern region of England including Cumbria, plus Merseyside, Cornwall and North Devon (see Figure A.2, in Appendix on p. 216). The advantage given to Development Areas in relation to financial assistance was that they reduced uncertainty, since firms could plan their investment in the knowledge that an area would not be stop-listed if unemployment fell below 4.5 per cent, as under the old approach.

Activities qualifying for the new investment grants were manufacturing, ship repair, construction, demolition, and mineral extraction, and the grants could also be made towards the provision of computers, hovercraft, ships and mining works. In the case of industrial buildings, an additional 10 per cent grant on top of the standard 25 per cent building grant was available to firms in the scheduled areas at Board of Trade discretion, and the existing 5 per cent initial allowance available nationally was increased to 15 per cent (Table 3.2). The new investment grants were not allowable against tax, so that the depreciation tax allowance was applied to capital expenditure net of grants, and in present value terms, the new system of subsidies and taxes was no more generous to firms in Development Areas relative to other areas than the one which immediately followed the 1963 Local Employment Act. However, the introduction of Corporation Tax in the intervening period had considerably diminished the effective subsidy under the 1963 legislation, and the new measures restored this (Bird and Thirlwall, 1967). Without assistance and under reasonable assumptions, the annual tax allowance against depreciation amounted to 28.2 per cent of the cost of plant and machinery in present value terms, but with the 20 per cent grant this rose to 40.7 per cent and with the 40 per cent grant to 53.1 per cent, so the real subsidy on this capital was around 12 and 25 per cent respectively. For buildings, the present value of annual depreciation allowance was 17.8 per cent, but with the 15 per cent initial allowance this rose to 22.0 per cent, and in Development Areas to 41.9 per cent where there was a combined 25 per cent building grant and 15 per cent initial allowance, giving effective subsidies towards the cost of buildings of 4.2 and 24.1 per cent respectively.[6]

Table 4.4 shows that gross expenditure on investment grants was substantial, at about £500m in the late 1960s, of which around £100m was in respect of the extra 20 per cent grant rate available in the Development Areas (see Table 4.5). In terms of grant equivalents, spending on these investment grants was around £330m at this time, compared with £450m on investment allowances and £75m on initial allowances. This compares with total spending on tax allowances in the early 1960s of around £700m

Table 4.4 Gross expenditure on national assistance, 1960–71 (£m, current prices)

	1960/1	*1961/2*	*1962/3*	*1963/4*	*1964/5*	*1965/6*	*1966/7*	*1967/8*	*1968/9*	*1969/70*	*1970/1*
Initial allowances (R)	185	190	220	230	254	200	241	293	338	411	1044
Investment allowances	380	432	446	556	636	542	164	33	5	–	–
SEP	–	–	–	–	–	–	40.3	129.9	27.4	1.4	0.2
SET refund	–	–	–	–	–	–	261.0	706.7	841.9	1253.3	1363.5
Investment grants	–	–	–	–	–	–	–	217.1	340.8	417.1	401.9
Total recoverable (R)	**185**	**190**	**220**	**230**	**254**	**200**	**241**	**293**	**338**	**411**	**1044**
Total non-recoverable	**380**	**432**	**446**	**556**	**636**	**542**	**465**	**1087**	**1215**	**1672**	**1766**

Notes: The table shows gross expenditure and takes no account of recoveries to the Exchequer. Figures for initial and investment allowances are reported on a calendar year basis, and so have been apportioned to financial years. Accelerated depreciation allowances have been deducted and are included in the figures for regional assistance as an explicit regional policy measure.
SEP = Selective Employment Premium; SET = Selective Employment Tax.
Sources: *National Income and Expenditure* (London: HMSO); *Financial Statistics* (London: HMSO); *Annual Reports on the 1966 Industrial Development Act* (London: HMSO).

(all at current prices), so that the switch from allowances to grants roughly maintained the level of support for investment.

An advantage given to investment grants over allowances was that they were available to all firms, including new and small firms which were not making taxable profits, but for firms in the Development Areas which were earning taxable profits the grants were only half as generous in the first two years as the pre-existing free depreciation (Wilson, 1967). Further, there was a delay in processing grant applications, which initially averaged fifteen months, but which was later brought down to twelve months (HC 329, 1969). In addition to the investment grants, discretionary loans and grants under the Local Employment Acts were retained, but, as Table 4.5 shows, combined spending on these was generally less than £20m per annum. Industrial Development Certificates, which had been extended to all industrial developments above 1000 square feet in 1964, were restored to their previous level in 1966, except in the south East and Midlands, where the limit was 3000 square feet. From 1965, permits were also required in the London region for office developments above 3000 square feet, known as Office Development Permits (ODPs).

DIFFICULTIES WITH INVESTMENT GRANTS

The 1966 Industrial Development Act sought both to promote faster economic growth and to maintain the effective subsidy in favour of the scheduled areas. Investment grants were seen as being the most effective means of achieving this, but in another respect the Act severely weakened the effectiveness of policy. Under the Local Employment Acts, BOTAC approval was sought, to ensure the commercial viability of projects, and an employment link was maintained through a grant-per-job limit, but the new investment grants had neither of these elements. This reflected the shift of policy towards economic growth objectives, but ultimately it was to undermine regional policy in particular, which was to be judged by its impact on employment. In fact, the shift in policy objectives in 1966 proved to be only temporary, and with a further squeeze on economic activity in July 1966, and a rise in unemployment from 290 000 in June 1966 to 540 000 a year later (see Table 4.1), the government was forced to superimpose the 'blackspot' approach on to the new system of regional incentives.

Special Development Areas were designated in November 1967, mainly in coal-mining localities, which as a result were not dissimilar to the old Special Areas. In these areas. additional assistance was available in the

Table 4.5 Gross expenditure on regional assistance, 1960–71 (£m, current prices)

	1960/1	*1961/2*	*1962/3*	*1963/4*	*1964/5*	*1965/6*	*1966/7*	*1967/8*	*1968/9*	*1969/70*	*1970/1*
Building grants	0.1	1.0	1.7	1.4	5.4	9.7	12.6	16.7	17.5	21.5	29.0
Discretionary loans	4.6	20.1	12.6	7.5	14.1	9.0	13.4	8.5	17.7	18.4	16.2
Discretionary grants	0.03	0.7	2.5	1.4	1.1	0.3	0.8	0.8	1.2	1.1	0.9
Plant/machinery grants	–	–	–	0.02	0.8	2.5	4.4	5.1	1.3	1.6	0.5
Accelerated depreciation	–	–	–	–	3.0	45.0	25.0	4.0	–	–	–
Investment grants	–	–	–	–	–	–	–	76.9	89.1	98.7	123.1
REP	–	–	–	–	–	–	–	35.0	103.3	108.8	109.2
SEP	–	–	–	–	–	–	–	–	25.6	27.1	7.4
Operational grants	–	–	–	–	–	–	–	–	–	–	0.2
Total	**4.7**	**21.8**	**16.8**	**10.3**	**24.4**	**66.5**	**56.2**	**147.0**	**255.7**	**277.2**	**286.5**

Notes: The table shows gross expenditure and takes no account of recoveries to the Exchequer. The figures for investment grants give amounts over and above the standard grant amounts available nationally at 20 per cent, later increased temporarily to 25 per cent. REP = Regional Employment Premium; SEP = Selective Employment Premium.
Sources: *Annual Reports on the Local Employment Acts* (London: HMSO); *Annual Reports on the 1966 Industrial Development Act* (London: HMSO); *Financial Statistics* (London: HMSO); Begg *et al.* (1975).

form of a standard building grant at 35 per cent, with low interest rate loans on the balance of building costs; operational grants at 10 per cent for three years calculated on the cumulative expenditure on the acquisition of eligible buildings, plant and machinery (net of grants); and rent-free periods on government factories up to a period of five years. An attempt to reflate the national economy led to an increase in the investment grant rate by 5 per cent across the country from January 1967. This was a temporary measure, and it meant that the investment grant rate in the Assisted Areas stood at 45 per cent for plant and machinery, but only 15.1 per cent in present value terms above that available elsewhere.

In this period, shipbuilding was receiving increased government support, and as well as the special assistance it was able to claim investment grants under the 1966 Industrial Development Act. However, the concern that foreign-owned firms incorporated in Britain were able to attract these grants meant that they were later restricted to those yards not having a detrimental effect on the UK balance of payments under 1970 Industrial Development (Ships) Act (Denton, 1976). Further exploitation of the grants by shipbuilding firms was uncovered by the Public Accounts Committee (HC 297, 1970), and the May 1970 Rochdale Report (Cmnd 4337, 1970) argued for the reintroduction of allowances in place of investment grants in the case of shipbuilding. This not only recognized that ships needed few UK resources, either in construction or operation, but that with 20 per cent investment grants and the credit readily available on up to 80 per cent of the cost of a ship through the guarantee scheme, shipbuilding firms had to put up little of their own money. Investment grants were abandoned altogether shortly afterwards, but little was made of the recommendation when they were reintroduced in 1972, and between April 1967 and March 1978, £609m was paid out in investment grants for shipbuilding, of which £475m was for ships constructed outside the UK.[7]

EMPLOYMENT TAXES AND EMPLOYMENT PREMIUMS

The attempts to marry faster economic growth with improvements in the balance of payments were generally unsuccessful, and in the mid-1960s frequent speculative runs on sterling forced the government into devaluation in November 1967 (Blackaby, 1978). As a deflationary measure to tackle an emerging trade imbalance and to raise revenue for expanded public sector activity, the Selective Employment Tax was announced in the 1966 Budget. This was levied as a flat-rate surcharge on employers' National Insurance contributions with broad distinctions relating to age and sex. It also sought structural adjustment of the economy towards those industries with a relatively high export content, and to this end the tax was refunded to all industries except services and construction, with a premium known as the Selective Employment Premium being paid at 37.5p per male worker, and a smaller sum for women and juveniles, payable to manufacturing firms and to institutions engaged in scientific research related to manufacturing (Hutton and Hartley, 1966). It was thought that the Selective Employment Tax would raise productivity, if only for the reason that firms would seek to maintain their service, but with less labour, which had become relatively more expensive (Reddaway *et al.*, 1973). The effect of the Selective Employment Premium on exports was calculated to be small, with the National Institute for Economic and Social Research estimating this as virtually zero (Price, 1978). Restrictions accompanying the devaluation meant that the premium was withdrawn for firms outside the Development and Special Development Areas just over a year after introduction, and abolished everywhere in 1971. Payments of the Selective Employment Premium were relatively small, reaching £130m in 1967/8 and then falling away (see Table 4.4), but the refund from Selective Employment Tax was substantial, running at over £1000m in the late 1960s.

The recession from mid-1966 led the government to doubt the effectiveness of its new regional policy as an employment measure, and in April 1967 a memorandum, which came to be known as the 'Green Paper', argued that 'it is impossible to foresee more than a limited reduction in the disparity in unemployment levels between the Development Areas and the rest of Britain, or a growth in employment fast enough to cut down migration from the Development Areas to a great extent' (Department of Economic Affairs, 1967). The Green Paper proposed a Regional Employment Premium for firms in the Development Areas, along the same lines as the Selective Employment Premium, which at that time was available nationally. This was seen as being more effective than infrastructure provision, for example, which would draw in labour and materials from outside the assisted areas. The government's view was that the subsidy would lead to greater competitiveness, rather than feed into increased prices or wages, so that 'a reduction in the disparity is likely to be achieved without adding effectively to inflationary pressures or leading to any worsening in the balance of payments' (para. 7). As such, the government believed that the subsidy could be self-financing in that it would not require any increase in taxation, and indeed, depending on the degree of success, could even lead to a reduction in taxation (Cmnd 3310 (1967) para. 29).

The Regional Employment Premium (REP) was introduced in September 1967, with firms in Development Areas able to claim this in respect of those employees eligible for the Selective Employment Premium. It was made at £1.50 per week for every full-time male employee, 75p per week for women and boys, and 47.5p per week for girls (and at half these rates for part-time employees), and was payable in addition to the Selective Employment Premium. The government proposed that the REP should run for a period of seven years; an initial proposal for a five-year duration was thought insufficient to encourage the setting-up of new firms. The combined subsidy was put at 8 per cent of the wages bill (McCrone, 1969), with REP put at about 7 per cent of average earnings of male manual workers (Moore, Rhodes and Tyler, 1977) or equivalent to a 5–6 per cent reduction in efficiency wages in manufacturing industry, or a 2 per cent devaluation of UK goods as a whole (Kaldor, 1970). Spending on REP was substantial, amounting to over £100m in the first full year, with an additional £25m on the Selective Employment Premium in the Assisted Areas (see Table 4.5). However, REP seems to have been an expensive way of creating jobs, and the uncertainty over its duration probably meant that it had a limited impact on investment, while its effect on employment is generally thought to have dissipated soon after it was terminated.

REP was maintained at around £100m for the first five years after introduction, and then increased, but the Selective Employment Premium was withdrawn from Development Areas in 1970 to pay for a £20m package of assistance for areas contiguous to the Assisted Areas. These 'grey areas', including parts of Lancashire, Yorkshire, Humberside and South Wales, made representations arguing that they would be adversely affected by the introduction of REP, and a government committee was established in 1967 (Cmnd 3998 (1969) Hunt Committee), leading to the designation of seven small Intermediate Areas under the 1970 Local Employment Act. In these areas, 25 per cent (and exceptionally 35 per cent) building grants and removal assistance for key workers was made available. The government also funded some factory construction and made 75 per cent grants available to local authorities for derelict land clearance. Under section 2 of the 1970 Act, the minister could further designate Derelict Land Clearance Areas in which assistance could be given towards the clearance of derelict land, and in 1970 parts of the North West, Yorkshire, Humberside and the north Midlands were designated as such.

A further measure to improve the balance of payments was loan and grant assistance under the 1969 Development of Tourism Act for the construction and improvement of hotels in the Assisted Areas. The scheme was available to projects commencing before April 1971, but open-ended, so that total expenditure of £57m far exceeded initial estimates. The Act also established the English, Scottish and Welsh Tourist Boards, and in addition to administering the above scheme, these Boards disbursed financial assistance to projects which provided or improved tourist amenities and facilities.

FURTHER PROTECTION FOR AGRICULTURE

The commitment to reduce trade restrictions under the General Agreement on Tariffs and Trade did not take effect until well into the 1960s, and in the 1950s and early 1960s non-Commonwealth trade was heavily protected. The direction and composition of British trade reflected this, with around a half of import and export trade conducted with Commonwealth countries, and for this the system of low tariffs known as Commonwealth Preference was in operation. It was mainly from these Commonwealth countries that Britain drew its agricultural imports, and as a result the domestic sector was particularly susceptible to fluctuations in world prices. Coupled with increased domestic farm output, this meant that the cost of open-ended support for agriculture through guaranteed prices was becoming erratic and expensive (Morgan, 1978), and in the early 1960s the government set about reforming agricultural support.

In March 1963 it was announced that the amount of domestic output qualifying for guaranteed prices would be restricted to 'standard quantities', to be given effect by the 1964 Agriculture and Horticulture Act. This legislation made provision for the introduction of minimum import prices to be enforced by levies on imports below the minimum price, but in practice a series of *ad hoc* measures came into force. Standard quantities were introduced for wheat and barley only, and the minimum import price was introduced only for major cereals. Negotiations in respect of similar measures for beef and lamb failed, while the volume of pig-meat imports was regulated by negotiated quotas (Morgan, 1978). However, the standard quantities for wheat and barley were later dropped, as the 1965 National Plan set targets to replace £250m of agricultural imports annually, which required additional output. Under the 1967 Agriculture Act, subsidies to improve basic services in rural and upland areas were to be administered by a Rural Development Board, and this supplemented a range of inducements to small horticultural and other farm businesses under the 1964 Act.[8] As a result, the pattern of assistance continued to shift away from profitability supports through price guarantees to the various incentive schemes, which, as a proportion of total agricultural assistance, increased from 44 per cent in 1960 to 64 per cent in 1970.

THE GROWTH OF INDUSTRIAL SUBSIDIES

The use of industrial subsidies as an instrument of policy became firmly established in the 1960s, and in Figure 4.1 we present grant equivalent estimates of this expenditure at constant 1980 prices. This shows an approximate fourfold increase in spending on industrial subsidies over the course of the 1960s, and in particular shows the dramatic rise in spending from 1967/8 following the introduction of the Selective Employment Tax refund. However, if this refund is excluded, then a rather different pattern emerges of a broadly constant level of expenditure over the decade, so that other than the introduction of this employment measure, the main

Figure 4.1 Expenditure on industrial subsidies in the 1960s

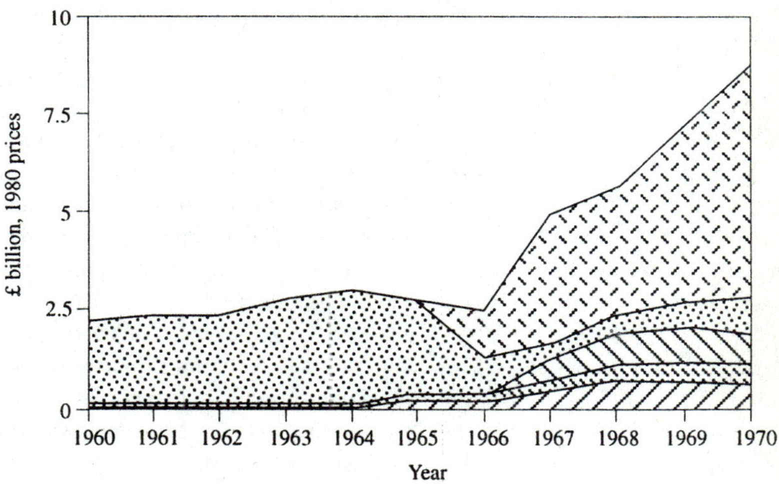

Notes: The figure shows expenditure in grant equivalents at constant 1980 prices. Financial years are shown as calendar years.

Key: Regional assistance; Sectoral and firm specific aid; National investment grants; Depreciation allowances; National employment subsidies

Source: Wren (1996b).

change was in the composition of assistance. This includes the withdrawal of the depreciation allowances for plant and machinery, to be replaced by nationally and regionally available investment grants, and the expansion of the assistance going to the civil aviation and shipbuilding industries.

As an explanation of these changes, the unsteady economic growth of the late 1950s and early 1960s was undoubtedly important, with repeated balance-of-payments crises, and unemployment which reached more than half a million at the time of recession. However, rather than abandon the measures that had failed to yield economic stability, the policy response was to sharpen their operation, so that relatively expensive investment allowances were replaced by a system of investment grants and a redistributive role was added to the stability objective of policy. This was coincident with a greater commitment to economic planning, and regional aid was increased in line with national economic growth objectives. A further worsening of conditions led to yet more intensification of policy, but this increased intervention was made within the context of an expansion of public expenditure, which as a proportion of national output grew from 37 per cent in 1964 to 44 per cent in 1967.

5 The Retrenchment and Reinvigoration of Industrial Subsidies (1970–4)

THE CUTTING OF SUBSIDIES

By June 1969 it had become apparent that the government had at last achieved a substantial balance of payments surplus, but this was as much due to devaluation as to any consequence of industrial policy. The Conservatives inherited this position a year later, but also inherited sluggish economic growth, wage inflation which reached 12–13 per cent during 1970 and unemployment at more than half a million (see Figure 5.1). The pre-election pledge was to transform the economy through increased efficiency in public services and by placing the onus on employers to resist excessive wage demands. The government also sought

Figure 5.1 Unemployment and inflation, 1969–76

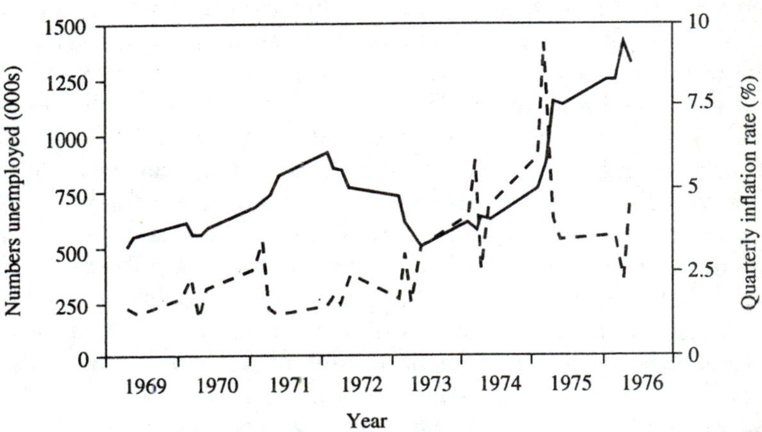

Notes: Unemployment figures (left scale) are for Great Britain and are unadjusted The inflation figures (right scale) are derived from the Retail Price Index and give quarterly inflation rates.

Key: Unemployment ——— Inflation - - -

Source: *Economic Trends* (London: HMSO).

to reduce non-discretionary assistance and profitability supports, and this was made abundantly clear by the then Secretary of State for Trade and Industry, who in Parliamentary debate in 1970 stated that 'the vast majority lives and thrives in a bracing climate and not in a soft, sodden morass of subsidised incompetence ... We believe that the essential need of the country is to gear its policies to the great majority of people, who are not lame ducks, or do not need a helping hand'.[1]

As such, a mini-Budget in October 1970 was more concerned with reductions in industrial subsidy than with general economic policy, abolishing the national and regionally differentiated investment grants on plant and machinery, along with the deficiency payments made to agriculture. It was announced that the Regional Employment Premium would be phased out, but that the original commitment would stand, and the scheme would terminate, after seven years, in 1974. The Budget also announced the repeal of the 1968 Industrial Expansion Act, which, along with the repeal of the Industrial Reorganization Corporation Act, was given effect by the 1971 Industry Act. There was in addition a shift in the financial support for local authority housing away from rents and towards supporting individuals, and subsidies to London commuter trains were withdrawn.

The October 1970 White Paper, *Industrial Incentives*, stated the view that 'the investment grants scheme has involved a high public expenditure cost without achieving its objectives' (Cmnd 4516, 1970, para. 2). In addition, it noted three specific disadvantages of these grants. First, investment grants benefit firms whether or not they are making profits, and can therefore result in uneconomic investment. Second, the previously existing scheme discriminated against the service sector, which was ineligible; and third, the scheme had imposed a considerable administrative burden, requiring the employment of around a thousand staff at an annual cost of over £2m. To restore the cash-flow of firms, Corporation Tax was cut by 2.5 percentage points and accelerated depreciation allowances were reintroduced. A first-year writing-down allowance of 60 per cent was introduced nationally for expenditure on new and secondhand plant and machinery, which, unlike the previously existing initial allowances, was not available in the first year in addition to the annual writing-down allowance and so was equivalent to a 35 per cent initial allowance.[2] This was extended to the service sector, and for mining, manufacturing and construction firms located in the Assisted Areas the allowance was increased to 100 per cent for new plant and machinery, to encourage the location and expansion of firms in these areas.[3]

While the assistance for plant and machinery was cut substantially, the much smaller support towards new industrial buildings was retained and strengthened, so that the initial allowances for industrial buildings were increased to 40 per cent in Development Areas (DAs) and Intermediate Areas (IAs), and to 30 per cent elsewhere, while building grants were increased to 45 per cent in Special Development Areas (SDAs) and 35 per cent in DAs, but kept at 25 per cent in IAs (see Table 3.2 on pages 36–7). The rate on operational grants, which had been available in SDAs since 1967 towards plant, machinery and building costs over the first three years, was increased to 20 per cent for wage and salary costs over the same period, but the discretionary assistance available under the Local Employment Acts remained intact (McCallum, 1979). In agriculture, the price guarantees were replaced by levies on imported food, and expenditure on the deficiency payments fell sharply, later reflecting Britain's entry to the Common Market.

INDUSTRIAL DISENGAGEMENT AND THE HELPING HAND

The policy of industrial disengagement was demonstrated in September 1970 when the subsidy to the Palmers ship repair yard at Hebburn on Tyneside was discontinued, and again in November 1970, when the government refused a bridging loan to the Mersey Docks and Harbour Board, but over the next year the resolve of the government was to be severely tested.

The first such case was Rolls-Royce, which had entered into fixed-price contractual obligations with the Lockheed Company in 1968 to supply its as yet not fully developed RB211 engine. Subsequent technological and design problems put a severe financial strain on the company, and the Industrial Reorganization Corporation became involved, providing a £10m convertible loan in May 1970 and promising a further £10m loan during 1971. The new government had exempted the aircraft industry from its non-interventionist stance, and in November 1970 a £60m loan package was to put together to complete the programme, including a government loan of £42m and a further £10m from the Bank of England.[4] But with further technical difficulties, the company petitioned for receivership in February 1971, and rather than see a 'lame duck' go under, the government provided a helping hand, on the grounds that the company's involvement in collaborative defence projects meant that it was too important to sacrifice. The aero-engine division of Rolls-Royce was taken into public ownership and the Lockheed contract renegotiated, but the estimated total cost of government involvement in the RB211 project, including Launching Aid at an exceptional rate of 70 per cent, was put at nearly £200m at current prices (Mottershead, 1978; Hayward, 1989).

The second case where the government at first resisted intervention, but subsequently became heavily involved, was Upper Clyde Shipbuilders. This company had been in financial difficulty since its formation in 1967, and when the government refused assistance after a further approach, the company petitioned for liquidation in June 1971. Credit guarantees in respect of the yard had already been suspended pending financial reconstruction, and in February 1971 a £4.5m loan was provided to help hive-off Yarrow Shipbuilders for the importance of its defence work. A group of experts was commissioned to examine the company's position, and this recommended that two of the four yards of Upper Clyde Shipbuilders should be combined to form Govan Shipbuilders, but that the other two yards, Clydebank and Scotstoun, should be closed. The recommendation was accepted, but after industrial action and several attempts to find a buyer, the government paid £10m in loans and grants to the Marathon Company of Texas to take over the Clydeside yard in order to supply the offshore oil industry. It also injected £35m, of which £17m was for losses on existing contracts, to form the new Govan Shipbuilders which included the Scotstoun yard (Broadway, 1976).

The consequences of allowing Upper Clyde Shipbuilders to collapse had evidently been too great and, coupled with the Rolls-Royce case, it precipitated a reversal in industrial policy. Subsequent assistance was forthcoming to the shipbuilding industry from late 1971, including £3.5m in Shipbuilding Industry Board grants to the financially troubled Harland and Wolff in Northern Ireland from 1970, and £4m in share capital from the Northern Ireland government in July 1971. Further grants of £13.9m were made to Harland and Wolff in May 1972 when a £35m modernization programme was announced involving £23.5m in central government loans and grants. Cammell Laird on Merseyside received £3m in loans in each of August 1971 and April 1972, and £14m in loans was agreed in September 1972 for modernization. The Local Employment legislation provided powers for assisting the Marathon Company, but most payments were made under the section 7 of the 1972 Industry Act (see below), and this Act was later used to take a substantial shareholding in the Marathon Company and to formalize government intervention in relation to the shipbuilding industry.

THE POLICY REVERSAL

Economic conditions continued to deteriorate from early 1970, and in early 1971 the government responded to rising unemployment by designating several new Special Development and Intermediate Areas, and by raising the rate on operational grants to 30 per cent. An attempt to stimulate the national economy was made in the April 1971 Budget, which reduced Corporation Tax and announced the gradual replacement of Selective Employment Tax (SET) and Purchase Tax with Value Added Tax (VAT), but these had little immediate impact and unemployment came increasingly to dominate economic policy. A series of reflationary measures followed, including an increase in housing improvement grants in June 1971 and a £100m programme of public works for the Assisted Areas announced in July 1971 to include capital spending on roads, schools and health facilities. Free depreciation was extended to service sector firms in DAs and SDAs, and the first-year writing-down allowances on plant and machinery for firms outside the Assisted Areas was increased from 60 to 80 per cent for expenditure incurred before August 1973. Interest rates were lowered twice during 1971, and in September 1971 ceiling limits on lending were removed, leading to a sharp increase in personal-sector borrowing. The government also became increasingly involved in bailing out the shipbuilding firms noted above, which by and large were located in the areas of high unemployment.

These measures failed to halt the rise in unemployment, which by March 1972 stood at more than 900 000 (see Figure 5.1). The government's anti-inflationary strategy also came apart, as the increase in unemployment did little to moderate private-sector wage increases, while the determination to reduce successive public-sector wage increases had been broken by the miners' strike. The latter prompted the government to control wage increases, first through negotiation and then through statutory intervention, but it was unemployment which promoted the most dramatic turnaround in policy. In early 1972 the government set out its plans for new measures to tackle regional unemployment, to formalize its support for industries and firms in difficulty, and to give a boost to manufacturing investment. Industrial subsidies were to play a key role in this, which contrasted strongly with earlier pronouncements, but the policy reversal occurred at exactly the time that previous measures appeared to be taking effect, and unemployment was to fall back by nearly half a million over the next eighteen months.

The proposals to stimulate industrial growth and to tackle regional unemployment were set out in the March 1972 White Paper, *Industrial and Regional Development* (Cmnd 4942, 1972), and given effect by the 1972 Finance Act and the Industry Act of August 1972. The White Paper stated the fourfold objectives of this programme: 'to promote and sustain faster economic growth; to secure the expansion and modernisation of

British industry; to attack the continuing and serious problems of regional imbalance; and to assist industry to meet the challenge of Europe' (para. 1), of which the 'overriding purpose is to attain a sustained and high rate of national economic growth' (para. 5). To facilitate this, the Budget proposed that the existing free depreciation on plant and machinery in Assisted Areas be available throughout the country and apply equally to new *and* secondhand equipment (so that the first-year writing-down allowance was increased to 100 per cent everywhere), and that the 40 per cent initial allowance on buildings to be similarly extended to the rest of the country.[5] Of course, this meant that the differential subsidy in favour of the Assisted Areas was eroded substantially (Scholefield and Franks, 1972), and to counter this the White Paper proposed the reintroduction of investment grants, which would replace the previously existing building and operational grants. The White Paper also proposed that the Regional Employment Premium should be phased out gradually from September 1974 rather than terminated suddenly at this date.

THE NEW REGIONAL POLICY

Regional Development Grants (RDGs) were introduced for capital expenditure on plant, machinery and buildings incurred after 22 March 1972, even though as little as eighteen months previously the government had ruled out investment incentives as being expensive and ineffective. The grants were available to firms engaged in mining, manufacturing or construction, and at rates of 22 per cent in SDAs, 20 per cent in DAs, and for buildings only at 20 per cent in IAs and Derelict Land Clearance Areas, but for a period of two years only in the case of the latter. Like the previously existing investment incentives, there was no formal direct link to job creation, but an important difference was that RDGs were allowable against tax. This meant that on plant and machinery the present value of the grant and tax savings from capital allowances combined was around 54 per cent in the Development Areas, against 34 per cent in non-Assisted Areas, of which 28 per cent was for the annual writing-down allowance. This represented an effective rate of subsidy of 26 per cent in the Development Areas and a differential in favour of the Development Areas of 20 per cent. The overall rate of subsidy in favour of buildings was much lower, but again the differential in favour of the Development Areas was around 19 per cent and the effective rate of subsidy was 30 per cent. The regional differential to plant and machinery was more generous than that which existed pre-October 1970, but was about the same on industrial buildings.

Discretionary loans and grants under the Local Employment Acts, which had been consolidated by the February 1972 Local Employment Act, were superseded by selective aid under Part II of the 1972 Industry Act. Regional Selective Assistance (RSA) under section 7 of the Act was available in any part of the Assisted Areas to projects which created, maintained or safeguarded employment. Eligible purposes under the Act were wide-ranging, but guidelines issued in October 1972 placed qualifying projects into two broad categories:

(a) Category A: New projects and expansions which create additional employment; and
(b) Category B: Projects which do not provide extra jobs (for example, modernization or rationalization), but which maintain or safeguard existing employment.

Assistance to projects in Category A could be given as a cheap loan, an interest relief grant or a removal grant. The interest rate subsidy was generally around 3 per cent a year, but could be as high as 10 per cent, while the removal grant covered up to 80 per cent of the cost of removal to an Assisted Area, including items such as plant and machinery, stocks and materials, and statutory redundancy payments. Service-sector firms were eligible for this assistance provided that they were not primarily serving local needs. Category B projects could obtain loan assistance at commercial rates, but only where finance could not reasonably be obtained from other sources, although this condition was not applied to Category A projects. In either case, assistance was related to the number of jobs involved, and to qualify for RSA an applicant had to demonstrate the viability of the firm and that the greater part of the project cost was provided from sources outside the public sector. In exceptional cases, such as where there was an imminent risk of significant redundancies, assistance could be given in any form, including a guarantee or share capital, but again this was related to the number of jobs involved. While these powers were similar to the discretionary assistance previously available under the 1972 Local Employment Act, Field and Hills (1976) note that they were wider in that they enabled the Secretary of State to give assistance in virtually any form and in any circumstance where assistance was likely to provide, maintain or safeguard employment in the Assisted Areas.

These section 7 provisions were used to support Govan Shipbuilders and Cammell Laird Shipbuilders, noted above, and for £3.5m in loans and grants to the Mersey Docks and Harbour Board in February 1973 for the purposes of rationalization. Schemes of assistance were also introduced under section 7, including the Service Industry Removal Grant Scheme in June 1973 to encourage service firms to relocate to the Assisted Areas. Under this, firms could obtain a grant of £800 in respect of each relocating employee (usually for up to 50 per cent of the total of jobs in place at the new location) and a selective grant covering rent costs in the new location for up to three years in IAs and five years in DAs and SDAs. This was in addition to that available under Category A. Building grants under section 3 of the 1972 Local Employment Act were replaced by the RDGs available for buildings, and discretionary assistance under section 4 was superseded by RSA, but otherwise the physical measures of the Local Employment Acts and the earlier Distribution of Industry Acts continued to apply. Grants for derelict land clearance were given a boost by the declaration of the Derelict Land Clearance Areas in the North Midlands in 1970, and a further scheme to clear derelict land was announced in February 1972, partly to help create employment. Temporary assistance was also made to local authorities under the Special Environmental Assistance Scheme, and as a make-work scheme this received £60m over a four-year period.

Details of gross expenditure on these various regional measures over the 1970s are presented in Table 5.1. Broadly, the table shows the decline in regional subsidy in the early 1970s, the increase after the 1972 Industry Act, and then a further decline from 1977, for the reasons described below. The table also shows that as spending on the investment grants lapsed, so expenditure on RDG grew quite strongly, and that by the mid-1970s it formed the major component of regional industrial assistance. By comparison, expenditure on RSA was modest, exhibiting a gradual shift away from loans to grant assistance, while spending on REP increased after a doubling of rates in 1974, but it was scrapped at the end of 1976.

A FRAMEWORK FOR NATIONAL ASSISTANCE

In addition to the new regional measures, section 8 of the 1972 Industry Act made discretionary assistance generally available to firms, known as National Selective Assistance (NSA). This could be made in any appropriate form to benefit all or any part of the UK economy, but could only be made where the firm had no alternative sources of finance, and so in this

Table 5.1 Gross expenditure on regional policy assistance, 1970–81 (£m, current prices)

	1970/1	*1971/2*	*1972/3*	*1973/4*	*1974/5*	*1975/6*	*1976/7*	*1977/8*	*1978/9*	*1979/80*	*1980/1*
Building grants	29.0	30.6	31.3	30.3	15.6	10.9	1.5	–	–	–	–
Discretionary loans (R)	16.2	14.8	20.4	8.2	0.4	–	–	–	–	–	–
Discretionary grants	0.9	1.2	1.5	0.9	0.6	0.01	–	–	–	–	–
Plant/machinery grants	0.5	0.6	0.01	–	–	–	–	–	–	–	–
Operational grants	0.2	2.4	3.8	5.3	4.3	2.5	–	–	–	–	–
Investment grants	123.1	89.6	67.6	29.5	15.5	5.5	2.4	0.6	0.6	0.1	0.5
REP	109.2	109.4	100.9	106.8	155.7	215.1	216.8	0.3	–	–	–
SEP	7.4	0.2	0.2	0.3	–	–	–	–	–	–	–
RDG	–	–	8.1	107.2	212.8	324.9	407.7	393.4	416.9	330.8	490.5
RSA loans and equity (R)	–	–	0.3	29.4	20.1	41.7	21.5	9.1	6.9	1.5	0.1
grants	–	–	0.07	4.5	15.1	22.3	20.6	41.2	91.3	73.7	48.1
SIRG/OSIS	–	–	–	–	0.2	1.0	1.7	2.2	3.1	3.4	5.4
Exchange Risk Guarantee Scheme (R)	–	–	–	–	–	–	–	–	42.5	123.6	90.6
Total recoverable (R)	**16.2**	**14.8**	**20.7**	**37.6**	**20.5**	**41.7**	**21.5**	**9.1**	**49.4**	**125.1**	**90.7**
Total non-recoverable	**270.3**	**234.0**	**213.5**	**284.8**	**419.8**	**582.2**	**650.7**	**437.7**	**511.9**	**408.0**	**544.5**

Note: The figures for investment grants give grant amounts over and above the standard grant rate amounts available nationally. In addition, there was some subsidy through the accelerated depreciation allowances which operated at a higher rate in the Assisted Areas in the early 1970s, totalling £189 million in grant equivalents (1980 prices). (R) indicates that the assistance is potentially recoverable. REP = Regional Employment Premium; SEP = Selective Employment Premium; RDG = Regional Development Grant; RSA = Regional Selective Assistance; SIRG = Service Industry Removal Grant; OSIS = Office and Service Industry Scheme.
Sources: *Annual Reports on the Local Employment Acts* (London: HMSO); *Annual Reports on the 1966 Industrial Development Act* (London: HMSO); *Annual Reports on the 1972 Industry Act* (London: HMSO); *Financial Statistics* (London: HMSO); Begg *et al.* (1975).

respect it was more restrictive than RSA. In effect, this systematized the previous *ad hoc* assistance that had been given by the Industrial Reorganization Corporation, under the 1968 Industrial Expansion Act, and in a series of one-off interventions since 1970. However, initially, it was little used, and was to be of more significance after a change of government in 1974. During the first year of operation, two offers of NSA were made, and in both cases the assisted firm was to require further financial support, as described below. One case involved £1.25m in loans and share capital to facilitate the merger of the machine tools manufacturers Kearney and Trucker and Marwin (Holdings) into a viable unit, and the other case involved £4.8m in preference shares to help form a new motor-cycle manufacturer, combining the interests of the Birmingham Small Arms Company (BSA) and Norton Villiers.

Several schemes of assistance were introduced under section 8 to tackle particular industrial problems, which were reminiscent of the late 1950s. The first such scheme was the Wool Textile Industry Scheme (later Stage I), which was open from July 1973 until the end of 1975, and designed to achieve greater efficiency in this sector by encouraging firms to modernize and to rationalize production. Funds totalling £15m were available in the form of grants at rates of 15 per cent for re-equipment projects (Category 1); 20 per cent for re-equipment and rebuilding projects (Category 2); and in the form of cheap loans for more comprehensive projects (Category 3). These rates applied after the deduction of any RDG. Assistance could also be obtained for the elimination of marginal capacity, while on certain types of equipment the applicant was required to scrap at least 90 per cent of existing equipment to prevent a recurrence of over-capacity, and to demolish any vacated buildings. The second scheme was the Offshore Supplies Interest Relief Grant Scheme (initially known as the Offshore Credit Scheme) which provided interest relief grants at 3 per cent per annum for up to eight years towards 80 per cent of the value of contracts. These were available to UK suppliers to the UK sector of the Continental Shelf. These suppliers were not eligible for ECGD facilities and this helped them to compete with overseas firms.

Part III of the Industry Act provided a general facility for assisting the shipbuilding industry. The major ongoing form of support introduced under this was the Home Credit Scheme, which superseded the guarantees provided under the 1967 Shipbuilding Industry Act, and guaranteed loans to UK shipowners for orders from UK yards, ostensibly to offset any disadvantage experienced as a result of other countries' export credit schemes. The terms for this were laid down by the OECD Export Credit Understanding for Ships, which meant that the credit could not exceed

80 per cent of the contract price, that the maximum period of the loan could not exceed seven (later eight) years, and that the minimum interest rate was 7.5 per cent.[6] The total limit on guarantees was fixed at £1000m, but could be extended by Order if necessary, and by April 1973 total net guarantees stood at £602m and there had been no defaults.

Following a dramatic slump in orders, a temporary profitability support in the form of the Construction Grant Scheme was offered in 1972 to avert collapses in shipbuilding. This provided grant payments to firms engaged in shipbuilding and mobile offshore installation at a rate of 10 per cent on the contract price attributed to the year 1972, and at 4 and 3 per cent for the years 1973 and 1974 respectively. The projected cost of this scheme was £50m, and in the case of Govan Shipbuilders the grant was deducted from a £35m package of assistance announced a few weeks earlier. In Table 5.2 we summarize assistance to the shipbuilding industry, including the one-off payments to this sector by the Shipbuilding Industry Board and through the facilities of section 7 (these *ad hoc* payments were later formalized within schemes). The table shows that much of the assistance to this sector was potentially recoverable, and that shipbuilding required ongoing support through the 1970s, which was maintained at a roughly constant level.

ADMINISTRATIVE MATTERS

To administer the 1972 Industry Act, an Industrial Development Executive (IDE) was set up under a new Minister for Industrial Development in the Department of Trade and Industry (DTI), which itself had been established in 1970 by the amalgamation of the Board of Trade and the Ministry of Technology. The DTI was given control over financial aid and industrial location policies even though the new Department of the Environment had been given lead responsibility for regional development. The DTI's Offices for Scotland, Wales and the English regions with substantial Assisted Areas formed part of the IDE, and were strengthened in anticipation of the Act by the appointment of Regional Industrial Directors. Industrial Development Boards in each of these Offices advised on industrial opportunities and on applications for selective assistance up to £500 000. Applications for larger amounts were referred to an Industrial Development Advisory Board (IDAB) in London, which also advised on industry-wide problems. This Board was supported by an Industrial Development Unit (IDU), composed of staff recruited from the City, industry and government, which helped to appraise and negotiate

Table 5.2 Gross expenditure on shipbuilding assistance, 1970–81 (£m, current prices)

	1970/1	*1971/2*	*1972/3*	*1973/4*	*1974/5*	*1975/6*	*1976/7*	*1977/8*	*1978/9*	*1979/80*	*1980/1*
Shipbuilders' relief	4.7	5.2	4.8	6.3	5.8	6.2	8.0	12.8	10.8	11.0	15.8
Home Credit Scheme (R)	235.2	91.2	171.3	97.0	226.3	182.2	145.9	134.2	205.3	148.1	225.2
SIB loans (R)	2.6	3.0	–	–	–	–	–	–	–	–	–
SIB grants	5.6	2.6	–	–	–	–	–	–	–	–	–
Section 7 loans (R)	–	–	6.0	10.6	22.2	29.0	0.6	7.7	–	–	–
Section 7 equity (R)	–	–	5.0	–	19.8	0.5	0.3	18.0	–	–	–
Section 7 grants	–	–	1.8	1.1	2.2	5.3	4.0	24.0	2.5	2.4	–
Construction Grant Scheme	–	–	12.0	18.0	12.0	4.2	1.0	0.5	0.3	0.1	0.05
Cost Escalation Scheme (R)	–	–	–	–	–	–	13.1	2.3	–	22.6	2.0
Refund Guarantees (R)	–	–	–	–	–	–	20.1	12.2	–	–	–
Intervention Fund	–	–	–	–	–	–	1.4	19.3	10.8	32.0	42.0
Total recoverable (R)	**237.8**	**94.2**	**182.3**	**107.6**	**268.3**	**211.7**	**180.0**	**174.4**	**205.3**	**170.7**	**227.2**
Total non-recoverable	**10.3**	**7.8**	**18.6**	**25.4**	**20.0**	**15.7**	**14.4**	**56.6**	**24.4**	**45.5**	**57.9**

Notes: The Home Credit Scheme includes guarantees made under the 1967 Shipbuilding Industry Act for 1970/1 and 1971/2. (R) indicates that the assistance is potentially recoverable. SIB = Shipbuilding Industry Board.

Sources: *Annual Abstract of Statistics* (London: HMSO); *Annual Reports on the 1972 Industry Act* (London: HMSO); *Annual Reports of the Commissioners for Customs and Excise* (London: HMSO).

applications for selective aid. The IDU also undertook studies of problems affecting industry and particular sectors, and was responsible for the disposal of assets built up by the former Industrial Reorganization Corporation. These Development Boards can be seen as successors to the BOTAC, which had been established under the 1960 Local Employment Act.[7]

In February 1971 the Trade and Industry Sub-Committee of the House of Commons Expenditure Committee was established, and this undertook two inquiries into industrial subsidies. The first study looked at the objectives and effectiveness of financial assistance, and was published as *Public Money in the Private Sector* in July 1972 (HC 651, 1972). This focused on the assistance provided over the previous decade, and in particular on the interventions in the case of *Concorde*, Rolls-Royce and the Upper Clyde Shipbuilders. In relation to these it recommended that the government should satisfy itself that the firm had the necessary financial, technical and managerial resources before providing support, and noted that the initial cost estimates for large-scale projects tended to be highly speculative and often overly optimistic. Tax incentives were outside the inquiry's scope, and on investment grants the report was mute, perhaps reflecting the recent abolition of these. In relation to regional assistance the report concluded that 'far too little information is available to Government on the effectiveness of regional incentives. Large sums are being spent with inadequate knowledge of how far they are contributing towards the desired objectives or whether the money could be better spent on alternative means of reaching them' (para. 265).

This same point was made more forcefully by a second report, *Regional Development Incentives* (HC 85, 1973) which, published in December 1973, followed the enactment of the 1972 Industry Act. This urged the government to commission studies into the costs and benefits of these policies, and was critical of frequent policy changes and of the need to retain confidentiality over assistance payments. The report also queried the emphasis of policy on unselective forms of assistance, noting that 'these are paid equally to those who would not otherwise have moved to or expanded in a development area and to those who either needed no such persuasion or who would have responded to a lesser form of assistance' (HC 85, 1973, para. 177). These remarks anticipated events of a decade later.

THE ARRANGEMENTS FOR NORTHERN IRELAND

Support for industry in Northern Ireland was provided mainly by the Department of Commerce, but the situation was complicated after Direct

Rule in 1974, since while Northern Ireland legislation was retained and amended, giving the Province a distinctive system of industrial support, some national industrial assistance measures also applied to this area. In relation to the Industry Act, section 8 sectoral schemes extended directly to the Province, but neither the Regional Development Grant nor section 7 assistance applied, because parallel schemes already existed under Northern Ireland legislation. A Standard Capital Grant worked in much the same way as the RDG, but with a 30 per cent rate which applied throughout Northern Ireland, compared with the maximum of 22 per cent for RDG. Also available in the Province was Selective Financial Assistance (SFA), which was offered at a rate of between 40 and 50 per cent, with the highest rates in the areas of greatest unemployment. This was made in a number of forms related to the fixed and working capital requirements of the project, but, unlike the British scheme, was not available in addition to the automatic capital grant assistance (HC 500, 1982).

The Department of Commerce dealt with job creation cases involving assistance of up to £1m, but in virtually all cases it had to consult with the Industries Development Advisory Committee (IDAC), which was an independent statutory body similar to the IDAB in Great Britain. The Local Enterprise Development Unit (LEDU), which was established in 1971 to assist the development of manufacturing and service firms with less than 50 employees, was given the responsibility of negotiating SFA in the case of these small firms. It also looked after co-operatives and the development of craft industries, for which it operated a start-up grant. It could give working capital grants in special circumstances to firms experiencing short-term financial difficulties, and make grants up to a rate of around 66 per cent for projects designed to improve profitability, and at up to 80 per cent for research and development.

EUROPEAN COMMUNITY MEMBERSHIP

Negotiations over UK entry to the former European Community (EC) were reopened in June 1970, and formal accession occurred at the beginning of 1973. The implications were felt most immediately for trade policy and agricultural support. In the case of the former, tariffs between the UK and EC were to be abolished in five stages up to 1977, and UK tariffs on imports from elsewhere were to be adjusted to bring them into line with the common external tariff. Commonwealth Preference for manufactured goods had already been abolished in January 1972, but certain transitory arrangements were made for this trade. Britain agreed to adopt the EC system of support for agriculture through the Common Agricultural Policy (CAP), which was administered by the European Agricultural Guidance and Guarantee Fund (EAGGF). This entailed fixing domestic intervention prices (as well as minimum import prices and levies for major products), so that the prices paid by consumers reflected EC production costs rather than world prices as under the old UK system of deficiency payments. To some extent, the UK had already moved in this direction, but membership of CAP still dislocated the agricultural sector in two respects. First, food prices rose rapidly after entry, representing a real increase of 20 per cent over the general rise in prices, and second, the emphasis of CAP was on profitability supports for farmers under the Guarantee section of EAGGF. As we have seen, UK policy had shifted towards providing incentives to farmers, but the Guidance section of EAGGF, which offered subsidies for land consolidation and investment aid, accounted for less than 5 per cent of total expenditure (Nevin, 1990).

At the time of UK entry, the EC had no formal regional policy, but finance was available through various funds which favoured the less developed regions, comprising: the European Investment Bank (EIB), which provided loans and guarantees on a non-profit-making basis to projects which were either located in less developed regions or of such size or nature that they were otherwise unable to obtain finance; the European Coal and Steel Community (ECSC), which provided loans to support activities capable of providing employment for redundant coal and steel workers, and retraining and resettlement grants for these workers, of which the latter required a matching grant from the relevant member state; and the European Social Fund (ESF), which reimbursed half of the cost of approved retraining and resettlement schemes.

A European Regional Development Fund (ERDF) was announced at an EC Summit in 1972 and came into being in 1975 for the purpose of correcting structural and regional imbalances which might affect the realization of economic and monetary union. It offered grants of up to 50 per cent of the assistance provided by a member state, and sometimes interest relief grants against certain loans, for the purpose of infrastructure provision or to assist with industry and tourism projects. Allocation of funds to countries was on a quota basis and this tended to favour countries receiving relatively little assistance under other funds, so that initially the UK received 28 per cent of the total. However, the ERDF bore little resemblence to a coherent EC-wide regional policy, with member states defining the areas for intervention and being responsible for submitting projects for funding, so that industrial support under the ERDF often served to recompense state governments for their own regional policy spending. This was partly by design, with the Council of Ministers circumscribing the scope of the ERDF in the original 1975 Fund Regulation to maintain their own distinctive regional policies, but it was also to become a significant source of conflict, as the Commission sought to assert its own EC-wide regional policy.

NATIONAL STATE AIDS

With the possible exception of the REP, which the government had planned to phase out in any case, the existing structure of UK industrial assistance was largely unaffected by accession to the EC. According to the Commission, state subsidies, or state aids as they were known, had a number of well-established characteristics: they were granted by a public body; involved some cost to the public purse; were of benefit to enterprises (in either the private or public sector); involved better-than-normal market conditions; were specific to certain sectors, regions or firms; and affected competition with other member states (Lehner *et al.*, 1991). In respect of these subsidies, the Treaty of Rome laid down that 'any aid granted by a Member State ... which distorts or threatens to distort competition by favouring certain undertakings or the production of certain goods shall, in so far as it affects trade between Member States, be incompatible with the common market' (Article 92.1). However, regional assistance and the selective interventions envisaged under the 1972 Industry Act were allowed under the exemptions in Article 92.3, as follows:

(a) aid to promote the economic development of areas where the standard of living is abnormally low or where there is serious underemployment;
(b) aid to promote the execution of an important project of common European interest or to remedy a serious disturbance in the economy of a member state;
(c) aid to facilitate the development of certain economic activities or of certain economic areas, where such aid does not adversely affect trading conditions to an extent contrary to the common interest; and
(d) such other categories of aid as may be specified by decision of the Council acting by a qualified majority on a proposal from the Commission.

In the case of shipbuilding assistance, an exemption from (c) meant that this form of aid was to be eliminated 'in so far as it served only to compensate for the absence of customs protection', but the Commission was reluctant to pursue this because of the cut-price competition from elsewhere, and a series of Shipbuilding Directives were issued permitting temporary aid to this sector up to some specified ceiling. Other exceptions under Article 42 allowed assistance to the agricultural sector including fisheries, and under Article 77 aids could be given to transport undertakings, either to meet the needs of co-ordination or where compatible with the concept of a public service. Article 4 of the ECSC Treaty declared that aids and subsidies to the coal and steel industries were incompatible with the Common Market and were to be abolished and prohibited, but Article 95 of the same Treaty enabled the Commission to permit specified aids to the coal industry (from 1965) and the steel industry (from 1980) for the purposes of rationalization (Lehner *et al.*, 1991).

A problem arose in distinguishing between state aids and general economic, social and fiscal measures which favoured particular firms, and although these 'general measures' were presumed not to be incompatible with the common market they could be dealt with under Treaty of Rome Articles 101 and 102, either by common agreement or by the adoption of Council directives. Under Article 93 of this Treaty, the Commission was required to keep under review all systems of aid and could require a member state to abolish or alter any aid which did not satisfy the above conditions. However, it was not until 1983 that the Commission announced its intention to recover illegal state aid from recipient firms, and 1985 before it adopted this systematically. Up to this time, much of its effort was concerned with giving exact meaning to the Articles, and on a number of occasions it came into conflict with the UK government.

A concern of the Commission was that member states' regional policies were leading to wasteful competitive bidding for internationally mobile projects, and in a communication to Council in 1971, subsequently adopted as a resolution, it set down four principles to ensure greater co-ordination of regional aid systems. These were: a single ceiling for aid intensity, so that assistance bore some relationship to the problem being tackled; transparency, so that the value of assistance could be measured readily in terms of investment cost; regional specificity, so that the areas for intervention were well defined (that is, neither whole national territories nor isolated geographical points); and sectoral repercussions, so that the amount of aid going to particular industrial sectors could be disentangled. These rules applied initially to the central geographical areas of the EC, where it was felt that the risk of aid distorting competition and trade was greatest. A ceiling on aid was set at 20 per cent of the grant equivalent net of tax expressed as a proportion of the investment cost, with a discount rate of 8 per cent and reference interest rate used to measure the grant equivalent of soft loans (CEC, 1971). This was developed by new rules in 1975 which fixed the grant equivalent in the United Kingdom at 35 per cent in Northern Ireland; at 30 per cent in the Assisted Areas to be observed within a period of three years; and at 20 per cent elsewhere (CEC, 1975). Both the 1971 and 1975 rules contained requirements regarding the geographical and industrial incidence of assistance; the latter to ensure that assistance did not go to industries with chronic excess capacity.

The attempt to render aid non-transparent or opaque which could not readily be measured incompatible with the Treaty of Rome were confounded by the large component such aid formed in the regional policies of some member countries, including the UK. In the UK, of particular concern to the Commission were the REP and RDG. REP came under close scrutiny because, as Maclennan (1979) notes, it 'seemed to infringe almost every canon of compatibility in that it constituted a continuing subsidy to operating costs available to all firms in the assisted areas and was unconditional on any investment activity, whether new investment or replacement investment' (p. 249). While the UK government questioned the use of capital costs as the sole basis for measuring the rate of assistance, and argued that REP would bring unused resources into use, the Commission's objections focused on the support it would give to otherwise uneconomic firms and the adverse implications this would have for trade. However, no action was taken over REP, since the UK government had made this a potentially troublesome element of membership negotiations, and the Commission was no doubt influenced by the time limit of seven years set for this subsidy (Maclennan, 1979). RDG was of concern because it was available against replacement investment, which was a normal commercial activity of firms, and it was argued that its grant equivalent would understate its true value to firms, who would take the continuing nature of the subsidy into account in their investment appraisals, but again no action was taken. Selective aid was acceptable to the Commission in so far as the exact terms for assistance were precisely set out, subject to satisfying the above criteria, and it was a 'once and for all' subsidy to non-replacement investment which enabled the firm to compete competitively.

THE REVIVAL OF INDUSTRIAL ASSISTANCE

Spending on industrial financial assistance accelerated rapidly in the late 1960s, so that by the end of this decade grant equivalent expenditure on these measures stood about at 5.4 per cent of gross domestic product (GDP). Such an expansion was probably unsustainable, but the attempt by the incoming government to eliminate the profitability supports and the automatic assistance ultimately proved unsuccessful, when it was faced with the prospect of one million unemployed. Nevertheless, as Table 5.3 shows, grant equivalent expenditure on industrial subsidies was cut-back by about a third by the mid-1970s. This was caused principally by the elimination of the nationally available employment subsidies, but in addition important shifts were effected in the pattern of assistance over this period. Grant equivalent spending on the tax allowances increased substantially with the adoption of free depreciation, which replaced the pre-existing nationally available investment grants, while capital-based grants became the principal element of regional policy. Support for the civil aviation and shipbuilding industries also continued to run at a high level.

The early 1970s saw important changes to the structure of industrial assistance, but probably of as much significance was the UK's membership

Table 5.3 Grant equivalent expenditure on industrial subsidies, 1965–76 (£m, 1980 prices)

	1965/6	*1967/8*	*1969/70*	*1971/2*	*1973/4*	*1975/6*
National Assistance						
Tax allowances	2 411	475	595	1 521	2 482	3 212
Investment grants	–	547	921	691	251	48
SET refund and SEP	–	3 335	4 502	3 116	408	8
Regional Assistance						
Tax allowances	178	15	–	27	47	–
Investment grants	43	265	298	257	408	612
REP and SEP	–	139	486	342	287	398
Sectoral Assistance						
Civil aircraft	93	213	292	400	235	211
Shipbuilding	22	30	143	47	108	125
Other	10	7	36	35	97	30
Total	**2 757**	**5 026**	**7 273**	**6 436**	**4 323**	**4 644**

Notes: The table gives expenditure in grant equivalents at constant 1980 prices for selected years. SET = Selective Employment Tax; SEP = Selective Employment Premium; REP = Regional Employment Premium. Support for agriculture is not included.
Source: Wren (1996b).

of the Common Market. The Treaty of Rome made state aid incompatible with the Common Market in so far as it distorted competition, and while the Commission specified ceilings on aid, the immediate impact of this on UK industrial assistance was extremely limited. Nevertheless, as the Commission gave meaning to the Treaty Articles, it was gradually to have an increasing influence on the pattern of UK state subsidy, although it was not until the mid-1980s that it clamped down on state subsidies and sought to recover illegal state aid. In the meantime, its main contribution was to fund various schemes of regional industrial support and promote adjustment in the coal and steel industries.

6 The Heyday of Industrial Assistance (Late 1970s)

ECONOMIC CONDITIONS

Unemployment peaked around March 1972, at about the time that the government had embarked on its programme of industrial expansion, and strong growth followed, so that by the end of 1973 unemployment had nearly halved to stand at just under half a million. Fiscal and monetary measures were taken during 1973 to curb demand, but such was the strength of growth that a deterioration in the balance of payments developed, despite currency depreciation following the floating of sterling in June 1972. These problems were compounded in October 1973 by steep increases in oil prices and by industrial action, which led to the abandonment of the statutory incomes policy. The Labour Party came to power in March 1974, and after a further election was returned to office in October of that year with a small majority. While the industrial action was settled quickly, the new government faced both a balance of payments deficit and inflationary pressures. It sought control of wage increases through voluntary restraint by trade unions and in return took a series of measures as its part of a 'social contract'. In the first of three Budgets in 1974, food and rent subsidies were increased by £570m, and further consumer subsidies were introduced in a July Budget to help curb inflation, which was running at 17 per cent.[1] REP, which had been reprieved when Labour came to power, was doubled at this time to help restore its real value.

LABOUR'S INDUSTRIAL STRATEGY

The broad industrial strategy of the Labour government was set out in the August 1974 White Paper *The Regeneration of British Industry* (Cmnd 5710, 1974).[2] This noted that financial inducements were no longer enough to address Britain's relatively low level of manufacturing investment and that 'a closer, clearer and more positive relationship between Government and industry' was required (para. 4). The framework for intervention, which had been established by the 1972 Industry Act, was to be retained and even strengthened, but in addition to this a number of new initiatives were proposed.[3] First, an extension of public ownership was to be undertaken, including the nationalization of the shipbuilding and aircraft industries, the extension of public ownership in the road haulage and construction industries, and the creation of a British National Oil Corporation. Second, it was proposed that various planning agreements would be established whereby voluntary three-year rolling plans would be drawn up between the government and major firms, to 'ensure that the plans of companies are in harmony with national needs and objectives' (para. 7). It was felt that the National Plan had faltered through a lack of private-sector co-operation, and these new agreements were a device to ensure co-ordination with government objectives (Sawyer, 1991). Third, a National Enterprise Board was proposed to 'secure where necessary large-scale sustained investment to offset the effects of the short-term pull of market forces' (para. 23).

Subsidies were to play a key role in the planning agreements, so that 'if in the course of these discussions it becomes clear that in order to align the company's plans with national needs some financial assistance is required beyond that which would in any case be available to the company by way of capital allowances, regional development aid and regional employment premium, the Government will be ready to provide ... discretionary financial assistance by way of loans and grants' (para. 12). In the event, nothing much came of this idea, and the only planning agreement to be concluded with the private sector was with the Chrysler Motor Company in January 1976 in the face of substantial redundancies (Fleming, 1980). This agreed maximum government assistance of £162.5m up to 1980, including £55m in loans, £35m in guarantees and £72.5m in grants towards losses, but Chrysler UK was sold to PSA Peugeot-Citroën in September 1978 without prior notification to the government, by which time £82m in loans and grants had been paid.

The National Enterprise Board (NEB) was charged with a number of roles, including assisting companies in short-term financial and managerial difficulties, assistance to help create jobs in areas of high unemployment, and the power to start new ventures and participate in joint ventures. It could provide finance in the form of a loan or grant, but as a rule and by agreement it would take a proportional share in the ownership of assisted firms.[4] Such was the confidence in public ownership that the White Paper stated that the NEB's 'main strength in manufacturing will come through the extension of public ownership into profitable manufacturing industry by acquisitions of individual firms' (Cmnd 5710 (1974) para. 24). Shareholdings obtained by the government under the 1972 Industry Act, and the remaining shares which had been acquired by the former Industrial

Reorganization Corporation, were to be vested in the NEB. Like the IRC, the NEB was given an active role in promoting industrial efficiency, but, unlike the IRC, the NEB would retain the shares it acquired.

The NEB was eventually established by the November 1975 Industry Act, which repealed certain of the powers relating to the provision of equity under the 1972 Industry Act, so that the Secretary of State was no longer required to take equity finance only as a last resort, nor was he/she prevented from taking a majority of shares in a firm or be required to dispose of these shares as soon as reasonable. Also at this time, the requirement that section 7 (Category B) and section 8 assistance under the 1972 Industry Act should only be given where it could not be provided appropriately by other sources was dropped. Gross external borrowing by the NEB could not exceed £700m, with a possible extension to £1000m, which was taken up in early 1978. However, the NEB's role was to be less free-ranging than had been originally envisaged, even in the White Paper, so that, according to Parr (1979), it became 'a state investment bank operating on commercial criteria, competitive with the private sector agencies and with an increasingly well-defined policy'. In opposition, it had been proposed that the NEB should be the vehicle for the taking into public ownership of the leading manufacturing, banking and insurance companies to counteract the power of large corporations, and that planning agreements would be a further device for harnessing remaining large private-sector firms (Labour Party, 1973b). In practice, the NEB had no compulsory share purchase powers, was subject to ministerial direction, and required government approval for share acquisitions in excess of £10m, where more than 30 per cent of a company's equity was involved, or where large loans, guarantees and joint ventures were to be undertaken. This was in part an attempt by the Labour government to water down pre-election commitments, which meant that legislation on the August 1974 White Paper was not pursued until February 1975 (Whitehead, 1985).

A large part of the NEB's portfolio was taken up with the government's rescue operations, so that of the holdings of £1009m at historic cost at the end of September 1978, £964m was in respect of eight transfers to NEB in early 1976, including British Leyland (£696m), Rolls-Royce (£203m), Herbert (£36m), ICL (£12m) and Cambridge Instruments (£6m).[5] The other thirty-eight holdings that NEB had built-up by this time cost £45m. As a consequence, a large element of the NEB's effort was taken up with dealing with these ailing companies, and its activities were further circumscribed in December 1977 when, after European Commission concern over unfair competition, ministerial guidelines required it to make a commercial return on capital of 15–20 per cent on investments other than

British Leyland and Rolls-Royce, and 10 per cent in the case of British Leyland (Maunder, 1979).

RESCUE OPERATIONS

This period is associated with a number of bail-outs of ailing companies, of which the most notable case was the financially troubled British Leyland (BL). BL had approached the government for assistance in 1974, and in December of that year it was provided with a guarantee of £50m. At the same time, the government established a team to assess BL's position and future prospects, which was headed by the Chairman of the NEB and included staff from the IDAB. The report was published in April 1975 in abridged form (HC 342 (1975) Ryder Report). It argued that vehicle production was an essential part of the UK's economic base, and that government intervention was justified on the grounds of BL's position as a major exporter, producer of import substitutes and employer. In some sense, this echoed reports in the early 1960s which similarly justified government intervention in the civil aircraft and shipbuilding industries for reasons of national importance. The report estimated that nearly £1300m over eight years (at 1975 prices) was required to make the company viable, and that 'a very large part of the funds can only be provided by the Government and ... there is an overwhelmingly strong case for the Government to provide the funds' (paras 9–10). The 1975 British Leyland Act provided for the government to purchase the existing £65m equity of BL and to take up a rights issue of a further £200m. Guarantees were extinguished, including another £100m in May 1975. The plans of Ryder Report proved to be overly ambitious, and in November 1977 they were shelved in favour of more modest plans. In total, around £1000m of public money went to BL before the end of 1979, and £1250m up to 1981, at current prices (Hindley and Richardson, 1983).

Other rescue operations had mixed outcomes, so that some companies were put on to a commercial footing, such as Ferranti, but others went into liquidation, most notably Alfred Herbert in 1980. Others still required ongoing support, including KTM Machine Tools and Norton Villiers Triumph, both of which had first received aid under the previous administration (Sawyer, 1991). Despite the declared aims of the NEB and partly because of the delays in its establishment, much of this assistance was provided under section 8 of the 1972 Industry Act, mainly in the form of loans and equity finance. KTM Machine Tools was formed in June 1973 with £1.25m in section 8 assistance, but it received a further £3.5m in equity and £1.9m in loans partly financed by ICFC in a financial reconstruction in June 1974, only to be taken over by Vickers in another financial reconstruction in August 1976, when further assistance of £1.9m was made. Perhaps the most notable case was that of Norton Villiers Triumph (NVT), which at times took on farcical proportions (Bruce-Gardyne, 1978), but is worthy of consideration since it is symbolic of failed government intervention.

Against the advice of the IDAB, NVT was formed in 1973 with £4.8m in government funds to help strengthen the British motor-cycle industry. The plan was that after one year the company should cease production at its Meriden plant and focus its activity on its Birmingham Small Heath and Wolverhampton plants. However, this prompted industrial action at the Meriden plant, which affected supplies to the other two factories, but the extent of intervention at this time was to give the workforce of the Meriden plant time to effect a buy-out. The solution of the incoming Labour government was more radical, and in July 1974 it established a workers' co-operative at Meriden, known as the Meriden Motor Cycle Co-operative, to which it provided £4.2m in loans and £0.75m in grants from March 1975.[6] The output of the co-operative was to be sold through NVT, which was also to carry out the marketing of the co-operative's output, but this solution provoked industrial action at the Wolverhampton plant, which saw its own position threatened.

In the course of 1975, market conditions deteriorated and both the Small Heath and Wolverhampton plants went into liquidation. The government provided a loan of £275 000 to the Birmingham plant to enable a limited number of activities to continue, and £200 000 to Wolverhampton Industrial Engines in February 1977 to take over the Wolverhampton plant. Of course, this also meant that a further rescue of the Meriden plant was now necessary, and in May 1977 a £500 000 write-off of NVT debt was made, to acquire its marketing assets, enabling the co-operative to trade as Triumph Motorcycles (Meriden) Ltd, while its stock of unsold motorcycles was sold to GEC for resale. A proposal to sell off Meriden to Armstrong Equipment, which undertook to employ 150 of the 462 workforce, fell through in 1980 because the government refused to release Meriden from certain of its obligations (including recoveries to the ECGD from the future sale of 2000 motorcycles held in stock). Later, it agreed to release Meriden from its outstanding loans and accrued interest, which stood at nearly £6m, if it fulfilled the terms of its agreement with the ECGD, but the company went into liquidation in 1983.

THE REVISED APPROACH AND SECTORAL INTERVENTIONS

The August 1974 White Paper had set out the government's policy towards industry, but in the face of rising unemployment, inflation and a balance of payments deficit, it sought a revised approach which would give greater emphasis to output and productivity. Rather than a new National Plan, the government sought a more flexible approach based on co-operation between government, industry and trade unions, which would not be discredited by 'unsustainable economic assumptions', setting out its plans in the November 1975 White Paper *An Approach to Industrial Strategy* (Cmnd 6315, 1975).

At the heart of the policy proposals were a series of sectoral studies to identify those areas of the economy most capable of achieving growth objectives, building on work already being undertaken through the National Economic Development Council (NEDC). Each sector study would either be overseen by an Economic Development Committee of NEDC or by the establishment of an *ad hoc* committee. Initially, thirty-seven sector working parties were set up (later increased to thirty-nine) under the aegis of NEDC, all within manufacturing, and these reported in August and December 1976. Of the problems specified, the government chose to focus on facilitating exports and industrial restructuring, including rationalization and product development (Cameron, 1979). The findings of the sector working parties were supposed to filter down to management and the workforce, but W. Grant (1982) notes that these groups may have amounted to little more than talking shops, with participants unwilling to suspend normal competitive practice for the sake of an industrial strategy. The main practical benefit seems to have been the introduction of numerous sectorally-based assistance schemes under section 8 of the 1972 Industry Act, but the effects of these may at best have been long-term, since twenty-three of the sectors covered by the working parties experienced import penetration up to 1979.

The objectives of each sectoral scheme reflected the circumstance of the industry, so that of the three schemes introduced in 1975, the Ferrous Foundry Industry Scheme sought to modernize plant, the Machine Tools Industry Scheme sought to improve efficiency and competitiveness through new products and processes, and the Clothing Industry Scheme sought to rationalize production and restructure. Fixed sums were allocated to each scheme (initially £20m, £25m and £20m respectively, for the above schemes), and the schemes were usually of one to two years' duration. As an example, the Ferrous Foundry Industry Scheme was open from August 1975 to December 1976, and received applications from 514 of the country's estimated 825 ferrous foundries. The ceiling on the available funds was raised twice to stand at £80m, and on the advice of the Ferrous Foundry Economic Development Committee the scheme was extended to cover ferrous die-casting. Offers were made in respect of 350 projects, involving assistance expenditure of £47.9m by March 1987 out of total project costs of £284.5m.[7]

By April 1978, a further ten schemes had been announced, covering the following industries: paper and board (final assistance expenditure £18.7m); poultrymeat processing (£7.3m); printing machinery (£8.8m); textile machinery (£6.3m); redmeat slaughterhouse (£13.0m); non-ferrous foundry (£11.8m); electronic components (£12.1m); instrumentation and automation (£6.8m); drop forging (£4.0m); and footwear (£3.4m). In total, £177m in grant assistance was made under the sectoral schemes, as set out in Table 6.1, but only in a relatively small number of cases was it necessary to increase the initial allocation because of demand. Final expenditure on the Wool Textile Industry Scheme, which was introduced in 1973, amounted to £16.2m, but of a total investment of around £75m, only £2.1m of this was for the purpose of eliminating surplus capacity, and this was thought to be disappointing. Following proposals of the Wool Textile Economic Development Committee, Stage II was announced in November 1976 to encourage rationalization and restructuring, and expenditure of this amounted to £6.2m.

A number of the sectoral schemes were evaluated in a series of assessments produced by the Government Economic Service. A general problem with the schemes was that they were introduced in a period of economic turbulence, shortly before the recession of the early 1980s, and in the case of the Ferrous and Non-Ferrous Foundry schemes this led to chronic over-investment (Lambert, 1985; Potter, 1985). In many cases it was found that the schemes did no more than accelerate investment, and it later turned out that, given the course of events, much of this would have been cancelled. Deadweight spending was a problem, with between a third and half of the supported projects not depending on the subsidy. In the case of the Clothing Industry Scheme, this accounted for 28 per cent of total investment in the sector over the life of the scheme, but was thought to have raised investment by only 15 per cent, and possibly at the expense of investment elsewhere in corporate groups (Lambert, 1983). Stage I of the Wool Textile Industry Scheme was thought to be more successful than Stage II in stimulating investment, but even here there were problems, since some firms reported that the scrapping requirement put them at a disadvantage because unit costs were often lower on older machinery (Potter and Davies, 1983). The Electronic Components Industry Scheme

Table 6.1 Expenditure on the sectoral schemes, 1976–86 (£m, current prices)

Scheme	*Opening date*	*Closing date*	*1976–78*	*78–80*	*80–82*	*82–86*	*Total*
Ferrous Foundry	5/8/75	31/12/76	10.6	24.1	13.0	0.2	47.9
Machine Tools	5/8/75	31/12/77	2.5	13.3	6.8	0.3	22.9
Clothing	15/10/75	31/12/77	2.0	8.9	2.9	0.1	13.9
Paper and Board	15/6/76	30/6/78	2.0	11.2	5.5	–	18.7
Poultrymeat Processing	4/8/76	31/3/77	0.4	5.1	1.6	0.2	7.3
Printing Machinery	13/8/76	31/12/77	0.6	5.0	3.2	–	8.8
Textile Machinery	13/8/76	31/12/77	0.07	3.5	2.8	–	6.3
Redmeat Slaughterhouse	9/11/76	30/11/80	0.2	2.6	5.2	5.0	13.0
Non-Ferrous Foundry	24/1/77	21/7/78	0.3	6.1	5.4	0.02	11.8
Electronic Components	24/1/77	31/12/78	0.2	5.4	5.3	1.3	12.2
Instrument/Automation	1/11/77	30/4/79	–	2.4	4.2	0.2	6.8
Drop Forging	8/11/77	30/6/79	–	0.7	2.8	0.5	4.0
Footwear	18/4/78	31/3/80	–	0.7	2.3	0.4	3.4
Total			**18.8**	**89.0**	**61.0**	**8.2**	**177.0**

Notes: Figures relate to financial years, so that 1976–8 indicates financial years 1976/7 to 1977/8 inclusive, etc.
Source: *Annual Reports on the 1972 Industry Act* (London: HMSO); *Annual Reports on the 1982 Industrial Development Act* (London: HMSO).

was heavily concentrated, with half the subsidy going to just two large firms, but the outcome appeared to be successful, partly because the recipient companies had existing strength (Gibbs and Aldridge, 1985). The take-up of the Textile Machinery Industry Scheme was poor, and the assessment concluded that this scheme was probably ill-conceived (Herron, 1986).

THE DEVELOPMENT AGENCIES

To devolve some decision-making, applications for section 7 assistance up to £1m could be handled by local DTI Offices from July 1974, and from July 1975 section 7 powers in Scotland and Wales were given to the Scottish and Welsh Secretaries and administered by the former Scottish Economic Planning Department and Welsh Office (the Department of Industry retained responsibility for certain projects with general UK implications). The Scottish and Welsh Development Agencies (SDA and WDA) were established shortly afterwards, in December 1975 and January 1976 respectively (the SDA is now known as Scottish Enterprise), and were given powers to intervene in industry in their areas along similar lines to the NEB in order to promote the growth and modernization of industry, but subject to achieving an adequate overall return. The Agencies took over the former Scottish and Welsh Industrial Estate Management Corporations and certain responsibilities for derelict land clearance. Their budgets were set at £200m and £100m respectively over five years, but much of this was earmarked for industrial estates and land reclamation, which formed the focus of their activity (McCallum, 1979). In the year ended March 1980, 8 per cent of the SDA's expenditure and 6 per cent (including some rural loans) of the WDA's spending was on industrial investment, but both agencies suffered from the closure of a number of companies, with the SDA achieving a rate of return of –0.8 per cent, which improved on the –14.3 per cent obtained a year earlier. The largest commitment of the SDA was to a rough-terrain vehicle manufacturer, Stonefield Vehicles, to which it had provided £4.7m before the company's collapse in August 1980. The Northern Ireland Development Agency (NIDA) was also established in 1976, with similar powers to the NEB, to assist companies by providing loans or guarantees or by taking shares. The Agency was responsible for sectoral analysis and for promoting the Province overseas.

The placate the English regions over these developments, Regional Boards of the NEB were established in North and North West England, with powers to invest up to £0.5m in individual companies. However, the NEB was not happy with this, and initially the activities of these Regional Boards were somewhat limited (HC 623, 1978; W. Grant, 1982). The functions of the Development Commissioners relating to Scotland and Wales were hived-off, so that the Small Industries Council for the Rural Areas of Scotland was transferred to the SDA and in Wales the Development Board for Rural Wales was established (now called Mid-Wales Development), with the Commissioners focusing their activities on England after this time. Elsewhere in Scotland, the Highlands and Islands Development Board operated from 1965 to improve the economic and social well-being of people in these areas. As well as constructing buildings it had extensive powers of loans, grants and equity participation, and became an important source of small grants to new and small businesses in these areas.

In England the role of the Development Commissioners was to advise government on disbursements under the Development Fund, which had been established before the First World War. The Commissioners did not directly undertake the work themselves, but rather initiated work through existing organizations, such as local authorities, the English Industrial Estates (EIE) in the Assisted Areas, and the Council for Small Industries in Rural Areas (CoSIRA). EIE had responsibility for factory construction in the English Assisted Areas, while CoSIRA provided management and technical advice, training facilities and a credit service for small businesses in rural areas. In 1975, the Commissioners were given the additional brief of creating 1500 jobs per annum in depopulating rural areas, focusing assistance on designated Special Investment Areas, while CoSIRA largely operated outside these areas where there were 'pockets of need'. However, direct financial assistance from these agencies was quite small, especially when compared with national industrial assistance. As an example, the Development Fund provided no more than £8.4m in loans and grants to other bodies to carry out development work in 1977/8 (HC 185, 1979).

THE FAILURE OF REGIONAL POLICY

As expenditure on the building grants and discretionary assistance under the Local Employment Acts wound down, so the changes to regional policy in 1972 started to take effect, and in 1974 regional industrial assistance spending stood at around £400m, rising to nearly £650m in 1976. Of this, around £400m was on the Regional Development Grant and £210m was on the Regional Employment Premium, but only about £40m was on

Regional Selective Assistance (see Table 5.1 on p. 81). However, no sooner had the new expanded regional policy taken root than economic conditions deteriorated, and unemployment and inflation became increasingly serious problems (see Figure 5.1 on page 73). An effort was made to curb inflation through a deflationary Budget in April 1975, which raised taxes and cut public expenditure, and a commitment was made to restrain wage and price increases in order to stave off a sterling crisis. However, unemployment rose sharply, from around 750 000 in March 1975 to 1.2 million (4.9 per cent of the labour force) by August, but since national reflation was ruled out and regional policy had effectively been undermined by these events, this gave rise to series of *ad hoc* measures.

At first, traditional methods were adopted, so that the Accelerated Projects Scheme provided interest relief grants to firms as the minimum necessary to bring projects forward through time. The scheme operated from April 1975 to July 1976 with the aim of generating additional capacity in anticipation of economic recovery, which would in addition help the balance of payments. Project capital cost normally had to exceed £2.5m, but such was the interest in the scheme that this was later lowered to £0.5m, including working capital. The deadline for the scheme was also extended, to the end of September 1976, and some funds were set aside for modernization projects. Applications, which totalled 350, were appraised by the Industrial Development Unit and submitted to the Industrial Development Advisory Board for approval. In the Assisted Areas the scheme tended to attract relatively capital-intensive projects, with more labour-intensive projects able to obtain support under Regional Selective Assistance (Chapman, 1978). Interest relief grants totalling £69.8m were offered towards 111 projects, involving expenditure of £586m. The average grant rate was 12.5 per cent, but this could vary between 3 and 20 per cent.

The Accelerated Projects Scheme proved to be no more than a stop-gap measure, and with a further rise in unemployment the government intervened directly into the labour market through its various special employment measures (see Gregg, 1990).[8] These did not just recognize that regional policy was not getting to the unemployment problem fast enough (Lindley, 1986), but that the full battery of regional policy instruments had failed to prevent unemployment rising above a million – the prospect of which had caused the previous government to reverse its industrial policy. As such, regional policy was no longer an option for tackling cyclical variations in unemployment, especially when unemployment was a problem across the country, and a new set of subsidies was laid over the existing pattern, including urban measures. In the case of the special employment measures, these represented the most direct means of raising labour demand and were frequently amended and expanded, so that by 1980 expenditure on these exceeded that on regional policy.

SPECIAL EMPLOYMENT MEASURES

The first significant special employment measure was the Temporary Employment Subsidy (TES), which was introduced from August 1975 under the 1973 Employment and Training Act, and terminated in March 1979 after repeated renewals. The scheme sought to improve efficiency through reorganization, paying a subsidy to firms to defer redundancies, thereby ensuring the co-operation of trade unions with this reorganization. It offered £20 per week in respect of each full-time job retained, up to a maximum period of twelve months, and was available to those firms threatening redundancies of ten or more employees. For the first two months it operated in the Assisted Areas only. Firms had to produce 'evidence of a decision in good faith' to declare an impending redundancy, and were subject to three-monthly reviews (Deakin and Pratten, 1981). In manufacturing, the subsidy per assisted employee amounted to around 32 per cent of the average weekly wage, and for firms which exhausted the subsidy by March 1979, a TES Supplement became available at £10 per week, up to a maximum of six months. In total, 540 300 jobs were supported under these schemes, and, as Table 6.2 shows, expenditure under these reached a maximum of £174m in 1977/8.

The European Commission was concerned about the amount of support being offered to the textiles, clothing and footwear sectors through TES, with over two-fifths of supported jobs in these sectors at November 1979 (Department of Employment, 1979). Hence, from March 1978, TES support to these sectors became limited to 70 per cent of employees in a firm for the first six months and 50 per cent thereafter. However, to compensate, the Short-Time Working Compensation Scheme (STWCS) was introduced from May 1978, which reimbursed 75 per cent of the normal wages to employees working short-time in the textiles, clothing and footwear sectors, to encourage these firms to adopt short-time working rather than redundancy. From this time, firms were also required to present a restructuring plan if they wished to receive the subsidy for more than six months, and the TES Supplement was limited to 50 per cent of a firm's labour force. TES and STWCS were closed for applications from April 1979, and were effectively superseded by the Temporary Short-Time Working Compensation Scheme (TSTWCS), which ran until March 1984. Again, this was designed to prevent redundancy and was similar to the

Table 6.2 Expenditure on the special employment measures, 1975–83 (£m, current prices)

Scheme	*1975/6*	*1976/7*	*1977/8*	*1978/9*	*1979/80*	*1980/1*	*1981/2*	*1982/3*
Wage subsidies								
TES	3	92	174	133	41	1	–	–
SFES	–	–	2	12	45	11	–	–
JIS	–	–	0.04	0.2	0.3	0.3	0.4	0.5
AES	–	–	–	0.3	0.4	–	–	–
Job creation								
JCP	1	35	73	77	5	–	–	–
STEP/CEP	–	–	–	9	51	46	86	307
Youth recruitment subsidies								
RSSL/YES	1	3	5	4	–	–	–	–
Youth employment and training								
WEP/YOP	–	1	33	63	122	212	401	747
Labour supply reduction								
JRS	–	2	15	22	85	136	135	212
STWCS/TSTWCS	–	–	–	1	24	365	260	189
Total	**5**	**133**	**302**	**321**	**374**	**771**	**882**	**1 455**

Note: The table gives gross expenditure. For an explanation of the schemes, see text. Some of the included schemes are discussed in Chapter 7. TES = Temporary Employment Subsidy; SFES = Small Firm Employment Subsidy; JIS = Job Introduction Scheme; AES = Adult Employment Subsidy; JCP = Job Creation Programme; STEP = Special Temporary Employment Programme; CEP = Community Enterprise Programme; RSSL = Recruitment Subsidy for School-Leavers; YES = Youth Employment Subsidy; WEP = Work Experience Programme; YOP = Youth Opportunities Programme; JRS = Job Release Scheme; STWCS/TSTWCS = (Temporary) Short-Time Working Compensation Scheme.
Source: Metcalf (1982), appendix II.

STWCS, except that it extended to any firm which withdrew an impending redundancy affecting ten or more employees. As economic conditions worsened, the take-up of TSTWCS rose dramatically, and at its peak was paid in respect of nearly one million individuals who were effectively sharing jobs, and expenditure stood at £365m (see Table 6.2). At April 1981, 963 100 individuals were covered by special employment measures, and of these, 711 600 were on the TSTWCS (Metcalf, 1982).

The above employment subsidies were designed to stem the flow of redundancies, but in addition recruitment schemes were introduced in attempt to address the high levels of unemployment experienced by some groups in the labour market. To tackle relatively high rates of youth unemployment, the Work Experience Programme (WEP) was adopted from September 1975, paying £18 per week to participants where firms provided an introduction to the working life for a minimum of six months, and the Recruitment Subsidy for School-Leavers (RSSL) was introduced from October 1975, paying £5 per week for up to 26 weeks to firms for each school-leaver recruited. The RSSL was later found to have a high deadweight element and a year after introduction was replaced by the Youth Employment Subsidy (YES). This was aimed at the long-term young unemployed, and paid £10 per week for up to 26 weeks to firms which took on a person under 20 years of age who had previously been unemployed for more than six months, but this scheme was also found to have a high deadweight element, with a net increase in employment of only 25 per 100 placements.

As well as the schemes to alter and increase private-sector demand for labour, the government became involved directly in work creation through the Job Creation Programme (JCP). This was introduced in October 1975 and paid for temporary employment at the appropriate local wage for up to twelve months for people aged 16–24 or over 50 years who would otherwise have been unemployed. The JCP sought to minimize the displacement effect of assistance, so that work was meant to have a social value and would not otherwise have been carried out, but since the subsequent employment benefits of this to the participants were questionable, then the scheme amounted to little more than 'make-work'.

These schemes were revised from April 1978, when the government sought a more integrated approach to tackling the problems of youth and long-term unemployment, resulting in a substantial expansion of the special employment measures. The YES was scrapped in favour of the Youth Opportunities Programme (YOP), which now incorporated the WEP as its major sub-scheme, known as Work Experience on Employers' Premises (WEEP), and the youth component of the JCP. For non-youths (that is, 19 years and over), the JCP was replaced by the Special Temporary Employment Programme (STEP), which provided employment for up to one year in projects of community benefit in areas of high unemployment. A total of around 11 000 places were provided on the STEP annually, with priority given to those aged 19–24 years who had been unemployed for at least six months, and those aged over 24 years who had been unemployed for at least a year. The STEP later expanded into the Community Enterprise Programme (CEP) and then further expanded into the Community Programme (CP) from October 1982. The YOP, which was later to develop into the Youth Training Scheme (YTS), paid a weekly allowance to people aged 16–18 years to engage in work experience, on- and off-the-job training, and various induction and preparatory courses, for a period of up to twelve months. Expenditure on YOP stood at £400m in 1981/2 (see Table 6.2), when there were 371 000 entrants on WEEP, 74 100 on community projects and 91 500 on work preparation, compared with a total of 29 000 participants on the former RSSL and 38 000 on YES.

The expansion of the special employment measures helped to promote the growth of the Manpower Services Commission (MSC), which had been established in January 1974 for the purpose of providing a national system of training and manpower supply. Community projects under STEP and YOP were sponsored mainly by local authorities and voluntary organizations, but these were approved by MSC-run area committees, and the MSC also had responsibility for the YOP, which by 1982 was the destination for more than one in two school leavers. The MSC acquired greater responsibility for training, although this is strictly outside the scope of this book. Early steps in this direction in 1972 were the Community Industry (CI) scheme, which provided grants to employers primarily to help the recruitment of young people to occupations requiring lengthy training, and the Training Opportunities Programme Scheme (TOPS), which sought to rationalize and extend the government's existing vocational training schemes. TOPS did not replace apprenticeships, but gradually took an increasing share of formal training places, so that in 1974 it provided about 45 000 places in addition to the 134 000 on traditional apprenticeships (Bowen, 1991).

FURTHER INVESTMENT AND EMPLOYMENT MEASURES

The special employment measures helped arrest the rise in unemployment, but further sterling crises from March and then from September 1976 resulted in severe cutbacks in public expenditure, and unemployment was to rise to around 1.5 million by mid-1977 (see Figure 5.1 on page 73). With the first sterling crisis, the government obtained a large credit from the Bank for International Settlements, set a target for money supply and in a Budget in July 1976 reined in public expenditure. Automatic industrial subsidies were a target for this, so that Regional Development Grants were no longer available to firms engaged in mining and construction, and from April 1977 grants were paid three months in arrears, while the Regional Employment Premium was effectively cut to a rate of £2 per employee, compared to £3 per adult male and £1.50 per adult female previously. However, a second sterling crisis a few months later led the government to apply for an International Monetary Fund stand-by loan, and the agreed terms for this were for a £1bn cut in public expenditure in 1977/8 and a further £1.5bn cut in 1978/9, together with the sale of £500m in British Petroleum (BP) shares. The Regional Employment Premium was a casualty and was abandoned with more or less immediate effect in a Budget in December 1976. In so doing, the government also removed a potential source of conflict with the European Commission (Bowers, 1991).

Within the context of tight monetary and fiscal policies, and inflation at around 15 per cent and rising, the government came to rely on financial assistance measures to combat and ameliorate certain aspects of unemployment, even though the recent economic experience had suggested that these kind of measures had failed. In the December 1976 Budget, £100m (later increased to £150m) was committed to the Selective Investment Scheme in order to promote investment. Unlike the Accelerated Projects Scheme, which had closed a few months earlier, this was not intended as a counter-cyclical measure and was not only available for the acceleration of projects, but rather for changes in the scale and nature of projects. Eligible purposes were drawn wide to include gains to productivity, technical developments and rationalization, and could extend to product development, licensing, training and the build-up of marketing facilities (Chapman, 1978). Assistance under the Selective Investment Scheme was made with reference to the sectoral strategies, negotiated as the minimum necessary for the project to proceed, and was paid as a grant contingent on performance.

The Selective Investment Scheme closed for applications at the end of June 1979, and of 766 applications received, 176 offers were made, involving assistance payments of £97.5m towards projected investment expenditure of £1041m. But of these, only eleven offers were made in respect of projects located in Scotland, Wales and Northern England, suggesting that firms in the Assisted Areas were able to obtain funding through the usual regional policy channels. Indeed, these eleven projects involved average assistance expenditure of £3.5m, compared with £0.4m on average for other projects, indicating that they were exceptional and would in any case have been dealt with by DTI offices in London.

Further *ad hoc* schemes continued to be added to the existing pattern of assistance, so that from January 1977 the Job Release Scheme (JRS) offered allowances to encourage early retirement, and in the March 1977 Budget the Small Firm Employment Subsidy (SFES) was introduced as an experimental measure to create jobs and help small manufacturing firms. The SFES was in addition to the existing Temporary and Youth Employment Subsidies, and paid firms £20 per week for each full-time job and £10 per week for each part-time job (21–35 hours per week) over and above that number existing at some given base date. Initially, the scheme was to run for six months, until December 1977, covering manufacturing firms with fewer than 50 employees in the Special Development Areas. However, as the results of a preliminary evaluation became known, it was extended for six months, and then expanded from July 1978 to cover all manufacturing firms with less than 200 employees throughout the Assisted Areas and also in the newly-designated inner city areas (see below). From January to June 1979, the scheme applied to the whole of Great Britain, with some non-manufacturing firms in designated areas eligible, and then from July 1979 to its abolition a year later it was confined to the Development and Special Development Areas.

Firms could claim the SFES for each job, up to a maximum of 26 weeks, but total expenditure on the scheme amounted to around £70m (see Table 6.2). An average of 40 000 jobs were supported by the subsidy, but the interim evaluation suggested that only a quarter of these were new jobs and that a further quarter were jobs brought forward (Department of Employment, 1978).

SHIPBUILDING

The government was faced with the same problems in shipbuilding that had dogged its predecessors. In 1974 it had faced the collapse of the Court Line, but the solution was to take its shipbuilding interests into public ownership for a consideration of £16m, including Sunderland Shipbuilders on Wearside, and the Appledore yard in Devon. Prior to acquisition, loans had been agreed with Sunderland Shipbuilders for reconstruction and modernization, £15m being paid; and a £9m loan was made to Austin and Pickersgill for modernization. The Labour government continued selective interventions, so that in its first few years of office it agreed assistance of £17.2m to Govan Shipbuilders to prevent redundancies in an area of high unemployment, and later converted £19m in loans to equity. Further aid was provided to the Cammell Laird modernization programme, which had run into difficulties through rising costs, and the government became the sole shareholder in Harland and Wolff. The downturn in demand also affected oil-rig construction, and here the government placed a speculative order with the Marathon Company, which had earlier taken over the Clydeside yard of Upper Clyde Shipbuilders, through a £6.5m loan to the British National Oil Corporation, and converted £6m in loans into share capital.

In the face of these continuing problems, and with inflation high, some general relief was afforded to shipbuilding in April 1976 through the Cost Escalation Scheme under section 7 of the 1972 Industry Act. This extended to UK shipowners and yards similar insurance cover to that provided by the ECGD for ships sold for export. The shipbuilder was required to bear cost overruns up to an agreed threshold, but then cover was provided on the remainder up to some ceiling in return for a premium. It was intended that the scheme should run for one year, but it was eventually terminated at the end of June 1980. Total premiums were £9.1m, and payments of £40.7m were made in respect of forty-eight policies.

The Bill to nationalize the aircraft and shipbuilding industries was introduced to Parliament in May 1975, but the shipbuilding industry was only taken into public ownership some two years later, after a protracted and sometimes controversial legislative process.[9] To maintain confidence and support shipbuilding in the interim, two new schemes were brought forward under the 1972 Industry Act. Both of these were introduced under section 7 of the Act relating to the Assisted Areas, rather than Part III relating to shipbuilding, since in this way the government could offer grant assistance at a rate of up to 30 per cent, and thereby avoid the aid ceiling imposed by the European Commission, and circumvent the requirement that aid should be eliminated as quickly as possible. The first scheme was the Refund Guarantees (Performance Bonds), which from April 1976 guaranteed stage payments made to UK shipbuilders, which went into liquidation prior to nationalization. The second scheme was the Intervention Fund, which from February 1977 offered £65m in grants for up to 30 per cent of the cost price of merchant ships in order to secure orders. The Intervention Fund was subject to close scrutiny by the Commission, and the government supported it by arguing that the assistance would enable cost reductions and improve efficiency. The initial allocation was soon taken up, and further amounts were negotiated with the

Commission, including £120m in October 1979. By April 1983 more than £200m had been paid in respect of 192 ships. Subsequent tranches were less generous than the first, and each case was subject to EC inspection to ensure that the assistance was linked to restructuring. The Fourth Directive on Aid to Shipbuilding required that intervention should be progressively reduced and linked to reductions in capacity.

Shipbuilding became heavily assisted in the 1970s, and details of this are given in Table 5.2 on page 84. Much of this support was either potentially recoverable or, as in the case of the guarantees under the Home Credit Scheme, involved little expenditure. Grant payments were made mainly under the Intervention Fund and the Construction Grant Scheme; the latter was introduced in the early 1970s to avert a collapse in shipbuilding. In Table 6.3 we present figures for gross expenditure on assistance over the period 1972–80 for each industrial sector. This includes loans and grants, but does not include the guarantees and tax allowances. It shows that shipbuilding was one of the most heavily assisted industries over this period, receiving more than one-tenth of the assistance, but that other relatively capital-intensive industries also received substantial amounts of aid over the period. In particular, the chemicals and metal manufacturing industries received nearly a third of the identified assistance, but despite this, both these industries experienced large falls in employment up to the early 1980s. In shipbuilding and repair, employment declined from 131 000 in 1980 to 77 000 in 1987, following the adoption of European Commission proposals in 1977 to nearly halve European shipbuilding capacity. This decline was partly anticipated by central government, and under the 1978 Shipbuilding (Redundancy Payments) Act it announced a programme of advance factory construction in affected areas and a scheme of redundancy payments for shipyard workers.

THE EUROPEAN COMMUNITY CONTRIBUTION

The economic crises of the mid-1970s boosted the industrial subsidy programmes of member states, and at first the European Commission took a lenient view, so that an operating subsidy to safeguard employment was permitted provided capacity was not increased, and that the subsidy was for the benefit of firms that were 'basically sound' (CEC, 1976). Member states were required to give prior notification of all general aid schemes, and concurrent notification of the more important assistance cases, but as the number of notified aid schemes increased substantially, from 21 in

Table 6.3 Sectoral incidence of assistance expenditure, 1972–80 (£m, current prices)

Industry grouping	*Regional aid*		*National aid*		*Total aid*		*Share of employment (1976)*
	RDG	*RSA*	*APS & SIS*	*Sectoral aid*	*£'m*	*%*	
Agriculture, forestry and fishing	–	0.1	–	–	0.1	0.0	1.7
Mining and quarrying	110	3	–	–	113	2.9	1.6
Food, drink and tobacco	260	22	7	12	301	7.7	3.1
Coal and petroleum products	179	0.3	20	–	199	5.1	0.2
Chemicals and allied products	589	34	83	–	706	18.0	1.9
Metal manufacture	446	22	7	58	533	13.6	2.1
Engineering	279	127	32	36	474	12.1	8.2
Shipbuilding and marine eng.	51	11	0.1	408	470	12.0	0.8
Other manufacturing	639	217	41	68	965	24.5	16.1
Construction	110	2	–	–	112	2.8	5.7
Services and utilities	–	22	–	–	22	0.6	58.6
Not classified	30	2	1	–	33	0.7	–
Total	**2693**	**462**	**191**	**582**	**3928**	**100.0**	**100.0**

Notes: The industrial groupings chosen correspond to the 1968 Standard Industrial Classification (SIC). Engineering comprises SIC Industrial Orders VII to IX; Other manufacturing comprises Orders XI to XIX; and Services and utilities comprises Orders XXI to XXVII. RDG = Regional Development Grant; RSA = Regional Selective Assistance; APS = Accelerated Projects Scheme; SIS = Selective Investment Scheme. Sectoral aid includes the Wool Textile Industry Scheme, the sectoral schemes in Table 6.1 and the shipbuilding assistance shown in Table 5.2 but excluding the loan guarantees. Tax allowances are not included in the table since no sectoral breakdown is available. RSA includes £127m in loans and a few equity cases, while £120m of the £408m in sectoral aid to the shipbuilding industry was in the form of loans and equity. The expenditure shown covers the financial years 1972/3 to 1980/1 inclusive.

Sources: *Annual Reports on the 1972 Industry Act* (London: HMSO); *Employment Gazette* (London: HMSO).

1970 to 137 in 1978, the Commission took a much tougher stance, placing more emphasis on the need to restore competitiveness and objecting to a large proportion of the proposed schemes (Curzon Price, 1990). In addition to setting the limits for the industrial assistance of member states, the Community also became increasingly important in financing various industry and infrastructure projects through its Structural Funds. In Table 6.4 we show spending on these measures for the UK, and this indicates that expenditure grew rapidly in the late 1970s, increasing from

Table 6.4 UK spending under community structural funds, 1973–9 (£m, current prices)

	1973	*1974*	*1975*	*1976*	*1977*	*1978*	*1979*
EIB Loans							
Industry	34	35	32	59	117	45	41
Infrastructure	–	41	155	201	203	241	436
ECSC Loans							
Industry	–	17	70	234	114	19	17
Infrastructure	–	17	78	89	57	162	150
Interest relief grants	–	1	2	2	5	4	10
ESF	29	32	62	66	149	74	127
ERDF							
industry	–	–	17	36	43	38	49
infrastructure	–	–	32	52	52	61	118
EAGGF Guidance Fund							
Industry	9	14	21	33	44	26	45
Infrastructure	1	1	1	1	2	–	1
Total assistance							
Loans	**34**	**111**	**337**	**583**	**491**	**467**	**644**
Grants	**39**	**48**	**135**	**190**	**295**	**203**	**350**

Notes: The average annual ecu-sterling exchange rate is used for each year to convert reported ecu figures to sterling. Infrastructure projects include assistance given for energy-related purposes. ECSC interest relief grants are reported for the Community as a whole, and these have been apportioned to the UK according to its share of ECSC loans. EIB = European Investment Bank; ECSC = European Coal and Steel Community; ESF = European Social Fund; ERDF = European Regional Development Fund; EAGGF = European Agricultural Guidance and Guarantee Fund.
Source: *European Economy*, no 6, July 1980 (Brussels: Commission of the European Communities).

£159m in 1974 to around £773m in 1976 and standing at almost £1bn by 1979.

The major source of EC funds was the European Investment Bank (EIB), which provided nearly £500m in loans in the UK in 1979, mainly towards major development and infrastructure projects, such as the Sullom Voe oil terminal in the Shetland Isles; various water-based schemes including the Dinorwic hydroelectric power station in Wales; the development of telephone links with continental Europe; and the development of the advanced passenger train (Department of Industry, 1980). The EIB had been established under Article 130 of the Treaty of Rome as an independent, non-profit-making body to help stimulate the development of less-favoured regions (the Assisted Areas in the case of the UK); to modernize and convert firms, and create new enterprises to offset structural change in certain industrial sectors; and to serve the common interest of the EC by increasing industrial co-operation and the use of advanced technology. To promote these roles, the EIB could make 50 per cent loans and guarantees to private and public enterprises and public authorities to finance specific investment projects. In addition, it could provide 'global' loans to various organizations that extended loans to small and medium-sized ventures. In general, the EIB did not make loans of less than £2.6m for any one project, but the Department of Industry, acting as an agent for the EIB, obtained a global loan to provide loans of up to £2.6m, mainly to new and small firms.

The major source of loans to UK industry in the 1970s was the European Coal and Steel Community (ECSC). These loans were either provided under Article 54 of the Treaty of Rome towards 50 per cent of fixed costs for the purpose of restructuring the steel industry, or under Article 56 to create new jobs for redundant coal and steel workers, but within a fifteen-mile radius of a coal or steel operation shedding labour. Loans were also offered to help resettle workers, and readaptation grants were available for retraining and resettlement. The ECSC was not a bank, so that it would borrow funds according to demand and re-lend these at the same rate. Industrial loans could receive an interest relief grant of 3 per cent per annum over five years if the project reduced energy costs or involved modernization without increasing production, and reconversion loans could also receive an interest rebate on a job-related basis but, as Table 6.4 shows, spending on these interest relief grants was small. Interest rate grants and administration costs were met from the ECSC's budget of around £100m per annum, which was raised from a levy on production, and in 1979 the UK received around £167m in loans from the ECSC.

A Structural Fund that was of much less significance for direct industrial support was the European Social Fund (ESF). This sought to improve employment opportunities by encouraging geographical and occupational mobility through training and retraining in the priority areas of problem regions, of young people, the handicapped, migrant workers and women. The Fund reimbursed 50 per cent of the cost of public sector training schemes and matched the public sector contribution to private schemes, but it did not provide support for capital expenditure. In 1979, spending in the UK was comparatively small at around £130m, but the ESF became a major contributor to the activities of the Manpower Services Commission in the early 1980s. The Guidance section of the EAGGF was mainly to improve the processing and marketing of agricultural and fish products. Grant payments of up to 50 per cent of project cost were made within investment programmes agreed with the Commission, but expenditure was small in the UK, at around £46m in 1979. The other main EC fund was the European Regional Development Fund, which was described in Chapter 5. Under this, the UK received around £167m in grants in 1979, about the same as in loans from the ECSC in that year.

In the early years of membership, the UK received a substantial share of the Structural Funds, amounting to around 29 per cent of the total in 1979. This was partly to recompense the UK for its relatively small proportion of the CAP Budget, which in 1979 stood at 8.9 per cent of the total. But since the CAP took 81 per cent of the EC budget in 1979 (excluding the activities of the EIB and ECSC), then this issue was to become a major source of contention in the early 1980s, leading to a rebate in the UK contribution to the EC. Table 6.4 shows that the major sources of EC support for industry in the 1970s were the loans from the EIB and ECSC, and while the grant assistance from the ERDF also appears to be substantial, this in fact served to recompense central government for existing UK regional policy payments, with a few large cases of assistance being submitted to the Commission each year for refund.

FROM REGIONAL TO URBAN POLICY

The economy was experiencing a mild recovery by May 1977, but the recession of the mid-1970s had altered the structure of industrial assistance fundamentally. Regional aid had failed to lead to the sustained and high rate of national economic growth envisaged in the March 1972 White Paper *Industrial and Regional Development*, and even failed in the more modest objective of holding down unemployment. Moreover, as unemployment increased and became a nationwide problem, so attention shifted away from regional policy matters, and towards the targeting of firms and people as the government sought more direct means of reducing unemployment and ameliorating some of the worst social aspects. Regional policy remained, but in its last few years of office the Labour government chipped away at various aspects of the policy, foreshadowing its eventual abandonment in the mid-1980s. By the summer of 1977 the plans to disperse civil service employment to the regions was at a standstill, ODPs had effectively been terminated in the face of a continued loss of employment from London, some Development Areas had been downgraded (the first time this had occurred since the 1966 Act) and the recommendations of the NEB to increase the differential subsidy in favour of the Development and Special Development Areas were met in only very limited measure (McCallum, 1979).[10]

Between 1975 and 1977, regional policy spending fell by 50 per cent in real terms as the effects of abolition of the Regional Employment Premium were felt and as a downturn in investment reduced the take-up of regional assistance. In May 1978, the ceiling on section 8 assistance was raised to £1000m from £850m, but the section 7 limit remained unchanged at £350m, even though a large £75m interest relief grant had been provided to the Ford Motor Company under this facility. The shift towards sectoral assistance as a means of strengthening industry further weakened the significance of regional aid, and it was perhaps no coincidence that the announcement of the abolition of the Regional Employment Premium coincided with the introduction of the Selective Investment Scheme, which in its effect heavily favoured the non-Assisted Areas.

However, it was not only that regional policy was ineffective, or that unemployment was rising across the country, which signalled the demise of regional aid, but that the very pattern of unemployment had changed. Nationally, employment had peaked in 1966, and the subsequent loss of jobs, particularly in manufacturing, which declined at average annual rates of 1.1 per cent over 1966–71 and 1.8 per cent over 1971–5, affected the major conurbations adversely. London experienced a 37.8 per cent reduction in manufacturing employment over the period 1959–75, and the six next-largest conurbations experienced an overall decline of 15.9 per cent over the same period (Fothergill and Gudgin, 1982). Industrial expansion was occurring away from these areas, leading to an urban-to-rural shift in employment, and as the rapid decline in coal-mining employment stalled, and as employment in the textiles and clothing industries was being shored up by the Temporary Employment Subsidy, so there existed a considerable diversity of circumstance within the Assisted Areas, leading some to argue for greater geographical selectivity in policy (Townsend, 1977). Existing regional policy was singularly ill-equipped to perform this task, since not only had IDCs – which could have been used to direct industry – been abandoned in the Development and Special Development Areas in 1972, but the differential subsidy in favour of Special Development Areas – drawn around only some of the large cities even within the Assisted Areas – was inadequate and the government had shown a reluctance to increase this. Thus a new set of urban policy assistance came to be added to the existing regional, national and special employment measures, and, with time, urban policy came to replace regional policy as the major spatially-defined development policy.

THE URBAN PROGRAMME

The origins of modern urban policy could be traced to the mid-1960s and were in part a response to the emerging concentrations of ethnic minorities in inner city areas, which were experiencing acute housing, employment and educational difficulties. The 1966 Local Government Act allowed for local authorities with a substantial immigrant population to receive special grants to employ extra teaching staff, and the 1967 Plowden Report recommended the establishment of Educational Priority Areas, with the intention that children with serious disadvantage should be given compensatory education. The 1967 Milner–Holland Report also advocated that certain areas with poor housing should receive special help and attention, but the real catalyst to policy was the so-called 'rivers of blood' speech delivered to Parliament in April 1968 by Enoch Powell, after which the government announced a working party to develop an urban programme. This drew heavily on the Plowden Report, and building on the provisions of the 1966 Local Government Act, recommended a policy of discrimination in favour of those local authorities experiencing multiple deprivation within their boundaries.

The Urban Programme was announced in July 1968, under which the government agreed to meet 75 per cent of the cost of eligible projects, with local authorities meeting the remainder from their own funds. Local authorities with high incidences of overcrowding, large families, unemployment, poor housing and other symptoms of deprivation were invited to submit projects for consideration, but spending was modest, amounting to £55.5m by the end of 1975. The programme was administered by the Home Office, and early schemes concentrated on social projects, but later leaned towards helping the deprived take better advantage of available services, and then still later concentrated on environmental schemes and projects supporting economic activity (Lawless, 1988). Twelve Community Development Projects were set up by the Home Office in 1969 to carry out experimental projects in small urban localities and, like the Inner Area Studies which were commissioned by the Department of the Environment on Lambeth, Birmingham and Liverpool in 1972, their conclusion was that urban deprivation arose from low levels of income resulting from economic decline, and it was this explanation that was to form the basis for subsequent urban policy interventions.

The real impetus to urban policy came in 1976 with scenes of violence at the Notting Hill carnival, which within a month led the government to commission a programme of urban aid (Parsons, 1988). The issue attracted considerable interest, and the proposals for a new and expanded Urban Programme were set out in the June 1977 White Paper *Policy for the Inner Cities* (Cmnd 6845, 1977). This drew heavily on the Inner Area Studies and proposed six initiatives to tackle the urban problem:

(a) reorganization of existing programmes and policies to help inner areas, including the adjustment of Rate Support Grant to take account of inner city needs;
(b) inner city areas to take precedence in the granting of IDCs after the Intermediate Areas;
(c) New Towns to take secondary place to that of declining cities, and to assist firms to locate in rather than out of inner cities;
(d) funding of the Urban Programme to be substantially increased from £30m in 1976/7 to £125m in 1979/80;
(e) the transfer of the Urban Programme from the Home Office to the Department of the Environment, and the expansion of the Urban Programme to include industrial, environmental and recreational measures as well as social projects; and
(f) the creation of special local and central government partnerships for some of the larger cities, and the designation of other inner areas in need of special help.

The proposals, which related to England, were given effect by the July 1978 Inner Urban Areas Act, which gave the Secretary of State for the Environment the power to declare as a 'designated district' any inner urban area with special social needs.[11] Local authorities containing these designated districts were then enpowered to make loans at commercial rates for the acquisition of land or the carrying out of work to land, and to allocate loans and grants of up to £1000 towards the cost of establishing a co-operative or common ownership enterprise. This assistance could be given throughout the administrative area, but only for the benefit of the designated district. Within the designated districts the local authority could also declare Improvement Areas of either a commercial or industrial nature, and within these areas offer loans and grants for improvements to the environment and amenities, and grants at rates not exceeding 50 per cent towards the conversion, extension, improvement or modification of commercial or industrial buildings. By 1984 more than 200 Industrial Improvement Areas had been declared.

The Inner Urban Areas Act permitted the Secretary of State to enter into an arrangement with district authorities where concerted action was required to alleviate special needs, and these were known as Partnership or Programme Authorities. Initially, five areas were selected as Partnership Authorities: Lambeth, Birmingham, Liverpool, Manchester/Salford, and London Docklands, the first three of which had been the subject of Inner Area Studies. Later, Hackney/Islington and Newcastle/Gateshead were added when these submitted proposals.[12] For these authorities the government could further designate Special Areas in which extra aid was available, comprising subsidized loans for site preparation and basic services, grants towards rent payments, and interest relief grants to smaller firms for the acquisition or carrying out of works to land. Fifteen Programme Authorities were designated, which had much greater autonomy from central government, and fourteen Other Designated Districts were declared, which could submit projects to government on a one-off basis. These, like non-designated local authorities, also received funding through the pre-existing Urban Programme, which remained in place and was known as the Traditional Urban Programme. For all eligible projects, central government provided a grant of 75 per cent towards the cost of the project. The main distinction between the different tiers of Urban Programme authority were their administration and level of funding. In its first full year of operation, £165m was allocated to the Urban Programme, of which £90m went to Partnership Authorities, £32m to Programme Authorities, and £33m to the Other Designated Districts and Traditional Urban Programme (HC 513, 1985).

LOCAL AUTHORITY FINANCIAL ASSISTANCE

The Urban Programme helped to promote the expansion of local authority loans and grants policies, which were to become an important source of funds for many small firms in urban areas, amounting to around £26m per annum in England in the mid-1980s (Armstrong, 1988).[13] These policies were primarily a response to rapidly-rising unemployment, but intervention by local authorities to promote employment was not new; it could be traced to the 1930s, and before that to the large municipalities of the late nineteenth century (Chandler and Lawless, 1985). Economic development was a non-statutory function of local authorities, and the powers to disburse industrial financial assistance arose in an *ad hoc* manner. Early powers to make contributions to bodies carrying on activities for the purpose of furthering trade, industry or commerce were available under the 1948 Local Government Act, but required Ministerial consent, while the 1963 Local Authority (Land) Act provided direct powers to give loans at commercial rates for the purposes of acquiring and developing land, and for the construction of industrial buildings.[14] Some local authorities sponsored their own Private Bills through Parliament, all of which expired by 1984, and important in this respect was the 1976 Tyne and Wear Act, which helped to form the basis for the 1978 Inner Urban Areas Act (Lawless, 1981).

General powers to incur expenditure for any purpose in the interests of an area or its inhabitants up to the product of an (old) penny rate existed under the 1963 Local Government (Financial Provisions) Act, but this was largely of an insignificant amount. However, section 137 of the 1972 Local Government Act raised the rate product limit to two (new) pence, and coupled with a general rating revaluation from April 1973, the available resources increased as much as fifteenfold (CIPFA, 1985).[15] Section 137 became a major source of funds for economic development, especially by some of the large metropolitan authorities created by local government reorganization in 1974, and while some uncertainty existed over its use in relation to financial assistance, this was cleared up by the 1982 Local Government (Miscellaneous Provisions) Act, which enabled local authorities to give industrial assistance in the form of loans, grants and guarantees. Later, the 1989 Local Government and Housing Act granted local authorities formal powers to promote the economic development of their area, and regulations issued soon afterwards allowed subsidies for a wide range of activities, but forbade wage subsidies except where they were either part of a government or EC scheme, or where the beneficiary had been unemployed beforehand. Nevertheless, even though over a third of local authorities were offering finance to industry in 1971 (JURUE, 1981), expenditure on industrial assistance by local authorities over much of the period was relatively small when compared with other programmes, amounting to £5m in England in 1976/7, and £7m in 1978/9 (Department of the Environment, 1980).

TECHNOLOGY SUPPORT

An important development towards the end of the Labour government's term of office was the support given to key technologies, and for the promotion of the awareness and take-up of these. Research and development had been supported since the Second World War by the National Research Development Corporation and later under the 1965 Science and Technology Act. With the move towards smaller-scale and more focused interventions in the late 1970s, technology became a natural outlet for this assistance. The Product and Process Development Scheme (PPDS) in 1977 brought together a number of schemes previously operating under the 1965 Science and Technology Act, offering assistance towards the cost of bringing new processes and products from the design stage to commercial exploitation.[16] The assistance was usually in the form of a 25 per cent grant and the government could also place pre-production orders for user trials. In exceptional circumstances, a 50:50 shared-cost contract could be offered, with the public contribution recovered through a levy on sales. By March 1979, 220 offers had been made under PPDS, involving £27.4m in assistance.

A number of specific schemes followed in 1978, including the Microprocessor Application Project (MAP), later known as the Microelectronics Application Project, and the Microelectronics Industry Support Programme (MISP). MAP was introduced under the 1965 Act as a quick response to concern over the relatively slow UK take-up of microelectronics technology, and provided 25 per cent grants towards projects embodying this technology, with an allocation of £55m. It also provided training, short courses and consultancy grants of £2000 to identify and establish feasible projects, of which around 1800 had been approved by the end of 1980. MISP arose partly from the work of the sector working parties (W. Grant, 1982), and provided assistance for the design and manufacture of silicon integrated circuits and for the development of such devices. The scheme was mainly funded under section 8 of the 1972 Industry Act, but the initial allocation of £70m was cut to £55m in late 1979 because at first the attitude of the incoming Conservative government proved to be only lukewarm to these measures.

The introduction of the technology-based schemes signalled an important change of direction for industrial assistance towards improving the competitiveness of firms, other than through measures to rationalize and reorganize capacity. Table 6.5 shows that expenditure on these measures was comparatively small during the Labour government's term of office, amounting to no more than £20m by April 1979, but these measures were

Table 6.5 Expenditure on new technology measures, 1977–82 (£m, current prices)

Scheme	*1977/8*	*1978/9*	*1979/80*	*1980/1*	*1981/2*
Product and Process Development Scheme	1.5	8.3	19.2	21.9	24.7
Microelectronics Application Programme	2.7	4.9	8.8	10.9	10.7
MAP training, short-course and consultancy	–	–	1.8	3.6	3.8
Microelectronics Industry Support Programme	–	–	1.2	1.3	3.7
Total	**4.2**	**13.2**	**31.0**	**37.7**	**42.9**

Note: MAP = Microprocessor Application Project.
Source: *Annual Review of Government Funded R&D 1983* (London: HMSO, 1984); *Annual Reports on the 1972 Industry Act* (London: HMSO).

to increase in significance over the following five years, and by the early 1980s expenditure was running at more than £40m per annum, with the PPDS accounting for more than half of this.

The financial constraints imposed on the National Enterprise Board by its holding of government rescue operations meant that it mainly initiated new ventures, and many of these were in high-technology areas. In 1978, these included Nexos Office Systems to develop advanced office equipment, and Insac to market software overseas, but the most notable case was Inmos International. This was provided with £25m to establish research facilities at Colorado Springs, USA for the development of a silicon chip with applications to telecommunications and industrial control systems, but the incoming Conservative government baulked at providing the second tranche of £25m, and only announced this in July 1980 after attempts had been made to offload the project to GEC. Production was established at Newport in South Wales in order to take advantage of £35m in regional assistance, and away from the firm's base in Bristol. The plant was sold to Thorn-EMI for £95m in 1984, and then to SGS-Thomson in 1989, which planned to move production to France. The case undermined the industrial strategy, since, as W. Grant (1982) notes, in establishing Inmos the NEB had failed to consult with the relevant sector working party on the grounds of commercial confidentiality, and this problem effectively undermined much of the working of these groups.

ASSISTANCE EXPENDITURE IN THE 1970s

The period of the 1970s is notable for a number of structural shifts that occurred in industrial policy. These shifts are evident from Figure 6.1, which gives spending over the period in grant equivalents at constant 1980 prices. The figure shows the dramatic decline in expenditure in the early 1970s, arising principally from the withdrawal of the Selective Employment Tax refund, but also from the elimination of the nationally available investment grants. We see the steady rise in expenditure over the middle part of the decade arising from the policy reversal, including the introduction and extension nationally of the free depreciation on plant and machinery, and the reactivation of regional policy. Finally, we see the decline in subsidy expenditure in the late 1970s, due mainly to the reduced take-up of the depreciation allowances in recession. The reduction in regional assistance is evident from the mid-1970s, following the sterling

Figure 6.1 Expenditure on industrial subsidies in the 1970s

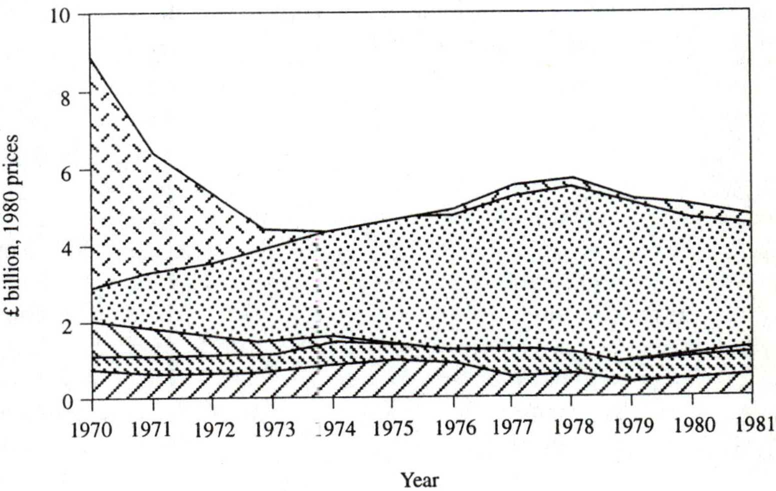

Notes: The figures show expenditure in grant equivalents at 1980 prices. Financial years are shown as calendar years.

Key: Regional assistance; Sectoral and firm specific aid; National investment grants; Depreciation allowances; National employment subsidies

Source: Wren (1996b), tables 1, 2 and 3.

crises, but there is in fact some increase in direct subsidy payments in the early 1980s associated with efforts to assist companies in difficulty.

Despite these changes in the scale and composition of industrial subsidy policy, the measures pursued at this time were essentially the same as those followed in the late 1960s, albeit at a much more intense level. What is perhaps surprising is that, given this experience, industrial subsidies should continue to be viewed as the key to reversing deteriorating economic conditions, and that, as conditions continued to worsen, the effectiveness of the measures were not called into question. Excluding the subsidy associated with the refund on Selective Employment Tax, real expenditure on industrial subsidies actually increased up to the late 1970s, and it was only the pressures on public expenditure that led to some reduction in spending. All the same, the period proved to be the watershed for industrial assistance policy, and the changes made at this time heralded the future direction of policy. These included greater selectivity in an attempt to improve effectiveness, including urban and direct labour market interventions, and efforts to improve productivity and efficiency under the various sectoral and technology-based schemes. The reductions in spending on the large-scale subsidies at the end of this decade also foreshadowed the more extensive cuts to be made in the 1980s.

7 Change and Continuity in Industrial Assistance (Early 1980s)

THE POLICY OUTLINE

The economic events of the mid-1970s forced the government into counter-inflation measures, including an incomes policy which traded tax cuts for reductions in wage inflation, and the introduction of a monetary target. Price inflation bottomed out at around 8 per cent in 1978, from 24 per cent three years earlier, but the incomes policy reduced the relative pay of public-sector employees and the attempt to catch up led to the 'winter of discontent', which was a precursor to the return of a Conservative government in May 1979 (Tomlinson, 1990; Allsopp, 1991). In this new climate the control of inflation through monetarism became the central tenet of policy, with the Medium Term Financial Strategy the mechanism for targeting the money supply and Public Sector Borrowing Requirement. Demand management was in effect discarded and the objective of full employment was effectively abandoned. Instead, the government sought to tackle the root cause of Britain's relative economic decline, and this required attention to the supply side of the economy. The aim was to improve efficiency, return nationalized industries to the private sector and liberalize markets so as to encourage entrepreneurship and the formation of new firms.

Within this context, the termination of industrial subsidies seemed a *fait accompli*, but while major changes were made, the first Conservative government continued the evolution that had begun with its predecessor, and small-scale assistance schemes became an important element of policy, giving both change and continuity (Grant and Wilks, 1983). The focus on the supply side did not deny the use of temporary subsidies to promote efficiency and the adoption of new technologies, and these measures became known as 'constructive interventions'. Similarly, temporary subsidies could be used to attract internationally mobile investment and to support projects of national or strategic importance. It was the permanent subsidies used to prop up the lame ducks and the ongoing blanket subsidies that most raised the hackles of detractors (Burton, 1979), and it was to these that attention was turned. The complete abandonment of automatic industrial assistance did not appear to be an option, especially as the economy was going into recession, and in the case of regional policy the government took the view that, on balance, 'the advantage lay in maintaining a policy which sought by a variety of instruments to encourage more industrial development in some parts of the country than would otherwise have taken place' (Department of Industry, 1981). Thus, as it turned out, the automatic subsidies were phased out gradually as the economy recovered from recession, and in the interim efforts were made to sharpen the differential subsidy in favour of the worse-off areas, to improve effectiveness and to prune spending.

THE REVIEW OF INDUSTRIAL AID

On gaining office, the Conservatives undertook an immediate review of industrial aid, and the results of this became known in July 1979. The main focus was regional policy, which the government sought to focus on the worse-off areas, partly to save on expenditure. The review proposed a major reduction in the coverage of the Assisted Areas from 40 per cent to 28 per cent of the working population to be staged in August 1980 and August 1982. While the three-tier system of designated area was maintained, the Development and Intermediate Areas were substantially reduced such that the Assisted Areas no longer covered the whole of Scotland, Wales and northern England, but were mainly confined to the conurbations in peripheral areas, coastal areas, the Highlands and Islands of Scotland, and to a new Development Area declared in the steel closure area of Corby, Northants in December 1979 (see Appendix Figure A.3 in the Appendix on page 217). The subsidy in favour of Special Development Areas was increased, but this was achieved by cutting the rate of Regional Development Grant in the Development Areas to 15 per cent and by disallowing RDG in Intermediate Areas on buildings and works from August 1980.[1]

As a further measure to reduce expenditure, an immediate Conservative step on gaining office was to defer approved RDG payments by four months from June 1979, which was to last until November 1982. This increased the average time between the receipt of RDG applications and payment to some seven to eight months, and was estimated to have reduced expenditure by £110m in 1979/80.[2] Industrial Development Certificates were also no longer required in the Intermediate Areas, but in any case these were being applied weakly and in January 1982 they were suspended and in effect abolished.

The review tightened the eligibility criteria for RSA with two new conditions:

(a) the provision of assistance should lead to a significant change in the nature or scale of the project, or a significant advance in timing or a desirable change in location; and
(b) the project should strengthen the regional and national economy and thereby provide more productive and more secure jobs (for example, by improving efficiency or by introducing new technologies or products).

These conditions were in addition to the requirements of project viability, the creation or maintenance of employment and that the greater part of the project should be funded from sources outside the public sector. The first new condition, requiring 'proof of need', reintroduced a condition of the 1945 Distribution of Industry Act that assistance could only be provided if funds could not be obtained on the requisite terms from elsewhere, which had been dropped by the 1960 Local Employment Act. In time, this condition extended to virtually every area of industrial aid, and one of its consequences was that assistance could generally only be given where a start on a project had not already been made. The second new condition, requiring that the project be of national interest, indicated that the redistribution of jobs through industrial relocation was no longer a major aim of policy. To cut down on administration costs, section 7 loans were only given in exceptional circumstances, with assistance provided mainly in the form of small capital grants. In 1980/1 there were no loan offers and 283 offers of capital grant, compared with just five grant offers two years earlier.

One motive for the changes to regional policy was to improve the employment effectiveness of policy. Reports of the House of Commons Expenditure Committee (HC 651, 1972; HC 85, 1973) had been critical that too little had been known about the effects of policy before changes had been made, but now the results of research and other evidence was becoming available and this suggested that jobs were sometimes being created at great cost, so the government sought better value for money. The Permanent Secretary of the Department of Industry told the Committee of Public Accounts (HC 623, 1978, Q. 3681) that the cost of each job created or maintained by section 7 of the Industry Act was £1200, which compared with flat-rate unemployment benefit of £1446 per annum, although, since 'proof of need' was not required nor tested for, this was more properly the grant-per-job. However, a year earlier, the Public

Accounts Committee had examined a number of oil industry projects qualifying for substantial amounts of Regional Development Grant. An oil terminal at Seal Sands on Teesside received around £36 500 in respect of each project job, and the figure was around £60 000 for each job which qualified for RDG (that is, oil refining rather than oil storage or movement). For the Rhosgoch Tank Farm on Anglesey the respective figures were £107 000 and £187 500, and for Flotta Terminal on Orkney they were £140 500 and £228 000 (HC 536 (1977) paras 3–9).

The Public Accounts Committee's conclusion had been that it was 'not cost-effective to pay large regional development grants on projects which would be located in the assisted areas anyway' (HC 536 (1977) para. 16), but the Labour government resisted this, arguing that the grant scheme sought the regeneration of industry rather than specific employment, and stressed the importance to the scheme of simple, objective criteria and continuity of the incentive offered.[3] While the changes announced in 1980 did not tackle the problems raised by the Committee directly, the smaller grant rates on RDG, the reduced coverage of the Development Areas and the new conditions on RSA sought some improvement in the overall effectiveness of policy, as well as a reduction in expenditure.

A measure that was left intact by the review was the regional assistance to the service sector, but this was because efforts had already been made to improve the effectiveness of this assistance a few months earlier. Changes to the Service Industry Removal Grant Scheme (SIRGS) in October 1976 made the scheme more generous by increasing the grant to £1500 for each employee relocated (up to 50 per cent of the number of new jobs created in the Assisted Areas) and by increasing the period over which the selective grant was payable in SDAs to 7 years from 5 years. A new grant of £1500 in SDAs and £1000 in DAs was also payable for each job created in these areas. Further changes in March 1979 revamped this scheme as the Office and Service Industry Scheme to make it more favourable to indigenous job creation. The selective component of SIRGS was abandoned and the £1500 removal grant limited to essential staff up to 30 per cent of the jobs being created. The job creation grant was raised to stand at £6000 in SDAs, £4000 in DAs and £2000 in IAs for each new job created within three years of the project's commencement, and the assistance could no longer be claimed in addition to other aid.

The other major change to policy centred around the National Enterprise Board. The July 1979 review announced that this would cease to act as general merchant bank and that it would lose its industrial restructuring role, so that support for companies in difficulty would only be provided on government initiative and on a temporary and tapering nature.

Further, the NEB's existing portfolio was to be disposed of to private ownership as soon as possible, while its investments in newly-established technology companies would be retained to allow these companies to develop before disposal. The NEB's North and North West offices could continue to make industrial investments in small firms, subject to maximizing the private contribution and disposing of these assets as soon as possible. The June 1980 Industry Act gave effect to these proposals, and similar provisions were applied to the Scottish and Welsh Development Agencies, so that these could continue to make investments from borrowing up to specified ceilings.[4]

At May 1980 the NEB had holdings in 69 companies at an historic cost of £1252m. Its major holdings were in British Leyland (£845m), Rolls-Royce (£234m), Herbert (£45m), Fairey Holdings (£18m), CIC Investment Holdings (£15m), Data Recording Instrument Co. (£12m), Inmos International (£11m), Insac (£7m) and Nexos Office Systems (£6m).[5] In 1980/1, the government received £54m for the sale of a 50 per cent stake in Ferranti, £22m for Fairey Holdings and around £90m for other small interests (Thompson, 1986).[6] But as the activities of the NEB were wound down, so the local authorities formed their own enterprise boards under section 137 of the 1972 Local Government Act. The first of these was the West Midlands Enterprise Board in 1982, which had a narrow industrial investment role, followed by the Greater London Enterprise Board in 1983, which pursued broader economic and social goals, and similar agencies were formed in Lancashire, West Yorkshire and Merseyside.

Other than the NEB, the structure of nationally available assistance was left intact by the July 1979 review, and the balance of this assistance was only to change gradually as old measures expired and new measures were added. It was announced that the discretionary aid under section 8 would continue to be available, but that the conditions would be tightened so that only those projects where there was a significant enhancement in either timing, scale or nature would be supported. Such conditions could be traced back to the Selective Investment Scheme, which required that projects would not go ahead in the same form without assistance, and to the Accelerated Projects Scheme, which sought to bring projects forward in time. These kinds of condition now applied to general industrial support, although they were less restrictive since they included projects which were changed either in timing, or in scale, or in nature. From 1984 this section 8 assistance became known as General Investment Support for Major Projects, and while spending built up to around £10m in 1986/7 it was relatively little used thereafter. As scheduled, the Selective Investment

Scheme closed for applications at the end of June 1979, but it was announced that outstanding applications under this would be examined more closely.

Most of the sectoral schemes had terminated by May 1979, with the exceptions being the Footwear and the Slaughterhouse schemes. Other measures were introduced to tackle particular problems, so that the Coal Fired Boiler Scheme was introduced in May 1981 to lessen the UK's dependence on oil by encouraging the manufacturing and agricultural sectors to switch from oil-fired to coal-fired boilers. This provided 25 per cent capital grants, with an initial allocation of £50m, later raised to £75m, but the scheme flopped and it was relaunched in the 1982 Budget as the Coal Firing Scheme, and extended to the service sector and to the conversion and replacement of existing oil- or gas-fired industrial equipment. To encourage the greater funding of tourism projects from private rather than public sources, the assistance available under section 4 of the 1969 Development of Tourism Act was extended to include interest relief grants, which, like other Tourist Board assistance, were available to commercial projects in the Assisted Areas. The relief was 3 per cent per annum for four years, covering up to half of capital costs, or three-quarters in the case of improvements and extensions.

UNEMPLOYMENT

The early 1980s were characterized by severe recession, and while the government possibly believed that any loss of output and employment from the implementation of its monetary policies would be both transient and small, in the event unemployment doubled in its first two years of office, rising from 1.3m in early 1979 to 2.6m by 1981, and reaching 3 million towards the end of 1982. As explanatory factors, the rapid appreciation of sterling up to early 1981 by as much as 50 per cent from a base in 1976, and 37 per cent from 1978 was undoubtedly important, but so was the non-interventionist stance of the government coupled with its targets for the PSBR and Sterling M3, which, though never fully realized, reduced the value of these variables below that which would otherwise have obtained (Tomlinson, 1990). Despite its policy stance, the government did not shirk from attempting to support companies in difficulty, especially as unemployment accelerated, but these were mainly confined to publicly-owned companies and were limited in their impact.

In June 1980 the government both provided additional funds to the state steel industry and mounted a £66.5m rescue operation for Harland and

Wolff, which required ongoing support of £93.5m up to April 1983. During a parliamentary censure motion in July 1980 it announced the additional £25m to Inmos to establish its production facilities, and around this time it converted loans to share capital and waived some levies on further development aid to Rolls-Royce in response to the adverse sterling–dollar exchange rate.[7] Later, it sought without success to rescue a Bowater paper-mill in South Wales, and for a period of two years from April 1981 it authorized £200m of guarantees on bank loans to ICL, subsequently extended for a further three years in November 1981.[8]

The changes to regional policy were announced before the rise in unemployment, so that the government preferred to intensify the existing special employment measures in its attempt to hold down unemployment. The inherited special employment measures comprised: the Temporary Short-Time Working Compensation Scheme (TSTWCS), aimed at preventing redundancy; the Small Firm Employment Subsidy (SFES), paid as a marginal employment subsidy to small firms; the Youth Opportunities Programme (YOP), which mainly provided work experience for 16- to 18-year-olds with some community work; the Special Temporary Employment Programme (STEP), which provided community work for those aged 19 years and over; and the Job Release Scheme (JRS), which gave allowances to encourage early retirement.[9] It was announced in February 1980 that these schemes were to be kept at roughly constant levels, but that the SFES, which had a high level of deadweight spending, was to be terminated from the end of March 1980, and the YOP was to expand to 260 000 entrants in 1980/1 from 210 000 a year earlier. However, as unemployment continued to rise, the planned 1981/2 budget for the special employment measures was raised in November 1980 from £350m to £600m to include a further 180 000 places on the YOP (mainly on the WEEP subscheme), the introduction of a Community Enterprise Programme to replace STEP, and for several minor changes to the TSTWCS and JRS. Spending on these special employment measures stood at £100m in 1978/9 (see Table 6.2 on page 105), but, as Table 7.1 shows, this had increased to £1500m by 1982/3.

The immediate manifestation of the recession was the rapid rise in youth joblessness as employers cut recruitment. The November 1980 announcement guaranteed a temporary job or training place to all 16- or 17-year-olds who had been unemployed for more than three months, and a direct attempt to raise the demand for youth labour was the wage subsidy provided by the Young Workers Scheme (YWS) from January 1982. This was paid to firms in respect of employees under 18 years of age and was inversely related to the wage rate, offering £15 a week for those with gross

Table 7.1 Spending on the special employment measures, 1982–91 (£m, current prices)

Scheme	*1982/3*	*1983/4*	*1984/5*	*1985/6*	*1986/7*	*1987/8*	*1988/9*	*1989/90*	*1990/1*
Job creation									
CEP/CP/ET	307	394	524	667	1 043	1 065	1 340	1 107	1 062
EAS	3	23	77	111	143	196	197	184	145
JSS	0.05	0.3	0.2	7	0.2	–	–	–	–
Youth recruitment subsidies									
YWS/NWS	41	58	41	32	27	15	6	–	–
Youth employment and training									
YOP/YTS	747	427	836	870	939	1 008	1 020	1 002	833
Labour supply reduction									
JRS	212	258	281	202	110	71	39	14	7
TSTWCS	189	60	–	–	–	–	–	–	–
Total	**1 499**	**1 220**	**1 759**	**1 889**	**2 262**	**2 355**	**2 602**	**2 307**	**2 047**

Notes: Figures are in gross terms, with spending for years before 1982 given in Table 6.2. Figures for JRS from 1988/9 are estimates from the Government's Expenditure Plans. The figure for TSTWCS in 1983/4 is an estimate based on the number of placements on this scheme. ET superseded CP and JTS in 1988 and YTS became Youth Training in 1990/1. The table does not include expenditure on Community Industry from 1972, which was primarily a training scheme. CP = Community Programme; ET = Employment Training; EAS = Enterprise Allowance Scheme; JSS = Job-Splitting Scheme; YWS = Young Workers Scheme; NWS = New Workers Scheme; YTS = Youth Training Scheme. For the definition of other included schemes, see the notes to Table 6.2.
Sources: *Government Expenditure Plans* (London: HMSO); HC 487i (1985); *Training Statistics*, Employment Department (London: HMSO, 1990).

earnings of less than £40 a week; £7.50 a week for those with gross weekly earnings in the range £40–£45; and zero otherwise. Since the mean wage of this cohort was around £50 a week and only one-third earned less than this, a subsidiary aim of this scheme was to drive down the wage to price youths back into work as an explanation of youth unemployment (Metcalf, 1982). The subsidy was payable in the first year of employment and was received by 174 300 individuals in 1982/3, but like the earlier youth wage subsidies, the RSSL and YES, it was found to have a high deadweight element of around five places in six (Rajan, 1985), which was the highest of all the special employment measures (Davies and Metcalf, 1985). Nevertheless, when the YWS ceased in March 1986 it was superseded by a similar scheme, the New Workers Scheme, which covered 18- to 20-year-olds on wages of less than £65 a week. This was eventually phased out in 1988.

The advantages given to the Community Enterprise Programme (CEP) over STEP in the November 1980 announcement was that it was available nationwide and not just in areas of high unemployment, would admit 18-year-olds if unemployed for more than six months, and was more permanent in that the scheme was scheduled to run for at least three years, at a projected cost of £332m. It also sought to encourage private-sector projects of community benefit and provide more opportunities for voluntary organizations to sponsor projects. Initially, 25 000 places were made available on CEP, as against 11 000 on STEP, but as long-term unemployment increased rapidly to stand at around a million in July 1982, CEP was expanded in October 1982 and renamed the Community Programme (CP). The CP provided mainly part-time work of up to a year's duration on projects of community benefit which would not otherwise have been undertaken within two years. It was open to those receiving state benefit who were unemployed for the previous two months and either aged between 18 and 24 and out of work for at least six of the previous nine months, or aged 25 and over and unemployed for at least twelve of the past fifteen months. Participants were paid the going wage for the work but subject to a ceiling on the average weekly wage (initially £60) and this not only meant that much of the work was part-time, but also severely limited the take-up by those long-term unemployed who had dependents. Most projects were organized by local authorities and voluntary organizations and included improving the environment by clearing derelict land and canals, energy conservation measures such as installing loft insulation and draught-proofing, and providing social amenities by renovating community centres and other facilities (HC 199, 1986). By the end of 1983, there were around 100 000 participants on the CP, and at its peak in 1986, when long-term unemployment stood at around 1.35m, there were nearly 250 000 participants (Jackman, 1987).

Finally, one failed scheme was the attempt to create employment by job sharing through the Job-Splitting Scheme (JSS). This provided a grant of £750 to split one full-time job into two part-time jobs, and partly to meet the cost of extra training. This scheme was scheduled to run from January 1983 to the end of March 1984. From July 1983 greater flexibility was imparted by allowing a gap of up to six weeks between the loss of a full-time job and its filling by part-time jobs, and by allowing people leaving government schemes to go directly into a split job with their present employer or elsewhere. However, the hope expressed at its launch that an extra 50 000 jobs would be created was overly optimistic, as at the end of May 1983 only 317 jobs had been split, and spending amounted to little more than £7m by 1986.

THE ENTERPRISE MEASURES

The special employment measures were a palliative to unemployment through a mixture of make-work and training schemes, but it was 'enterprise' that was seen as the key to reversing economic decline, and as unemployment reached levels not seen for fifty years, so these became the chief means by which the government sought to create new jobs. The first such measure was the announcement in the April 1980 Budget of the Enterprise Zone experiment to 'see how far industrial and commercial activity can be encouraged by the removal of certain tax burdens, and by relaxing and speeding up the application of certain statutory or administrative controls' (Department of the Environment, 1981). The Zones gave a deregulated environment to encourage enterprise and promote industrial expansion, and offered exemption from Development Land Tax to both new and existing firms (which was normally levied at a rate of 60 per cent on the receipts from the disposal of land, but was later abolished) and relief from local authority rates on industrial and commercial premises. The existing 40 per cent initial allowance on buildings, which had been extended from the Assisted Areas to the whole country in 1972, was increased to 100 per cent in these areas, and exemption was given from Industrial Training Board levies and where applicable from the requirement of an Industrial Development Certficate. Simplified planning regimes were put in place, although control over developments which were either noisy, polluting or hazardous was retained in each case, and the Enterprise Zones were either relieved or given priority in certain administrative matters.

The relevant local authority was given responsibility for each Zone and, following negotiations, eleven first-round Enterprise Zones were declared in 1981 and 1982. The selection criteria required sites of approximately 500 acres each in derelict inner areas, but partly owing to the lack of such land on a large compact scale, the Zones varied markedly in characteristics, with some at split sites and the Wakefield Enterprise Zone located 10 miles out of town and covering just 170 acres. The Zones were experimental in nature, and were given a life-span of ten years from the date of designation, but even before a preliminary three-year evaluation had been carried out, a further fourteen Zones were declared in 1983 and 1984.[10] A lesson from the first-round Zones was that reclamation and infrastructure work caused delay and added substantially to costs, so that the second-round Zones favoured greenfield sites with good access. Originally, the initiative was seen as a measure to promote long-term economic growth, but with rising unemployment they were used in a manner similar to the old 'blackspot' approach. The announcement of the first-round Zones generally coincided with unemployment debates, while the second-round Zones were located near areas of high unemployment and were introduced along with the Community Programme (Talbot, 1983). Later, the government announced that any new Zones would be introduced only in exceptional circumstances, but several were designated in the late 1980s and early 1990s in the wake of industrial closures affecting particular areas.

A second area-based initiative to promote enterprise were the Freeports, now known as Freezones. Like the Enterprise Zones, these were experimental in nature, and were to be closely monitored and reviewed after five years. The main benefit given to the Freeports was that goods could be imported, processed and exported to areas outside the European Community free of Customs levies, but since duties could be offset against exported goods in any case, the Freeports offered little real financial advantage and were not very successful. Six sites were selected at a mixture of air and seaports, located at Belfast, Birmingham, Cardiff, Liverpool, Prestwick and Southampton, but by August 1986 there were only around 450 jobs located at the sites, compared with an estimated extra 10 000 jobs on the Enterprise Zone sites after a similar period (Roger Tym and Partners, 1984). Half these jobs were at the Belfast site, where close proximity to the airport seems to have been most important, while the Cardiff site had generated no extra activity by this time, and the Birmingham site was still being developed. Part of the problem was that UK trade was directed towards Europe, but the selection of the sites reflected various political interests and they were located away from the east coast; in the case of the Liverpool Freeport many of the imported goods came via Heathrow Airport (Moreton, 1986). The original supporters of the Freeport idea described the working of the Freeports at this time as an 'almost unrelieved failure' (Davies and Butler, 1986), although the life of three of the zones was later extended for a further ten years.

Other measures to promote enterprise were concerned with improving the access of new and small firms to finance. An 'enterprise package' in the 1981 Budget introduced the Small Firms Loan Guarantee Scheme (SFLGS) to test for a gap in the provision of medium-term loan finance to small firms, initially as a three-year pilot scheme from June 1981. The guarantee covered 80 per cent of approved loans up to £75 000 (but normally above £5000), repayable over two to seven years, for which the firm paid a 3 per cent premium that raised the interest rate by 2.4 per cent. The scheme operated in England, Scotland and Wales, and was later extended to Northern Ireland. It was designed to be self-financing and operated through some thirty participating banks and commercial institutions, which were responsible for vetting the potential viability of applications. The limit for guaranteed loans was set at £150m, but following a strong response – 3351 applications were received by April 1982 in respect of £113.7m in bank loans – this was raised to £300m in 1982 and to £600m in the following year. The early failure rate of guaranteed loans was high, running at around one-third of loans in mid-1984, prompting the government to reduce the guarantee rate to 70 per cent and to increase the premium to 5 per cent, but this reduced the take-up substantially, so it was necessary to relaunch the scheme in 1986 with a reduced premium of 2.5 per cent. Following another dip in take-up, the guarantee was raised to 85 per cent and the premium lowered to 1.5 per cent in 1993. By April 1990, nearly 25 000 guarantees had been offered under the scheme, covering loans to a value of £812m.

The 1981 Budget also introduced the Business Start-up Scheme, later known as the Business Expansion Scheme (BES). This provided tax relief for individuals investing in certain new small companies, initially available up to £10 000 per person per annum, but then doubled in each of the 1982 and 1983 Budgets to stand at £40 000. The BES initially proved successful, raising around £75m from 10 000 individuals for 400 companies in its first year of operation, with over half the amount going to new or newly-established firms. However, by the end of the decade it became clear that 'a laudable scheme had been transformed into a tax avoidance vehicle for the wealthy' (Storey, 1994, p. 228), and it was abolished at the end of 1993. In a similar way, the Loan Guarantee Scheme was initially thought to be successful in demonstrating to the clearing banks that there existed profitable opportunities for lending to small firms, but scepticism was later expressed about its rationale (National Economic Research Associates, 1990). In Table 7.2, gross figures for expenditure on these enterprise measures are compiled, showing that they involved significant sums of money and were maintained throughout the 1980s.

To reduce the risk of business start-up, the Enterprise Allowance Scheme (EAS) was announced in November 1981, initially on an

Table 7.2 Enterprise and urban policy measures, 1978–91 (£m, current prices, annualised expenditure)

	1978–81	*1981–4*	*1984–7*	*1987–91*
Enterprise Measures				
Enterprise Zones	–	52	110	139
SFLG Scheme	–	157	37	77
BES	–	95	158	290
Urban Policy Measures				
Urban Programme	153	271	296	244
UDCs	–	65	88	330
Derelict Land Grant	23	53	74	65
UDG / URG / City Grant	–	2	20	36
ICTFs and CATs	–	–	–	20

Notes: The table shows gross Exchequer expenditure on an annualised basis for each of the periods shown. Enterprise Zone expenditure comprises the estimated total cost of rate relief, capital allowances and additional infrastructure costs. These figures are not available after 1985/6, so that real expenditure has been assumed to run at a constant level from this time. The Department of the Environment (1995) puts the net present value cost of the first-round Zones at nearly £550m in 1990/1 prices by the early 1990s. The figures for the Small Firms Loan Guarantee (SFLG) Scheme give total guaranteed loans in each year, while those for the Business Expansion Scheme (BES) give total funds raised in each year. Figures for the BES are reported for years 1983/4 onwards, but it is known that that BES raised £75m in its first year of operation in 1981/2, and the annualized figure is based on these. For other measures gross expenditure on the programme is given, including Urban Development Corporations (UDCs), Urban Development Grant (UDG), Urban Regeneration Grant (URG), Inner City Task Forces (ICTFs) and City Action Teams (CATs). Freeports are not included in the table since spending on these is not separately reported by the Customs and Excise. Expenditure is reported for financial years, so that 1978–81 indicates the financial years 1978/9 to 1980/1 inclusive.

Sources: *Annual Reports on the 1982 Industrial Development Act* (London: HMSO); *Inland Revenue Statistics 1991,* Board of the Inland Revenue (London: HMSO); Cm 2207, (1993); *Government Expenditure Plans,* (London: HMSO), Department of the Environment (1987a); Martin (1990).

experimental basis in Coventry and parts of north Kent and north-east Lancashire, but was later expanded nationwide from the beginning of August 1983. Subsequently known as the Business Start-up Scheme (the same name as an earlier scheme), it provided an allowance of £40 per week for a maximum of 52 weeks to people unemployed for at least 13 weeks (later reduced to 6 weeks) who had at least £1000 to invest in a suitable new business venture. The scheme was aimed at those who might be deterred from starting a business by a loss of entitlement to unemployment or supplementary benefit, so applicants had to be in receipt of one of these benefits, and for this reason it is usually included as a special employment measure; expenditure is shown in Table 7.1. Up to ten individuals could combine to form a new business under the EAS, but in practice most were sole traders in conventional small-scale service activities such as shops, cafés, hairdressing, motor repairs, light haulage, general building repairs and maintenance, the design and manufacture of clothes, furniture manufacture, and contract cleaning (Gregg, 1990).

In the mid-1980s, 87 per cent of entrants completed their year on EAS, and of these perhaps well over half were still trading two years later, but in the late 1980s only about half survived for more than six months. At the scheme's peak, there were nearly 100 000 participants, with gross spending at more than £100m per annum, but under the assumption that benefit would otherwise had been paid, its net cost to the Treasury was in fact negative (Jackman, 1987). However, the apparent success of EAS has to tempered by a possibly high level of deadweight and the loss of initial capital and debt acquired by some of the failed enterprises. The change in the scheme's name reflected its transfer to the Training and Enterprise Councils, and at that time applicants no longer needed be in receipt of unemployment benefit nor to have £1000 to invest. Survival rates appear to have increased, but commentators still questioned whether such schemes were in the best long-term interest of the economy (Storey, 1993).

URBAN MEASURES

As regional policy gave way to urban, so a number of important innovations occurred in policy. What turned out to be the major urban policy initiative of this period was the power given to the Secretary of State for the Environment under the 1980 Local Government, Planning and Land Act to designate areas in the metropolitan districts of England and in inner areas of London as urban development areas. In these areas, Urban Development Corporations (UDCs) could be appointed to secure regeneration 'by bringing land and buildings into effective use, encouraging the development of existing and new industry and commerce, creating an attractive environment and ensuring that housing and social facilities are available to encourage people to live and work in the area' (section 136). The UDCs were given the power to acquire, hold, manage, reclaim and dispose of land, carry out building work, ensure the provision of basic services, and to fund public bodies to carry out this work where necessary. While they were required to provide a code of practice for consultation with the local authorities, they could acquire land compulsorily, were responsible for development control, could decide planning applications and operate outside their immediate boundaries, so that they became effectively the development agencies for these areas, but without the transport and housing responsibilities (Buck, Gordon and Young, 1986).

The London Docklands Development Corporation (LDDC) was established in 1981 in eight square miles of parts of Newham, Southwark and Tower Hamlets, and in the same year the Merseyside Development Corporation (MDC) was created in 865 acres of riverside sites in Liverpool. The respective budgets were £60–80 million and £25–30m per annum, and they could also use the receipts from the sale of land, which in the case of the LDDC amounted to £38m in 1986/7 (Parkinson and Evans, 1990). Table 7.2 shows spending by the UDCs and indicates the rapid expansion of this measure. However, in the 1980s, the Urban Programme continued to be the mainstay of urban policy, and there was some real increase in expenditure on this up to the mid-1980s.[11] Part of the impetus for this was undoubtedly the riots of the early 1980s, but expenditure was modest, averaging less than £3m per annum for each Programme Authority in 1983 and less than £20m for each Partnership Authority.

Despite this, the number of projects supported through the Urban Programme was substantial, amounting to around 12 000 at any one time, with about 2000 new projects approved each year from around 5000 applications (HC 513, 1985). The supported projects were spread across the designated areas, and most involved physical measures, with the government seeking a 70/30 per cent split between capital and revenue spending, but could also involve industrial assistance. Some changes were made to the management of the Urban Programme under Ministerial Guidelines issued in July 1981 and further guidelines in 1982 and 1983, but the management of the policy remained a concern to both the National Audit Office (HC 513, 1985) and the Committee of Public Accounts (HC 81, 1986). Moreover, the Urban Programme came under scrutiny from the Treasury, which had an inherent dislike of central-government-funded programmes implemented by bodies outside its direct control.

The involvement of the private sector in both the design and implementation of policy became an increasingly important aspect of urban policy, partly reflecting the perceived solution to the urban problem, but also recognizing the relatively small scale of public funds. For some schemes, the ratio of private-to-public expenditure became an important intermediate objective, and in other cases the government sought explicitly to raise private funds above the level which would otherwise have occurred, to obtain 'leverage'. The attraction of private funds was clearly important in the case of the UDCs, which initially had limited budgets and could undertake physical planning measures only, but the amount of private investment going to these areas was largely determined by local economic conditions. Greater private-sector involvement was also sought in the Urban Programme, and in the wake of the Merseyside riots in 1981 a Financial Institutions Group was set up, comprising twenty-six managers seconded from the financial service sector, with civil service support (Haughton and Roberts, 1990). The role of this group was to scrutinize existing policy and examine ways in which the private sector could be more actively involved in urban regeneration.

The Financial Institutions Group was responsible for several new initiatives before it was disbanded in 1982. One of these was Inner City Enterprises in April 1983, which drew its capital through share issue, and sought viable property development opportunities of community interest in Urban Programme areas. However, of greater significance was the Urban Development Grant (UDG) scheme launched in April 1982, based on a similar American scheme and designed to 'promote the economic and physical regeneration of inner urban areas by levering private sector investment into such areas' (Department of the Environment, 1983). Part of the objective was to foster private and public relationships, so that a developer and local authority would first agree a project and level of assistance, and then approach the Department of the Environment for funding. If successful, the government reimbursed 75 per cent of the local authority's approved expenditure, but, like other assistance, the UDG was intended to be the minimum necessary for the project to proceed in the given form, and other conditions were laid down detailing eligible projects and requiring that the project should contribute to economic, social or environmental conditions (Martin, 1990).

Priority was given to UDG projects in areas either in or close to Urban Programme areas, Urban Development Areas and Enterprise Zones, and initial interest was such that 262 UDG bids were received within the first six months, involving a reported £200m in public money and £500m in private funds (Department of the Environment, 1983). However, the drop-out rate was high – partly because the appraisal process took much longer than the projected 90 days – and only £6.6m was spent out of the first year's budget of £70m. Total expenditure reached £87.5m by April 1988, when the scheme was replaced by the City Grant. Similar arrangements also existed in Wales, and in Scotland the equivalent scheme was administered by the Scottish Development Agency and known as Leg-up: Local Enterprise Grants for Urban Projects.

The use of financial assistance extended to other areas of policy, so the 1980 Local Government, Planning and Land Act combined previously available measures to form the Derelict Land Grant (DLG), which was offered to both the private sector and public bodies. This superseded the grants for derelict land clearance which had been available to local authorities in the Assisted Areas since 1959, and similar grants to local authorities elsewhere under the 1966 Local Government Act. The DLG was made the responsibility of the Department of the Environment and redirected, so that whereas previously aid had often been used to remove coal-mining slag heaps to reclaim land for open space, agriculture or forestry in mainly rural areas, priority was now to be given to schemes that cleared land for industry, commerce or housing in run-down urban areas.[12]

Around the same time, the government designated more than a hundred localities in England as Derelict Land Clearance Areas. The DLG grant rate was 80 per cent (100 per cent in the case of local authorities) in the Assisted Areas and Derelict Land Clearance Areas, and 50 per cent elsewhere, although there was a higher rate of 75 per cent for local authorities in scenic areas outside the above designated areas. The non-local-authority component increased steadily from £0.6m in 1981/2 to £9.6m in 1987/8, when, as Table 7.2 shows, overall expenditure was running at about £75m per annum (Department of the Environment, 1987b; HC 27, 1989). The scheme was widened in June 1991 to allow sites to be reclaimed for environmental improvement as well as development, with an enhanced grant regime to encourage take-up by the private sector.

CONSTRUCTIVE INTERVENTIONS

At first the government was lukewarm to the technology measures introduced by the outgoing Labour government, so while it maintained the assistance under the MAP and PPDS schemes, it cut £15m from the MISP allocation going to infrastructure companies in the 1979 review of public expenditure, and made the selective interventions in the case of Inmos and ICL only reluctantly. Further, when the Advisory Council for Applied

Research and Development (ACARD, 1979) recommended that a much greater degree of government involvement was necessary to promote technological change, the response of the Secretary of State for Industry was unenthusiastic, arguing that 'experience in this country and elsewhere has shown that the creation of a climate favourable to enterprise and risk-taking remains the principal contribution that the government can make to technological change'.[13] It was only with a change of Secretary of State in 1981 that the policy changed, and the government became actively involved in promoting investment in the new technologies through a number of new schemes, which became known as the 'constructive interventions'.

The constructive interventions were directed towards improving the competitiveness of firms through the introduction of new technologies, and were initially concentrated on particular industrial sectors. In February 1980, the Advisory Council for Applied Research and Development (ACARD, 1980) reported that computer-aided design and manufacture was underutilized by industry, and to address this the Computer-Aided Design/Computer-Aided Manufacturing (CADCAM) and the Computer-Aided Design/Computer-Aided Manufacture and Test (CADMAT) were introduced in 1982. These interventions sought the greater utilization of such technologies in the mechanical, electrical engineering and electronics sectors, and were allocated £6m and £9m respectively. CADCAM supported awareness seminars and courses at centres of CADCAM expertise, and assisted firms willing to demonstrate systems to potential users. CADMAT offered awareness seminars, training courses, demonstrations and capital grants from July 1982 for up to a third of the cost of hardware/software, plus contributions towards installation and training costs. A further £12m was allocated to this area in 1982 through the Computer Aided Design and Test Equipment Support (CADTES) scheme to encourage capital investment in support of computer-aided design, manufacture and testing. This offered grants at a rate of up to one-third to firms with over 200 employees, with a maximum grant amount of £60 000 and a lower limit of £6000. From July 1983 another £10m was available for consultancy studies, with 50 per cent grants of up to £50 000 covering project planning and implementation, and £3000 grants for feasibility studies.

Further measures directed at the engineering sector were the Flexible Manufacturing Systems (FMS) scheme which was allocated £35m from June 1982 for new systems combining microelectronics and mechanical engineering yielding economies of scale in batch work, and the Small Engineering Firms Investment Subsidy (SEFIS I) which from March 1982 provided discretionary assistance to firms with up to 200 full-time employees towards, at most, two items of equipment in order to accelerate and promote the use of certain types of advanced metal working machinery.[14] At a time of recession, when firms were cash constrained, the take-up of SEFIS I was rapid and the scheme closed for applications less than two months after opening, by which time the initial £20m allocation and a further £10m had been committed. A second scheme followed a year later (SEFIS II), which relaxed eligibility conditions and paid a further £48.2m in grant assistance.

A gradual shift in policy from the support of industrial sectors to the general promotion of new technology was acknowledged by the Secretary of State for Trade and Industry, who noted in September 1983 that 'key technologies have been singled out for support because they have applications to many industries. In this sense, and indeed with the increasing emphasis upon the R&D and innovation component of government assistance, policy has shifted from a sectoral to a horizontal basis'.[15] Some further schemes in this direction were the Fibre Optics Scheme (later known as the Fibre Optics and Opto-Electronics Scheme), which provided support towards the design and development of fibre optics and related technologies, and the Robot Support Programme, which provided assistance for the manufacture and installation of industrial robots. In November 1982, the MAP scheme was extended for three years with an additional £30m allocation, and in June 1983 an allocation of £40m was made to the new Innovation Linked Investment Scheme (ILIS), which offered 20 per cent investment grants to small and medium-sized firms to produce or adopt significantly improved products or processes, and provided assistance at a rate of one-third towards market appraisal studies. A development which proved something of a trail blazer for later programmes was the experimental Joint Opto-Electronics Research Scheme (JOERS) which funded collaborative research projects between industry and higher education.

The shift in the government's attitude to the support of technology extended to other areas of policy, so that in September 1982 the government announced it was willing to assist projects in the aerospace industry. The mechanism for this was Launch Aid under the 1982 Civil Aviation Act, and, reflecting the failure of the government to recover assistance from this sector under earlier schemes, the Act required projects to be commercially viable to enable the government to obtain a satisfactory real rate of return on its investment through a levy on sales. At the time of the introduction of Launch Aid the government was already providing some development help to Rolls-Royce, which at this time was publicly-owned and, as Table 7.3 shows, gross spending on this facility was to stand at

Table 7.3 DTI support for industrial research and development, 1981–8 (£m, current prices)

	1981/2	*1982/3*	*1983/4*	*1984/5*	*1985/6*	*1986/7*	*1987/8*
Industrial innovation							
Alvey Programme	–	–	1.5	5.5	12.7	26.9	28.1
Information technology	12.1	27.1	27.7	35.7	26.8	18.5	10.4
Electronics	11.1	13.0	21.8	37.4	38.1	27.0	25.3
Mechanical and electrical engineering	3.9	10.8	13.8	24.2	26.1	17.5	14.6
Textiles, chemicals, materials	10.3	9.2	13.7	13.4	12.6	11.2	9.9
Metals and minerals	6.3	4.3	5.9	5.5	5.8	7.0	6.7
Maritime and shipbuilding	3.9	5.4	7.1	6.2	6.5	5.5	4.9
Vehicles	7.7	8.1	11.1	12.0	9.5	6.7	5.7
Biotechnology	–	0.4	0.7	2.9	5.9	5.2	4.7
Other	4.6	10.1	19.1	3.2	8.3	8.5	8.4
Total	**59.9**	**88.4**	**122.4**	**146.0**	**152.3**	**134.0**	**118.7**
Launch Aid							
Airframes	–	–	–	46.5	73.0	86.0	92.5
Helicopters	–	10.0	10.7	17.8	8.6	5.7	9.6
Total	**0.0**	**10.0**	**10.7**	**64.3**	**81.6**	**91.7**	**102.1**

Notes: The table shows government support provided by the Department of Trade and Industry (DTI). The total figure for industrial innovation in 1987/8 is actual expenditure, but the breakdown is projected spending. The Launch Aid figures exclude aero-engine aid given to Rolls-Royce, which at that time was in the public sector. There were no recoveries on this Launch Aid by 1988.
Source: *Annual Review of Government Funded R&D* (London: HMSO).

around £100m per annum by the late 1980s. Support for the *Concorde* project was ongoing, but a review at the end of 1981 favoured a phased run-down of the project, rather than a cancellation, which would have been more costly.[16]

The breakdown of the government's support for technology through the Department of Trade and Industry is shown in Table 7.3, and is organized on a sectoral basis, but with some details of spending on particular schemes (see also Table 6.5 on page 122). Table 7.3 shows that the engineering and electronics sectors were major recipients of this assistance, but that other sectors received some of the more general support. Expenditure on the various schemes grew steadily, from £13.2m in 1978/9 to £60m in 1981/2, and to over £100m by 1983, leading to a gradual shift in the overall balance of national industrial support. Partly to accommodate this, the limit on section 8 assistance was raised to £1800m under the 1982 Industrial Development Act, having already been raised by £250m to £1350m in January 1980.[17]

THE FRAMEWORK FOR TECHNOLOGY SUPPORT

The Department of Trade and Industry was responsible for about 15 per cent of the government's civil research and development expenditure (HL 20, 1986). The bulk of the support for general industrial research and development was met through the Product and Process Development Scheme (PPDS) under the 1965 Science and Technology Act, and £137m in assistance had been offered to 821 projects by April 1982. Research Requirement Boards had been established to act as proxy customers for applied research supported by the Department, and these were streamlined in May 1981, and subsequently integrated with the PPDS following a Rayner review of the DTI's financial support for research, development and technology in 1982. At the same time, the assistance for research and development projects under the 1965 Science and Technology Act, including the PPDS, and the various technology-based investment schemes under section 8 of the 1982 Industrial Development Act were brought together under the general heading of Support for Innovation.

Other developments included the merger of the National Enterprise Board with the National Research Development Corporation (NRDC) to form the British Technology Group (BTG) to further promote industrial competitiveness. The NRDC was established in 1948 to encourage the exploitation of research which was either sponsored by the government or unable to attract private funds, and its remit clearly overlapped with the revised brief of the NEB.[18] The BTG was required to pursue a catalytic role in its investments, and its standard package consisted of a five-year unsecured low-interest loan of up to £50 000, with a three-year moratorium on capital repayments. Under government guidelines it assisted small firms and focused mainly on the Assisted Areas in England. In 1982 it announced its intention to invest £20m in these areas over four years and also extended its assistance to include cash injections of up to £100 000 in return for a levy on sales. BTG became involved in joint initiatives with the English Industrial Estates Corporation and the Small Firms Service (see below), and in January 1983 it provided an additional £15m in equity finance to Inmos to build-up production facilities at its Newport site. In 1992, BTG was sold for £28m to a consortium led by its management and including financial institutions and universities.

In Northern Ireland, a similar role to that of the NEB was performed by the Northern Ireland Development Agency, but to increase accountability it was combined in 1982 with those parts of the Department of Commerce dealing with industrial development to form the Industrial Development Board (HC 500, 1982). At around the same time, the Department of Manpower Services was merged with the remaining functions of the Department of Commerce to form the Department of Economic Development (DED). As well as dealing with employment and training matters, the DED had responsibility for Standard Capital Grants, Selective Financial Assistance, the provision of sites and industrial premises, research and development support, inward investment and measures relating to the aircraft and shipbuilding industries.

An account of the operation of economic development policies in Northern Ireland is given in Harris (1991), and gross expenditure on the various industrial support measures over the period 1978–83 is given in Table 7.4. This table shows the large amount of aid provided to Harland and Wolff and to Shorts, and the significant role played by selective assistance compared with the automatic capital grants in the form of the Standard Capital Grant. The Selective Financial Assistance was made at rates between 40 and 50 per cent, compared with 30 per cent under the Standard Capital Grant, in order to make the Province competitive with the Irish Republic, which offered corporation tax at rates of 10 per cent. However, there were several notable failures of this selective policy, including the De Lorean Motor Company, which received £77m in assistance but closed in 1982 with the loss of 2600 jobs, and the Lear Fan Aircraft Project, which received £55.7m in public funds but went into liquidation in 1985 taking with it the promise of a further 2800 jobs.[19] In reviewing the Lear Fan case, the Committee of Public Accounts was

Table 7.4 Industrial support in Northern Ireland, 1978–83 (£m, current prices)

Purpose	*1978/9*	*1979/80*	*1980/1*	*1981/2*	*1982/3*
Factories and sites	11.4	16.0	15.5	10.8	14.9
Industrial promotion	1.1	0.9	0.5	1.0	1.9
Selective Financial Assistance	61.3	70.4	83.7	68.5	75.5
Standard Capital Grants	27.2	18.4	39.8	41.7	45.7
Northern Ireland Development Agency	15.6	5.4	6.8	3.7	6.8
Local Enterprise Development Unit	3.9	5.0	4.8	4.9	6.5
Marketing assistance	0.02	0.05	0.2	0.3	0.5
Harland and Wolff	13.5	22.5	42.5	46.0	47.5
Short Brothers	–	12.5	7.3	11.7	6.3
Total Assistance	**134.0**	**151.1**	**201.2**	**188.6**	**205.6**

Notes: Figures for 1982/3 are estimated outturn. Selective Financial Assistance includes support for research and development. Prior to April 1979 Short Brothers received assistance under Selective Financial Assistance.
Source: HC 500 (1982).

critical of the Department of Commerce, arguing that the substantial job opportunities involved had weakened its perception of the risks inherent in the extensive use of new technology (HC 223, 1986). After the shake-up of the development agencies, further significant assistance was announced for Northern Ireland in March 1983, to stimulate the economy and to make it more attractive to inward investment. This comprised a Corporation Tax relief grant of up to 80 per cent for new approved projects, 100 per cent de-rating for industrial premises, a grant scheme to help firms attract good management, an advisory service to industry on production methods and processes, and a 30 per cent grant for approved energy conservation projects.

STEEL RATIONALIZATION

The intention of the European Commission to be tougher on subsidies was made known in May 1981, but from this three types of state aid were exempted, which were seen as being consistent with the Community's general economic objectives. These were: horizontal aid, which operated across sectors, including assistance for small and medium-sized businesses; assistance for the development of new products; and the support for traditional industries in difficulty, such as shipbuilding, textiles and steel. While the Commission introduced special arrangements for shipbuilding and later sought to ease adjustment in areas affected by textiles closures, in the case of the steel industry it actively encouraged rationalization. Voluntary quotas and guideline prices had been put in place for the steel industry in 1977 which proved to be ineffective, but as demand continued to fall, compulsory production quotas were imposed in 1980 to achieve market stability. A code for assistance to the steel industry was also introduced at this time, requiring aid to contribute to restructuring as well as being completely transparent and having minimal distortionary effects on competition.

In this context, the UK introduced several sectoral schemes that were reminiscent of the earlier attempts to rationalize industry. The Private Sector Steel Scheme provided funds towards redundancy payments as part of a reduction in capacity or restructuring, and towards closure or restructuring costs. Applications had normally to be received before October 1982, but in respect of unforeseen closures they could be received up to July 1984 or until the allocation of £22m was exhausted. The take-up was strong and the allocation later increased, so that by the time the scheme closed in March 1984 total payments had been £31.9m, of which a substantial part went towards modernization projects. A more direct reference to the activities of the Bank of England in the 1920s was made by the Steel Castings Rationalization Scheme. This was a voluntary scheme promoted by the Lazard Brothers merchant bank. It involved firms paying compensation to those firms choosing to close, the amount of compensation being based on the volume of sales in a recent period, to which the government contributed £7.1m.

In addition to these schemes to restructure the private steel industry, the government continued to make over substantial sums to the British Steel Corporation in the form of public dividend capital as an ongoing subsidy. In the face of such subsidies, the EC member states agreed to phase out state investment and operating assistance to the steel industry by the end of 1985, with any aid in the interim being linked to reductions in steel-making capacity. In the UK this amounted to £806m, £743m and £396m in the years 1982/3, 1983/4 and 1984/5 respectively, and a further £355m grant payment was made to British Steel in 1984 to cut capacity, resulting in the closure of some large establishments.[20] Payments to redundant steel-workers under the readaptation scheme of the European Coal and Steel

Community continued to be made, and over the period 1974–84 more than 100 000 UK steel workers were assisted under this. Spending in the UK on this scheme stood at £8m in 1978/9, peaking at £112m in 1981/2, but then falling back to £56m in 1983/4.

The rationalization of the steel sector and the closure of some large plants prompted the government to designate the affected areas for special assistance, operating through the traditional methods of regional policy. In December 1979, the Corby employment office area was designated a Development Area, and the area around Shotton in North Wales was upgraded to a Special Development Area. Later, and shortly before the changes to the Assisted Areas map in August 1980, similar treatment was given to the areas around Port Talbot, Newport, Cwmbran and Scunthorpe. For the steel closure areas of Consett and Scunthorpe, the government provided an extra £10m in derelict land clearance grants and £19m for advance factory construction to be undertaken by the English Industrial Estates Corporation, while in South Wales it announced £48m for a two-year crash programme of land acquisition, derelict land clearance, site development and factory construction to be undertaken by the Welsh Development Agency (WDA) and the Cwmbran Development Corporation. The WDA had taken over responsibility for factory construction from the Welsh Industrial Estate Management Corporation and, in addition to government grants, it drew on outside sources to fund its construction programme. Several hundred factories were constructed, and as the economy picked-up from 1983 so the ready supply of factories coupled with the preferential regional assistance made South Wales an attractive location for inward investment.[21]

The Scottish Development Agency (SDA) took a different approach from its Welsh counterpart, and became actively involved in various area-based initiatives. As in Wales, the Urban Programme and other central government urban policy measures did not extend to these parts, and so, at the behest of the Scottish Office, the SDA was given responsibility for co-ordinating major urban development projects. It reluctantly took a lead role in the Glasgow Eastern Area Renewal project, seeing its main role as promoting competitiveness in industry rather than as a job creation agency in areas of high unemployment (Keating and Boyle, 1986). However, sudden job losses in steel at Garnock Valley, and a spate of industrial closures at Clydebank, led it to set up Task Force areas and to establish an Area Programme Development Division to launch initiatives in areas which were experiencing difficulties or showed good potential. As such, its activities came to revolve around four development functions: industrial investment, of which its early record was mixed; inward investment, in which it built up a significant presence; sectoral initiatives in electronics, pharmaceuticals and energy; and the area-based initiatives.

EUROPEAN COMMUNITY FUNDS

The European Regional Development Fund was a source of conflict between the Commission and member states, since the Fund served essentially to recompense member governments for their own regional spending.[22] To address this, the Commission attempted some partitioning of the different regional policies, so it proposed that regions adversely affected by Community policies or divided by national boundaries should be subject to EC policy, but that regions experiencing underdevelopment or requiring temporary assistance to restructure industry should best be the subject of member states' own regional policies (CEC, 1977). For this purpose, a non-quota section was proposed, outside the predetermined quota described above, to direct aid to regions of Community interest. It was intended that this non-quota element should be substantial, but in the event it accounted for only 5 per cent of the ERDF budget, and the unanimous approval of the Council of Ministers was required to determine included projects (Nevin, 1990). This meant that the effective control of Community regional policy remained with the member governments, and a further reform was later necessary.

The budget for the ERDF was determined by negotiations between the Commission, the European Parliament and member states, and the funds were allocated to member states according to predetermined quotas (see Armstrong and Taylor, 1993). The UK share of the Fund was around a quarter, and within the context of an enlarged budget the amount received increased from around £128m in 1980 to £182m in 1984 (see Table 7.5). Proposals for specific non-quota regional aid were adopted in October 1980, and these provided funding over a five-year period to help areas affected by the decline of traditional industries and areas of special need such as the border areas of Northern Ireland. A total of £33.5m was allocated to the UK under this scheme, including sums in mid-1982 to convert disused buildings and provide services for small and medium-sized firms in steel and shipbuilding areas.

The major source of European Community finance for investment continued to be the European Investment Bank, but, as Table 7.5 shows, much of this went towards infrastructure. To encourage the take-up of EIB funds by industry, the government offered exchange risk cover from January 1978 to firms undertaking projects creating jobs in the Development,

Table 7.5 Community financial support in the UK, 1980–8 (£m, current prices)

		1980	*1981*	*1982*	*1983*	*1984*	*1985*	*1986*	*1987*	*1988*
Loans										
EIB	industry	92	15	44	31	34	91	80	23	102
	infrastructure	286	109	247	307	156	179	274	523	404
ECSC	industry	77	40	68	60	50	93	34	63	121
	infrastructure	126	1	94	95	1	1	3	3	3
NCI	industry	–	–	–	18	6	10	–	–	66
	infrastructure	–	19	–	39	21	10	12	10	–
Euratom		–	–	–	26	–	–	71	77	–
Total loans		**581**	**184**	**453**	**576**	**268**	**384**	**403**	**699**	**696**
Grants										
ERDF		128	145	135	169	182	298	368	447	400
ESF		88	111	167	140	227	108	313	340	357
ECSC interest relief grants		11	1	7	2	2	7	1	10	6
EAGGF Guidance Fund		57	62	38	85	69	67	57	15	–
Fishing		4	5	6	5	6	8	16	8	8
Total grants		**288**	**324**	**353**	**401**	**486**	**488**	**755**	**820**	**765**

Notes: The average annual ecu-sterling exchange rate is used for each year to convert reported ecu figures to pound sterling. Infrastructure projects include assistance given for energy-related purposes. ECSC interest relief grants are reported for the European Community as a whole and have been apportioned to the UK according to its share of ECSC loans. Euratom loans are for nuclear power projects. Figures for ESF in 1987 and 1988 are estimates. NCI = New Community Instrument. For the definition of other included schemes, see the notes to Table 6.4.
Sources: Loan details and ECSC interest relief grants from *European Economy*, July 1989 (Brussels: Commission of the European Communities). Grant figures are annual payments through the general budget, and are taken from *Eurostat Review* (Luxembourg: Statistical Office of the European Commission).

Special Development Areas and Northern Ireland in return for a 1 per cent premium. The scheme was set to run for one year, but was extended in 1979 when a similar measure was introduced for loans from the ECSC. The latter measure operated through the Industrial and Commercial Finance Corporation (ICFC), and the ECSC provided £10m in guarantees for the firms creating jobs in those parts of the Assisted Areas affected by rundowns in the coal and steel industries. Later, the two measures were combined as the Exchange Risk Guarantee Scheme under sections 7 and 8 of the 1972 Industry Act, which added the condition that eligible projects should satisfy the normal criteria for Regional Selective Assistance. While the scheme was applied primarily to manufacturing, it was extended to tourism from August 1980.

As the EIB approached its overall lending ceiling, a further tranche of money was agreed in 1981 under a New Community Instrument (NCI).[23] This was used to support infrastructure projects contributing to regional development and/or of Community interest, and investment projects carried out by small and medium-sized businesses. Around the same time, the government agreed to provide exchange risk cover on a £5m global loan obtained by ICFC for loans of up to £50 000 for small firms, and similar facilities were extended under the Exchange Risk Guarantee Scheme to global loans obtained for small firms by the clearing banks and by the Scottish and Welsh Development Agencies. The maximum size of loan was £100 000, later raised to £250 000, and the minimum loan size was £5000, but this was later raised to £15 000. Loans from the EIB and ECSC covered by this amounted to £61.5m over the period 1981/2–1982/3, and in case of ECSC loans, a 3 per cent interest rate reduction over the first five years was available if a sufficient number of jobs was created. Loans were also available for nuclear power projects under Euratom.

The European Social Fund gave substantial support to the vocational and retraining courses organized by the Manpower Services Commission (see Table 7.5), but also provided support for some small-scale financial assistance schemes, including numerous wage subsidy schemes established by local authorities to aid the recruitment of unemployed people.[24] An unusual regional assistance measure under section 7 of the 1972 Industry Act was the In-plant Training Scheme (later known as Training Grants), for which the Social Fund provided half the funds. This was introduced on an experimental basis in April 1980, and funded 40 per cent of the eligible training and wage costs of manufacturing projects providing a minimum of 25 jobs in the Development and Special Development Areas where training was an essential part of a project and accounted for a significant proportion of total project costs. The restrictions on the number of jobs, on service industry projects and the Intermediate Areas were removed in late 1981, when spending ran at about £20m per annum, but the scheme was effectively terminated in 1986 following changes to the ESF rules. The final item of expenditure shown in Table 7.5 is the support under the EAGGF, which offered 50 per cent grants to help modernize the fishing industry and to help meet the capital costs of fish farming projects.

MODIFYING INDUSTRIAL SUPPORT

The perception is that industrial subsidies were cut back in the early 1980s, but while important modifications were made to the pattern of industrial support, the overall structure of industrial assistance was left remarkably intact in the Conservatives' first term of office. Attempts were made to rein in regional aid and improve effectiveness, including a scaling-down of the Assisted Areas, and the activities of the National Enterprise Board were also curtailed, but otherwise industrial assistance continued the evolution begun by the preceding Labour government. The dramatic rise unemployment undoubtedly went against a general industrial disengagement, so that regional aid was sharpened to focus on the worse-off areas, the Urban Programme was maintained, and the special employment measures were expanded, with spending on the latter increasing fourfold in the early 1980s.

As the worst of the recession passed, there was considerable innovation in policy, with the introduction of numerous technology-based schemes, the creation of Urban Development Corporations and the introduction of new 'enterprise' measures, including the Enterprise Zones, the Freeports, the Small Firms Loan Guarantee Scheme and the Enterprise Allowance Scheme. The enterprise measures were intended to be experimental, but they were maintained throughout the remainder of the decade, while at the same time industrial closures prompted the designation of areas for special regional assistance akin to the old 'blackspot' approach. The overall level of industrial subsidy declined only gradually in the early 1980s, and much of this was caused by the reduced take-up of assistance arising from the dramatic loss of manufacturing capacity in the recession. Indeed, direct subsidy payments, excluding the accelerated depreciation allowances, in reality increased up to 1981, and it was not until the return of a Conservative government that a radical overhaul of this assistance was attempted.

8 The Recasting of Industrial Support (1983–Present)

ECONOMIC RECOVERY

By the middle of 1983 the economy was starting to grow strongly, inflation was low and falling, and the expansion of the service sector continued to mitigate the job losses in manufacturing. But unemployment was high – and was to remain at around three million for the next four years – and this rise in joblessness had influenced the pattern of industrial assistance in two main ways. First, the effect of recession on government finances and the failure to bring public expenditure under control had meant that new resources were focused on ameliorative labour market measures, so that where new measures were introduced these were generally on a small scale.[1] Second, the severity of the recession meant that the Conservative government was unable to abolish the large-scale blanket subsidies going to the manufacturing sector in the form of the automatic regional capital grants and the accelerated depreciation allowances. With the resumption of strong economic growth and a fresh mandate, attention now turned to the elimination of these subsidies.

THE ELIMINATION OF THE BLANKET SUBSIDIES

Two major changes were made to industrial subsidy policy in this period, the first surrounding the Regional Development Grant scheme. An interdepartmental team chaired by the Treasury had been established in 1982 to review regional policy, and the government's plans were published in the December 1983 White Paper *Regional Industrial Development* (Cmnd 9111, 1983). The spur to the rejuvenation of regional policy in the early 1970s was high unemployment, but now the much higher level of unemployment meant that 'there is no general shortage of labour in any region' (para. 13), so the economic argument for regional policy was no longer self-evident and 'the case for continuing the policy is now principally a social one with the aim of reducing, on a stable long-term basis, regional imbalances in employment opportunities' (para. 16). Thus a substantial redirection of regional policy was proposed, to focus 'on encouraging new and indigenous development in the Assisted Areas, rather than simply transferring jobs from one part of the country to another' (para. 20) and 'to exclude from regional selective assistance those relocation projects where there is no net increase in jobs' (para. 35).

In nine reports from 1973, the Committee of Public Accounts had been critical of the arrangements for administering, monitoring and evaluating regional assistance, and of the poor value for money obtained from the Regional Development Grant in some cases. Addressing these concerns, the White Paper recognized that nearly £20 billion had been spent on regional policy measures since the early 1960s, but that 'the cost per additional job created in the Assisted Areas in the 1970s was around £35 000 at 1982 prices' and that 'many of these jobs would otherwise have come into existence elsewhere in the country and should thus best be described as "transferred"' (para. 8). It proposed that 'the incentives must be made much more cost-effective than at present, with greater emphasis on job creation and selectivity, and less discrimination against service industries' (para. 20). The Regional Development Grant was a symbol of central government's commitment to the regions, and rather than abandon it altogether, the White Paper proposed changes that would relate the grant rate to capital expenditure or to the number of jobs involved; relate assistance to approved projects rather than qualifying premises; impose a cost-per-job ceiling on the assistance amount, other than in small firms; and extend the scope of qualifying activities.

The changes were made known in November 1984 and they followed the proposals quite closely. The revisions made RDG available at a fixed rate of 15 per cent against eligible capital spending, but imposed a grant-per-job ceiling of £10 000, to restrict the amount of assistance going to projects that created few new jobs, effectively ruling out completely projects with no job effect. The ceiling increased the administrative complexity of the scheme, and so was not to apply to projects involving less than £500 000 of expenditure which were implemented by firms with less than 200 employees. These changes were seen as making the scheme more cost-effective while maintaining the predictability of assistance. Around this time, the results of research were also becoming known, and it was found that the metal manufacture and chemicals sectors received nearly 30 per cent of regional aid over 1966–76, but that policy in fact led to a loss of jobs in these sectors (Moore, Rhodes and Tyler, 1986), so that the grant-per-job ceiling can be seen partly as a response to this.

To reduce the bias of RDG in favour of capital-intensive investment, a £3000 grant for each new job created could be claimed in preference to the capital grant. This was subject to European Community rules that the project should include some capital investment (which was not necessarily eligible for RDG) and that the job grant could not exceed 40 per cent of the capital investment in the case of manufacturing firms. Other changes that made the scheme payable in respect of the qualifying activity of the project meant that service firms could claim RDG in respect of manufacturing projects, and the scheme was extended to a number of service activities. In addition to this, the project also had to create new capacity (or expand existing capacity), so it was no longer available in respect of replacement investment.

The second major change to industrial subsidy policy occurred in Nigel Lawson's first tax reforming Budget, in March 1984. This reduced the rate of Corporation Tax from 52 to 35 per cent and sought greater fiscal neutrality in the tax treatment of investment financed from different sources. In his Budget speech the Chancellor argued that there was little evidence that investment incentives had strengthened the economy, but rather that 'too much of British investment has been made because the tax allowances make it look profitable, rather than because it would be truly productive. We need investment decisions based on future market assessments, not future tax assessments'.[2] Accordingly, the 100 per cent first-year allowances on plant and machinery and the 40 per cent initial allowances on industrial buildings, which had been introduced nationally in 1972, were phased out over a three-year period. To reflect the true rate of economic depreciation, these were replaced by an annual allowance on plant and machinery at a rate of 25 per cent on a reducing-balance basis, and on buildings by a 4 per cent annual allowance on a straight-line basis. The depreciation allowances were by far the most important element of industrial subsidy and, as Table 8.1 shows, the nationally available assistance was virtually eliminated as a result of these changes; by the end of the decade it consisted of just a few small schemes. The reform cut back the subsidy and achieved a reduction in the variability of tax rates between different forms of asset, but its effect was to increase the overall tax rate on new investment. Under reasonable assumptions, Kay and King (1986) calculate that the changes increased the average marginal tax rate on corporate investment from a value close to zero to between 35 and 40 per cent.

THE REVISED REGIONAL POLICY

The November 1984 changes sought to improve the effectiveness of the Regional Development Grant, but in addition made a number of important changes to regional policy. Following the reduction in Assisted Area

Table 8.1 Gross expenditure on national assistance, 1980–91 (£m, current prices)

	1980/1	*1981/2*	*1982/3*	*1983/4*	*1984/5*	*1985/6*	*1986/7*	*1987/8*	*1988/9*	*1989/90*	*1990/1*
Initial allowances (R)	638	562	549	525	385	245	105	–	–	–	–
First-year allowances	14 569	14 727	14 999	14 288	10 478	6 668	2 858	–	–	–	–
Investment grants	0.5	–	–	–	–	–	–	–	–	–	–
Accelerated Projects Scheme	3.7	10.9	6.5	0.4	–	–	–	–	–	–	–
Selective Investment Scheme	20.5	32.8	11.9	8.2	5.0	1.9	–	–	–	0.7	–
Energy Conversion	6.7	9.3	7.0	–	–	–	–	–	–	–	–
Support for Major Projects	0.2	1.4	4.4	7.2	11.9	10.2	10.3	3.8	2.1	1.4	1.7
Coal Firing Scheme	–	0.1	1.8	4.2	10.1	12.3	11.1	4.3	1.9	1.0	0.04
Consultancy Initiatives	–	–	–	–	–	–	–	–	10.8	35.6	41.2
Total recoverable (R)	**638**	**562**	**549**	**525**	**385**	**245**	**105**	**–**	**–**	**–**	**–**
Total non-recoverable	**14 601**	**14 782**	**15 031**	**14 308**	**10 505**	**6 692**	**2 879**	**8**	**15**	**39**	**43**

Notes: Tax allowances are reported for calendar years and so have been apportioned to financial years, and are not reported after 1983, so they are assumed to taper to zero over three years. The General Investment Support for Major Projects was superseded by the Assistance for Exceptional Projects in January 1988. Some of the business consultancy assistance is included as regional spending and shown in Table 8.2.

Sources: *National Income and Expenditure* (London: HMSO); *Annual Reports on the 1982 Industrial Development Act* (London: HMSO).

coverage in 1980 and 1982, the Assisted Areas map was redrawn and now increased in coverage from 28 to 35 per cent of the working population, but this was achieved by the inclusion of the West Midlands conurbation to help ensure that the UK allocation of ERDF money was fully taken-up.[3] In addition, the Special Development Areas were withdrawn. Regional Selective Assistance was no longer available to relocation projects where there was no net increase in jobs, a grant-per-job limit was imposed in the administration of this assistance, and a 'claw-back' clause introduced whereby the grant was repayable if the project assets were not retained for a period of three years after the last asset had been provided, or if the assisted jobs did not remain in place for eighteen months after the last job had been filled or asset provided. Regional Selective Assistance could be claimed throughout the Assisted Areas, but the Regional Development Grant was available in the Development Areas only. Service firms were made eligible for mainstream section 7, so that the Office and Service Industry Scheme was discontinued, and the British Technology Group was relieved of its regional investment role through its North and North West offices in order to focus on technology transfer.

As a result of these changes, spending on regional assistance was expected to fall by about £280–£300m from 1987/8 onwards, with around half of this saving arising from the RDG revisions and the remainder from the changes to the Assisted Areas. Under transitional arrangements firms could claim the old RDG for projects commencing before 29 November 1985, but the take-up far exceeded expectations, leading to a moratorium on payments from January 1985 until February 1989. This delayed payments of approved grants for a period of four months, to keep spending down to £500m in 1985/6 from a level of £600m which would otherwise have obtained, but it could not prevent a surge in spending as firms brought projects forward to take advantage of the more favourable terms under the old scheme, and the provision for public expenditure on regional incentives for 1987/8 was raised by 10 per cent to reflect this. To further reduce expenditure, a delay of two months in the payment of the revised RDG was introduced from January 1987, and this was only relaxed after the scheme had been terminated. As Table 8.2 shows, gross expenditure on regional incentives peaked at nearly £800m in 1982/3, but then fell steadily to £450m in 1987/8 and for a time the revised RDG scheme became the principal instrument of policy.

Before the new regional policy became operative, the Committee of Public Accounts commented on the proposals in the 1983 White Paper. This commended the decision to make regional policy more selective, with an emphasis on job creation, but the Committee expressed reserva-

Table 8.2 Gross expenditure on regional measures, 1980–91 (£m, current prices)

	1980/1	*1981/2*	*1982/3*	*1983/4*	*1984/5*	*1985/6*	*1986/7*	*1987/8*	*1988/9*	*1989/90*	*1990/1*
Exchange Risk Guarantee (R)	90.6	62.0	39.1	97.2	72.3	7.5	28.0	54.0	70.0	130.0	101.0
Investment grants	0.5	0.2	0.04	–	–	–	–	–	–	–	–
RDG	490.5	616.8	689.6	438.9	410.7	319.7	196.3	118.7	75.5	41.3	18.7
RSA–Loans and equity (R)	0.1	0.1	0.01	–	–	–	–	–	–	–	–
–Grants	48.1	75.1	92.1	74.1	78.3	116.1	141.6	154.3	182.2	175.4	188.2
OSIS/SIRG	5.4	5.7	5.2	8.8	6.1	6.1	3.3	2.4	1.3	0.1	–
In-plant Training	0.2	1.8	2.5	4.0	7.9	15.7	8.3	6.3	2.1	3.0	1.6
Business Improvement Scheme	–	–	–	–	0.2	8.4	14.6	18.4	15.5	11.4	2.1
Revised RDG	–	–	–	–	–	38.6	116.4	151.9	221.8	162.6	110.9
REG–Investment	–	–	–	–	–	–	–	–	1.1	5.9	8.6
–Innovation	–	–	–	–	–	–	–	–	0.3	2.2	4.0
Consultancy Initiatives	–	–	–	–	–	–	–	–	1.0	3.2	3.7
Total recoverable (R)	**91**	**62**	**39**	**97**	**72**	**8**	**28**	**54**	**70**	**130**	**101**
Total non-recoverable	**545**	**700**	**792**	**526**	**503**	**505**	**480**	**452**	**501**	**405**	**338**

Notes: The In-plant Training scheme helped meet training costs with new investment projects satisfying the requirements for Regional Selective Assistance. Around half of the expenditure on the Consultancy Initiatives was in the Assisted and Urban Programme Areas, and only the increased grant amount of two-thirds against one-half is shown here. The remainder is given in Table 8.1.

Sources: *Annual Reports on the 1982 Industrial Development Act* (London: HMSO); *Government Expenditure Plans* (London: HMSO).

tions over the lack of information on the effects of individual policy instruments (HC 378, 1984). They recommended that a review of the revised policy should be begun before the proposed five-year period, with the result that an evaluative study of the Regional Selective Assistance was announced in 1985 (King, 1990). Other commentators questioned the ability of the public sector to carry out a policy of selective assistance (R. M. Grant, 1982), while others criticized the complicated nature of the RDG revisions that made the scheme far less predictable (Pettigrew and Dann, 1986). In practice, the revised RDG operated as a marginal subsidy to employment, with 91 per cent of the 3298 grant payments by February 1986 made in the form of £3000 job grants, so in effect the Regional Development Grant as an automatic capital subsidy was terminated in November 1984 (Wren and Swales, 1991).

By 1986, 12 000 projects had been approved, for £360m in grants, under the revised RDG scheme, and a preliminary review reported that the complexity of the new rules had been well understood (Department of Trade and Industry, 1986a). However, the National Audit Office review of the scheme was less enthusiastic, reporting that there may have been a significantly higher level of fraud under the revised scheme and that 'suspected fraud was particularly prevalent where grants were job-related and in the service sector' (HC 346, 1988, para. 4). In 1986, twenty cases of suspected fraud had come to light, involving £1m in grants, and a further twelve cases had been unearthed in the first three months of 1987. This compared with only 54 confirmed fraud cases under the old RDG scheme since 1972, of which 34 had arisen since 1982, and involving only £100 000 in total. The government accepted that the revised scheme was more open to abuse, and in March 1987 established a working group to consider the extent of such fraud and possible counter-measures, but the scheme was abandoned in January 1988 and no new applications were accepted from April 1988.[4]

COLLABORATIVE RESEARCH PROGRAMMES

Worsening performance in information technology and signs of increased competitive pressures from abroad led to the formation of the Alvey Committee in March 1982 to advise on the scope for a collaborative research programme in information technology. It argued that a programme was essential to preserve and strengthen the UK's capability in information technology (Department of Industry, 1982), and did so at a time when the government had shown its willingness to intervene in industrial innovation.[5] The report's recommendations were largely implemented, and the Alvey Programme was established in 1983, co-sponsored by the DTI, the Science and Engineering Research Council and the Ministry of Defence. Its budget was fixed at £350m over five years, of which £200m was to come from public funds, including £50m for academic research. Projects were selected under the four sub-programme areas of enabling technologies comprising software engineering, intelligent knowledge-based systems, man-machine interfaces, and very large-scale integration, of which the latter was already planned by the Ministry of Defence. Academic work was funded in full, but industry projects were funded at a rate of 50 per cent.

To administer the programme, an Alvey Directorate was established in the Department of Trade and Industry, staffed partly by industrial and academic secondees. Nearly all the funds were exhausted by the time the programme was half-way through, with 92 per cent of the budget taken by 192 collaborative projects involving an average of three to four industrial, academic and/or government institute research partners, and the remainder by 117 academic projects where industrialists took an interest only. The evaluation reported that the Alvey Programme had largely met its technological goals, encouraged collaboration and broadened the UK base in information technology research and development, but that the commercial gains would at best be long-term (Department of Trade and Industry, 1991). The report also highlighted various barriers to the commercial exploitation of research, including shortages of capital, changes in strategy by partner firms after projects had commenced and poor management of the interface between production and research and development.

Subsidizing joint production by encouraging collaboration generally went against EC competition policy, even though Articles 85–94 of the Treaty of Rome recognized the benefits to be derived from direct Community support of research and development, and from private sector collaboration in such activity. Many of the early Community initiatives focused on pre-competitive research and development, including the European Strategic Programme for Research in Information Technology (ESPRIT). As with the UK Alvey Programme, it was concern over a trade imbalance in the broad area of information technology and a perceived technological weakness in industry that prompted action, although the real spur may have been lobbying by firms prominent in the industry (Curzon Price, 1990). The Commission committed £6.5m to pilot a number of projects in 1983, and in 1984 the Council of Ministers adopted ESPRIT with an overall budget of around £900m. The programme funded up to 50 per cent of the cost of pre-competitive research and development projects involving at least two participants from different member states in the areas of advanced microelectronics, office automation, computer integrated manufacturing, advanced information processing, information exchange systems, and software technology. The scheme was set to run for four years, and in 1988 it was succeeded by ESPRIT II, which ran for a further four years with an overall budget of £2000m, of which the UK contributed £200m.

The Bide Committee was established in 1986 to examine what should follow the Alvey Programme, but funds for a similar purpose became available under ESPRIT II, and in many ways this became the successor scheme. The Alvey Directorate took the lead for the ESPRIT programmes in the UK, and sought to avoid duplication at the individual project level. In 1988 it made £29m available over three years for a UK programme for the support of collaborative projects in information technology through the Information Engineering Directorate, which by then included the Alvey Directorate. In addition, £55m was provided over five years by the Science and Engineering Research Council for related academic research, mainly in partnership with companies. This was complementary to ESPRIT II and picked up projects unable to obtain funding under the EC programme.

The apparent success of ESPRIT led to a number of EC programmes designed to foster collaborative arrangements between educational institutes, research bodies and industry across the EC. The Commission argued that these were necessary to fund projects which could not be carried out at the state level, but they were also useful for establishing the EC as a single economic and political entity. The new programmes were largely technology-based and usually directed towards specific industrial sectors and firms, although ESPRIT was the largest. The Research in Advanced Communications for Europe (RACE), at around £300m, was designed to establish a strong EC manufacturing base in broad-band communications and put in place an advanced telecommunications infrastructure, for which thirty-two consortia were announced in March 1986. The Basic Research in Industrial Technologies for Europe (BRITE), at £300m, sought to rejuvenate traditional industries by applying new technologies, and was open from 1985 until 1988. This was extended up to 1992, when it was combined with the EURAM scheme, which dealt with advanced materials. The Strategic Programme for Innovation and Technology Transfer (SPRINT) sought to improve the competitiveness of small and medium-sized enterprises by encouraging co-operation across member states, with financial assistance for conferences, workshops and collaborative arrangements. Other programmes were devised with suitable acronyms, including that for unconventional energy sources (JOULE: Joint Opportunities for Unconventional or Long-term Energy Supply); biotechnology (BAP: Biotechnology Action Programme) and the food industries (FLAIR: Food-linked Agro-industrial Research).

Several European-wide initiatives were established outside the EC receiving direct support from member governments. In 1985 the European Research Co-operation Agency, known as EUREKA, was established, on French initiative, as a European response to the American Strategic Defence Initiative. This involved eighteen countries for the purpose of providing support for substantial co-operative ventures between European firms applying new technologies to the development of new civilian products. Assistance was provided by member governments to their own firms, and in the UK this was available under the Support for Innovation programme which offered 50 per cent towards the share of applied research costs and up to 25 per cent of the share of development costs. After one year, twenty-six projects involving UK collaborators had been announced, with project costs ranging from £1m to £70m, and after three years seventy-four agreed projects had UK participation, with a total value of £1200m.

The second major European collaboration was for the development and production of aircraft through the Airbus Industrie consortium. This drew together partner companies from Britain, France, Germany and Spain, and was designed to yield a strong European presence in the civil aerospace industry, which was dominated by American firms. British Aerospace had a 20 per cent stake in Airbus Industrie, undertaking work on the Airbus A300 and A310, and after the government turnaround on support for commercial aerospace it was offered £250m in Launch Aid towards its share of the design and development costs of the Airbus A320. Of this, £50m was repayable on a fixed schedule over the period 1990–2 and the remainder through a levy on sales. In May 1987, a further £450m public funding for British Aerospace was announced as part of its development costs of the Airbus A330 and A340, but no further aid was granted to British Aerospace until June 1993, when it sought a further £200m in Launch Aid to develop a new family of turboprop aircraft for the regional airline market at an overall estimated cost of around £400m–£450m.

The Launch Aid given to British Aerospace is shown in Table 7.3 on p. 144 under the heading airframes, amounting to £298m by April 1988. The American aerospace industry was unhappy both about this and about the other European support afforded to the Airbus project, and made frequent representations. In 1993 the US administration requested that total Launch Aid for Airbus be cut from 33 per cent to 20 per cent of the development costs, but the funding satisfied the GATT and, since the assistance was not given towards production costs, it also satisfied the European Commission.

REDIRECTING TECHNOLOGY SUPPORT

The policy for supporting the use of new technology continued to evolve, so that as existing schemes under the Support for Innovation programme exhausted their allocations, so new measures were introduced. In early 1984 SEFIS II and CADTES were terminated, and the ILIS scheme was withdrawn because other assistance was available on less onerous terms, so that only £3.5m of the £40m allocation had been offered. The Flexible Manufacturing Systems allocation was increased by £20m, and £120m was made available for the Microelectronics Industry Support Programme 2 up to 1990 as a successor to MISP.[6] The money for FMS was for consultancy and installation projects, with coverage extended to the use of advanced manufacturing technology including robotics, so that when the Commission approved of the extra funding in August 1984 the Robot Support Programme was incorporated into the FMS scheme and these became known as Support for Advanced Manufacturing Technology. Like the earlier scheme, MISP 2 was designed to ensure that the electronic equipment industry had access to advanced microelectronics devices and provided selective assistance of up to 25 per cent (later 20 per cent) of eligible costs towards the development of products and processes, investment in plant and machinery, and product launch and market capability.

Assistance under the Support for Innovation programme was not subject to proof of need and the take-up was strong. This was attributed to the recovery of firms from recession, but it was also clear that applications were being diverted from closed areas and schemes with tougher criteria. Thus shortly before the result of the regional policy review became known in November 1984, which no doubt would have placed greater pressure on the Support for Innovation programme, it was announced that a review of this assistance was to be undertaken, and in the meantime no new applications were to be considered under a range of measures.[7] The results of the review became known in March 1985 and they changed policy in two important respects. First, technology-based investment schemes were put under the same scrutiny as regional and other nationally-based investment assistance; and second, the balance of technology support was set to shift from investment schemes towards advisory assistance in order to increase firms' awareness of new technologies.

Following the review, shorter-term projects had to be innovative, there had to exist realistic market opportunities to ensure successful commercial exploitation, and the project had to represent a significant advance either for UK industry or for the sector concerned. The principle of additionality was applied, so that assistance had to be necessary for the project to go ahead in the form and time-scale proposed. Longer-term applied research projects had to improve industrial performance or provide a technology from which a new product or process might be developed. Maximum grant rates were specified as 25 per cent of eligible costs for projects undertaken by a single firm and 50 per cent for longer-term collaborative research projects, where the results would either be shared or made more widely available. Eligible costs up to £5m would be supported and a minimum of £100 000 was specified, although this could be relaxed in the case of small firms, and higher grant rates were available for advisory-based assistance.

Table 7.3 on page 144 shows that spending on the technology measures peaked at around £150m in 1985/6. However, and perhaps naturally, firms were critical of the additionality condition, and several witnesses to the House of Lords Select Committee on Science and Technology argued it would favour struggling firms which could not otherwise obtain finance (HL 20, 1986, para. 5.29)! Similar points were made in respect of the Microelectronics Application Project, a scheme devised to speed the take-up of microelectronics technology, but in this case additionality meant that the firm could not commence work until after the application had been vetted, and this took an average of six months (Policy Studies Institute, 1985).

As a second strand, the review sought to change the direction of policy 'to increase the proportion of aid going on advisory services, the encouragement of best practice, improvement in the supply of key skills, and collaborative research'. As such, the emphasis was to shift from investment to a policy based on information and advice, and on increasing awareness and collaboration between firms, so that the government came to refer to these as 'support' rather than 'assistance'.[8] Moves had already been made in this direction through the Alvey Programme and through the DTI's Technical Advisory Service. The latter sought to encourage technology transfer by the provision of advice to small and medium-sized firms, and comprised the Manufacturing Advisory Service, which since 1977 had helped firms improve manufacturing efficiency and was run by the Production Engineering Research Association; the Design Advisory Service, which was operated by the Design Council since 1982; and the Quality Assurance Support Scheme, which offered investment support to help implement consultants' recommendations.

The March 1985 review grouped these various advisory schemes together under the heading of the Business and Technical Advisory Service (BTAS), which made grants available at a rate of 75 per cent towards the cost of up to fifteen person-days consultancy for manufacturing organization and techniques, product quality, design and technical matters. The assistance was available to small and medium-sized firms and extended to the service sector. The popularity of BTAS was such that efforts were made to restrict take-up in 1986, when spending was running at £20m per annum compared with £5m on the constituent schemes in 1982. From this time, the consultancy project had to form part of an overall business plan; eligibility was restricted to independent firms; the grant rate was reduced to two-thirds; projects had to last for a minimum of eight days' duration; and firms could obtain at most one consultancy grant in the areas of manufacturing, design and quality assurance.

Subsequent measures in 1986 – which was designated 'Industry Year' – continued the shift in policy. The National Electronics Research Initiative in March 1986 enabled pre-competitive industrial collaborators to work together at a single site with the government meeting up to 50 per cent of the cost of support staff, services and new capital equipment. In April 1986 the Small Firms Merit Award for Research and Technology (SMART) staged a competition whereby twenty Phase One awards of up to £37 500 were available to proposals which demonstrated innovation in important areas which could be translated into commercial success, and in the second phase, grants at 50 per cent in the second year and at 25 per cent in the third year for projects showing promising progress. The competition was held annually, so that 150 Phase One awards were available by 1990, but only to companies with less than 50 employees. In 1992, £60m was committed, to enable the scheme to continue for a further three years, by which time the number of Phase One awards was increased to 180 and the maximum value of awards was £45 000 in the first phase and £60 000 in the second phase.

A number of small-scale initiatives followed, including £4.5m in June 1986 for the purchase of advanced textiles equipment by higher education institutions, £2m in July 1986 through the Support for Electronics Manufacture towards computer-assisted production equipment and software in smaller electronics firms, and £1m in September 1986 for software engineering demonstrator projects. The LINK initiative was launched in December 1986 to speed the development of ideas through to processes and marketable products. LINK was allocated £210m over five years, but this was not new money, as the scheme drew on existing programmes in mainly defence-related areas. A total of £83m was earmarked for the first five programme areas, and as at August 1990, twenty-four programme areas were approved, involving £160m in government funds. The government agreed to meet half the cost of collaborative projects between industry and the scientific community, comprising at least one firm and at least one higher education institution or research establishment. The model for LINK was the Alvey Programme, but it extended across the range of new technologies, including areas as diverse as biochemical engineering, high-speed machinery, food processing and refrigeration.

SMALL FIRM ADVISORY ASSISTANCE

At the time of the general re-evaluation of industrial assistance in November 1984, certain refinements were made to the enterprise measures referred to in Chapter 7. Changes had already been made to the Small Firms Loan Guarantee Scheme in 1984, but with failures reaching 40 per cent, against an anticipated rate of 8 per cent, the scheme was restricted to secured loans, and the greater involvement of the Small Firms Service and local enterprise agencies (see below) was sought in preparing business plans and providing support. By 1984 the Enterprise Allowance Scheme had assisted nearly 50 000 individuals, and a further £72m was announced for this, representing a 25 per cent increase in funding.[9] Around this time, the life of the Co-operative Development Agency was extended for a further six years, but funding was kept at the existing level to encourage the agency to become self-financing. The Agency was established in 1978 and funded with £900 000 over three years to represent and promote the formation of co-operatives, but its budget was cut to £200 000 per annum in 1981 to encourage it to be more selective and to focus on promotional work.

To the policy of encouraging enterprise and improving the access of small firms to funds, a third strand was added in the form of advice to improve the competitiveness of firms. Large firms were generally excluded from this, on the grounds that they could obtain sufficient technical expertise from their own sources, and this view was later to extend to financial assistance in the round. Nevertheless, these large firms were an important source of advice for new and small firms, and in the early 1980s numerous local enterprise agencies and trusts were established to advise small firms on finance, premises and related problems, and these were often staffed by secondees from large firms (Deloitte, Haskins and Sells, 1984). The enterprise agencies received support from local authorities and banks, and to expand on this initiative financial assistance became available under the 1982 Industrial Development Act to local enterprise agencies and other such organizations providing advice to people carrying on or proposing to carry on a business. This was provided on a pump-priming basis over one to three years, after which time the agency was expected to rely on private contributions. To further promote this, government grants were made to Business in the Community, which was sponsored by large companies, local authorities and trade unions, and which in addition to establishing enterprise agencies, encouraged private-sector involvement in local regeneration.

Up to this time publicly-provided advice tended to be offered through public agencies, of which the Small Firms Service was the main agent. This had been set up in the early 1970s to act as an information service for small businesses through a network of regional Small Firms Centres, to which a further network of 80 Area Counselling Offices was added in 1978 to meet more detailed enquiries and offer specialized guidance. These centres were staffed by experienced industrialists operating on a self-employed contract basis, providing up to ten days' free advice to small businesses in any one year regarding a range of management problems. This service was expanded in 1983 with the nationwide adoption of the Enterprise Allowance Scheme, and in 1984 it handled around 300 000 inquiries and nearly 25 000 new counselling cases. Similar services operated in Scotland and Wales, managed by the Development Agencies and the government came increasingly to rely on these services to provide support and to screen small-firm applicants for its assistance schemes.

In addition to the Small Firms Service and the promotion of local enterprise agencies, a departure around this time was the provision of financial assistance to firms to obtain advice from their own private-sector sources. Of course, this was not entirely new, since as early as 1967 the Shipbuilding Industry Board made grants for advice on regrouping, and the MAP scheme made £2000 consultancy grants to identify feasible projects, but now this assistance was available generally and extended beyond feasibility studies. From 1984 the Business Improvement Scheme (see below) extended a range of consultancy assistance to various management functions in certain parts of the country, and from April 1986 two new schemes were introduced, offering advice to small and medium-sized firms in the areas of marketing and for the evaluation of research and development proposals in the automotive-related industry. Under these, firms could obtain two days' free consultancy for an initial appraisal and then, subject to this, a 75 per cent grant towards a further thirteen days of advice, and this later formed the model for the subsequent expansion of advisory assistance under the 1988 *Enterprise Initiative*. The direct origins for this new area for policy were both the various measures under the Technical Advisory Services described above, which, when brought together under BTAS, offered 75 per cent grants towards up to fifteen person-days' consultancy, and the grants for consultancy under the Robot Support Programme and Flexible Manufacturing Systems, which, when merged, also offered 75 per cent grants. As we see, these various technology and management areas of advisory support were later brought together under the *Enterprise Initiative*.

REGIONAL AID FROM THE EUROPEAN COMMUNITY

By the mid-1980s the European Commission had toughened its stance on state aid, and a proposed £20m investment scheme for small firms in the textiles, clothing, knitting and footwear industries was not allowed to proceed. Rather than support industries in difficulty, which had implications for competition, the Commission preferred to promote industrial restructuring by helping the areas affected by structural decline to diversify through improved infrastructure, loans and grants and other measures under its Structural Funds. Hence, in November 1984 it announced £89m from the European Regional Development Fund for UK areas affected by run-downs in steel, shipbuilding and textiles. In England and Wales this was known as the Business Improvement Scheme (BIS), and with a further £12.5m from the UK government, it made £63m available to help establish and improve the efficiency of small firms, and the remainder for environmental improvements and the conversion of disused buildings into premises for small businesses.[10] The scheme was set to run for a period of five years until March 1989, although in the event it was closed for applications at the end of 1988. Importantly, from the Commission's point of view, it was in addition to UK regional policy spending, although as it approached termination date it was effectively assimilated into mainstream UK industrial policy.

Most of the small firm assistance under BIS was for consultancy-based studies, with 55 per cent grants of up to £1500 available in the areas of business appraisal, marketing strategy, translations of market information, business planning, budget and control systems, financial restructuring, licensing and for the investigation of the merits of computer and related equipment. A group of small firms could join together to take advantage of common services and obtain a 55 per cent grant towards operating costs over a three-year period, and a 70 per cent grant was available for the cost of feasibility projects leading to a new product or process, and for market research. This assistance was available to new or small independent firms with up to 200 employees, and could be claimed by most manufacturing and service firms, but excluding those in steel, shipbuilding and textiles except where diversifying into new activities. In addition, firms providing services to small firms in the eligible areas could obtain assistance, but this seems to have been little used.

Smaller firms with up to 25 employees could claim 20 per cent grants towards the cost of buildings, plant and machinery, up to a maximum of £25 000, for investment needs identified by a consultancy study. This was in addition to the revised Regional Development Grant, but not Regional Selective Assistance, and since the areas eligible for BIS assistance closely resembled the traditional UK Assisted Areas (and in some parts were drawn as such), then in effect automatic capital grants continued to be available to these very small firms, even after the November 1984 revisions to regional policy. The BIS package was used to provide extra assistance to areas experiencing economic distress, and in March 1986 it was extended in coverage to the declining fisheries areas of Hull, Grimsby and Blackpool; in July 1986 to the declining tin-mining area around Penzance and St Ives in Cornwall; and in March 1988 to the depressed area of Thanet in Kent.

The BIS was part of a second series of measures adopted under the non-quota section of the European Regional Development Fund, and an extension to this provided a further £9.5m for Northern Ireland and £8.5m for the declining fisheries areas in northern England. Spending on BIS amounted to £70m by 1991 which, as Table 8.2 shows, is modest compared to some other regional policy measures, and its main significance lay in the direction it gave to general industrial support measures. Further, the non-quota section failed to redirect the ERDF, and in most years part of the allocation had to be transferred to the quota section because of poor take-up as member states resisted a facility under direct EC control. As a result, the distinction between the quota and non-quota sections was abandoned in 1984, and in its place 'indicative ranges' came into force, whereby the amount received by a member state above some minimum quota level was determined by the quality of applications, including the extent to which the EC's interests were served (Armstrong, 1989). The UK was initially given an indicative range of 21.4 to 28.6 per cent, against 23.8 per cent previously, but this was later revised as 14.5 to 19.3 per cent following the accession to the Community of Spain and Portugal.

The failure of the non-quota section to assert Community control over regional policy meant that the Commission remained concerned that much of the ERDF continued to support regional and national projects in the

Assisted Areas which would otherwise have gone ahead. Further, the large number of unrelated projects receiving assistance made the policy look both disparate and unco-ordinated, and actually helped facilitate the substitution of ERDF money for national funds, so that the Commission sought a more integrated approach which would bring together its sectoral and regional measures. Experimental co-ordinated schemes, known as Integrated Operations, had been initiated in the depressed urban areas of Naples and Belfast in 1979, and further Integrated Mediterranean Programmes began in France, Greece and Italy in 1985 (Mellors and Copperthwaite, 1990). These comprised co-ordinated packages of jointly agreed initiatives designed to alleviate a clearly defined problem, and these Integrated Development Operations Programmes (IDOPs) were now set to form the model for the Community's economic development work.

Under the 1984 reform a distinction was drawn between those programmes initiated by the Commission and those National Programmes of Community Interest (NPCIs). Public bodies involved in infrastructure provision, including local authorities in the UK, could apply via their sponsoring government department for 50 per cent ERDF funding as part of an integrated national programme. The first three NPCIs were announced in 1986 and all were in the UK, including £66.7m to clean up the Mersey Basin; £68.2m for infrastructure, industrial development, vocational training, energy, environment and tourist measures in Strathclyde; and £18.1m for a range of infrastructure and economic promotion activities in the Shildon area of County Durham following the closure of the British Rail Engineering Ltd wagon works (Department of Trade and Industry, 1986b). Further NPCIs and IDOPs were announced for Mid Glamorgan (£32.9m), the Tees corridor (£18.8m) and Northern Ireland (£3.3m) in January 1987, and for Birmingham (£113m) and West Lothian (£26.7m) later that year. Member states were required to submit a five-year national development plan, and submissions for assistance were in line with this. In addition, the EC continued to finance industrial investment through its contributions to national regional policy measures, so the reform had not gone very far in wresting control of regional policy matters from the member states.

INDUSTRIAL CLOSURES AND THE 'BLACKSPOT' APPROACH

A recurrent theme of UK economic development policy is the use of the blackspot approach to designate for special assistance areas experiencing high unemployment. This was not only the case for the Development

Districts of the early 1960s, but applied also to the Special Development Areas from 1967, the use of Assisted Area designation in the late 1970s, and to the second-round Enterprise Zones of the early 1980s. As the rundown of traditional industries accelerated in the recession a more effective approach was sought which could deliver a range of assistance and economic development measures at the local level to ensure that the benefits were well targeted. The Urban Programme offered a model of a locally delivered national spatial policy, but rather than fund the local authorities, the government chose to channel its support through various agencies which were established by existing or former nationalized industries involved in making the redundancies.

British Steel Corporation (Industry) Ltd was formed by the British Steel Corporation in 1974 and, following a number of closures, it was reconstituted in 1982. In order to attract mobile investment it engaged in marketing and publicizing designated Steel Closure Areas, of which there were eleven in 1983 and eighteen in 1988.[11] In these it offered advice and some rent assistance to be competitive with the English Industrial Estates Corporation, but its main function was to arrange packages of assistance from local, national and supranational bodies for employment creation (Buswell, 1983). The agency sought to pump-prime so that as soon as an initiative had been firmly established it disengaged, passing on its marketing functions to enterprise trust and other local bodies. Expenditure by the agency fell from £9.5m in 1982/3 to £5.3m in 1983/4, and then to zero thereafter as it sought a self-financing basis for its activities (Owen, 1988).

The coal industry lost 125 000 jobs between 1981 and 1987, and at the time of the miners' strike NCB (Enterprise) Ltd was established by the National Coal Board with £5m to assist new companies or relocations in areas affected by coal-mining job losses and to help former miners find new work, either through retraining or through business start-up. Known as British Coal Enterprise Ltd from August 1986, the agency provided assistance in the form of rent subsidies and loans, and also helped to convert buildings no longer required for mining. The loans carried some subsidy and were the main element of support. In 1985/6 447 loans totalling £8.8m were made and 737 loans totalling £18m in 1986/7 (Owen, 1988). The agency was part-staffed by secondees from banks and accountancy firms, and in addition provided managed workshops and support for local enterprise agencies, and offered training packages. Finance for the initiative was increased to £20m in 1985 and £40m in 1986, by which time an additional £66m had been attracted from banks, local authorities and government grants. The supported projects tended to be one-man businesses run by ex-miners investing their redundancy payments, and serving highly localized markets.

The closure of the British Rail Engineering Ltd (BREL) wagon works at Shildon in County Durham with the loss of 2500 jobs prompted a rather different approach. Here, following discussions between central government, BREL and the relevant district local authority, the Shildon and Sedgefield Development Agency was established with £1.6m in funds over three years to promote employment in the local area. It offered a range of assistance, including capital grants, operating subsidies, loan guarantees and a job subsidy of £30 a week for a year for firms taking on an ex-BREL employee. The initiative helped to generate the ERDF non-quota funding mentioned above, and a similar arrangement was put in place following the closure of the BREL works at Horwich near Bolton.

Further special measures were taken in 1986 for areas affected by redundancies in shipbuilding and tin-mining. British Shipbuilders Enterprise Ltd was established with £5m as a subsidiary of British Shipbuilders to provide financial assistance and advice on training to individuals wishing to start up in business. In North East England this was supplemented by £1m from the Manpower Services Commission for retraining and by £4m under various urban policy measures. Similar measures were taken in west Cornwall after the government concluded that financial assistance to the Geevor tin mines would not yield a viable operation. Instead, a £1m area-based scheme along the lines of the Business Improvement Scheme was introduced, and an office opened to promote this and other available assistance. Later in 1986, an interest-free loan of £15m and loan guarantees of up to £10m were made to a subsidiary of Rio Tinto-Zinc (RTZ) under section 8 to restructure and save the Wheal Jane and South Crofty tin mines. However, by 1994 only the financially troubled South Crofty mine remained, and the government agreed to write off its loan contingent on a successful share issue.

PRIVATIZATION

Privatization fitted in well with the general strategy since not only did it bring private sector management to sometimes ailing public enterprises, but the receipts helped to reduce the Public Sector Borrowing Requirement, and the responsibility for these firms was devolved away from central government.[12] In its first period of office the Conservative government sold companies which were not public corporations, but were those in which it held shares, including British Petroleum, Amersham

International, Cable and Wireless, and certain holdings of the National Enterprise Board. In its second term, the public utilities of gas and telecommunications were privatized, and at the same time the government sought to hive-off the profitable parts of formerly ailing firms while putting remaining parts on a sounder financial footing.

Jaguar Cars was sold off in 1984, and in 1986 the government invited bids for the Rover Group of British Leyland, including Land Rover, Freight Rover and Leyland Trucks. DAF, in which the Rover Group had a 40 per cent holding, purchased Freight Rover and Leyland Trucks in 1987, but the government was unable to cast off total responsibility, so when DAF experienced financial difficulties in 1993 it was eventually forced to provide a subsidy to effect a management buy-out of Leyland Trucks. British Leyland received £2230m in government funds over the period 1975–84 and the government was prepared to meet further obligations of £1600m on the understanding that British Leyland would meet subsequent requirements from private sources, including privatization receipts.[13] In the event, £680m was given in 1987 to support the privatization of the truck and bus subsidiaries, and £547m was provided as a net payment to British Aerospace in 1988 to take over remaining parts of the Rover Group, comprising Austin Rover and Land Rover. Under the original deal, British Aerospace was to pay £150m for the company and the government agreed to write off the group's debts of £800m. However, the European Commission ruled that £231m of this would be working capital and that an assumed level of debt of £100m would be reasonable so as not to distort competition. This potentially jeopardized the deal, so the Commission agreed to supply £78m in regional aid to help bridge the gap, but in addition the government paid £44m in 'sweeteners' to British Aerospace, which the Commission later ruled to be illegal. In 1994 British Aerospace sold the Rover Group to BMW for £800m.

Through management buy-out and the promise of some orders, the sale of the warship yards of British Shipbuilders was completed in March 1986, including Vickers Shipbuilding and Engineering Ltd, Yarrow Shipbuilders, Vosper Thorneycroft, Swan Hunter, Cammell Laird and a number of smaller concerns. However, merchant shipbuilding was depressed in the face of cut-price competition from abroad, and these yards were organized on a regional basis to be made ready for privatization, with the formation of British Shipbuilders Enterprise Ltd in May 1986 a precursor of this. The Commission sought to cut the state aid, but, given the depressed state of the world market, a Fifth Directive on Aid to Shipbuilding was extended for two years from 1984, enabling temporary aid to be made to shipbuilding. Further, the proposals for a Sixth Directive drew a distinction between aid, which sought structural adjustment; and production aid, which offset the difference between European costs and the prices charged by Far Eastern yards. This was effective for a period of four years from 1987, and was different from previous directives in that it recognized that subsidies were essential for Community yards to compete with those elsewhere. As such, the ceiling for shipbuilding aid at 28 per cent was calculated on the basis of the cost difference and reviewed annually.

The Sixth Directive provided a breathing space in which the government could further support and restructure the industry. In 1987, £114m was made to British Shipbuilders to offset the collapse of several of its customers, and, following a Commission review, the rate of subsidy on the Intervention Fund was increased to 20.5 per cent (25.5 per cent in Northern Ireland) with an extra 2 per cent available in Shipbuilders' Relief. In addition, higher rates of subsidy could be paid where there was no Community competition or where the maintenance of defence capacity was involved, but subsidy could not be paid where a yard was privatized or scheduled for such use. Table 8.3 shows that spending on the various support measures was maintained through the 1980s and even increased in the late 1980s with general recovery, so in 1989 a proof of need condition was introduced to the loan guarantees under the Home Credit Scheme to curb spending. However, from 1987 the assistance became progressively less generous, and a Seventh Directive in 1992 reduced the aid ceiling to 13 per cent.

When the move towards selling off the remaining parts of British Shipbuilders came in 1988 it had less than one-fifth of UK shipbuilding employment. The Govan shipyard was sold to the Norwegian firm of Kvaerner and negotiations were under way for the sale of other yards, including Clark Kincaid at Greenock to a management buy-out, the Appledore yard in North Devon, and the Ferguson yard at Port Glasgow.[14] However, offers for North East Shipbuilders Ltd (NESL), which included the former Sunderland Shipbuilders and Austin and Pickersgill, were unacceptable on the grounds of viability and the government announced these yards for closure. To ameliorate the job losses an Enterprise Zone was declared with a life of ten years with a budget of £28m, which, like other zones, offered a simplified planning regime, rate relief and 100 per cent capital allowances on all new industrial and commercial developments. In addition, English Estates (formerly English Industrial Estates Corporation) was given £7m to carry out advance factory construction in the area, £5m was available in financial inducements for job creation projects, and a further £5m was made available for counselling and retraining measures.

Table 8.3 Gross expenditure on shipbuilding measures, 1980–91 (£m, current prices)

	1980/1	*1981/2*	*1982/3*	*1983/4*	*1984/5*	*1985/6*	*1986/7*	*1987/8*	*1988/9*	*1989/90*	*1990/1*
Shipbuilders' Relief	15.8	8.8	18.3	14.0	13.5	22.7	8.4	11.0	8.7	10.3	12.1
Home Credit Scheme (R)	225.2	298.2	181.7	157.1	130.0	240.1	28.8	77.3	204.4	140.0	213.1
Construction Grant Scheme	0.05	0.3	–	–	0.5	–	–	–	–	–	–
Cost Escalation Scheme (R)	2.0	0.7	–	–	–	–	–	–	–	–	–
Intervention Fund	42.0	49.0	48.0	36.2	20.1	25.9	6.6	31.6	51.4	37.7	17.4
Total recoverable (R)	**227.2**	**298.9**	**181.7**	**157.1**	**130.0**	**240.1**	**28.8**	**77.3**	**204.4**	**140.0**	**213.1**
Total non-recoverable	**57.8**	**58.1**	**66.3**	**50.2**	**34.1**	**48.6**	**15.0**	**42.6**	**60.1**	**48.0**	**29.5**

Sources: *Annual Abstract of Statistics* (London: HMSO); *Annual Reports on the 1982 Industrial Development Act* (London: HMSO); *Annual Reports of HM Customs and Excise* (London: HMSO).

By agreement, state aid to the steel industry ceased at the end of 1985, and while the government anticipated that the British Steel Corporation would continue to need state finance thereafter, strong demand moved the Corporation into profitability and it was privatized in 1988. Public money made over to the British Steel Corporation in the form of subscriptions amounted to £5151m between June 1979 and 1986, and in addition it received substantial amounts of Regional Development Grant. Other formerly ailing companies in the aeronautics industry were sold around this time, including the aeroengine division of Rolls-Royce in 1987 and Short Brothers in 1989 to a Canadian company called Bombardier Inc.

Gross spending on industry-specific support measures (excluding shipbuilding) is shown in Table 8.4. This shows that expenditure fell away sharply in the mid-1980s from a peak of around £634m in 1981/2 to virtually zero by 1987. Much of this was to do with the privatization of British Leyland, but assistance was also withdrawn from other areas as the various sectoral schemes of the previous Labour government finally wound down (see Table 6.1 on page 100). Two long-standing measures which had been introduced in the early 1970s, the Mineral Exploration Grants and the Offshore Supplies Interest Relief Grant scheme, were terminated, and the Eady levy for film production, which had been established in 1957 and extended in 1981 to cover cinema films shown on television, was also ended. This was coupled with the reduction in nationally available assistance, and was only partly compensated for by the increase in subsidy under the technology, enterprise and urban measures.

EFFECTIVENESS IN URBAN POLICY

Expenditure on urban policy was maintained in the mid-1980s, and undoubtedly factors which favoured this were the inner city riots in 1985 at Handsworth and in London. Instead, the focus was on better value for money through increased effectiveness and the targeting of benefits on the disadvantaged residents. Best practice guidelines were issued in 1985, partly to pre-empt criticism by the National Audit Office, and City Action Teams (CATs) were set up in the same year in each of the five Urban Programme Partnership Areas to achieve better co-ordination between the relevant government departments. In 1986, Inner City Task Forces were announced, made up of civil servants, to test initiatives in training and employment in some parts of the urban areas.[15] Eight Task Force areas were established, and a further eight were added in May 1987, with each having a life longer than the original intention of two years. The funds for

Table 8.4 Gross expenditure on industry assistance, 1980–91 (£m, current prices)

	1980/1	*1981/2*	*1982/3*	*1983/4*	*1984/5*	*1985/6*	*1986/7*	*1987/8*	*1988/9*	*1989/90*	*1990/1*
International Computers Ltd (R)	–	200	–	–	–	–	–	–	–	–	–
Mineral Exploration Grant	0.7	1.4	0.7	0.5	0.6	0.7	–	–	–	–	–
Sectoral schemes	45.8	17.1	6.8	1.6	0.6	0.02	–	–	–	–	–
Offshore Supplies IRG	27.9	22.2	24.1	22.6	17.7	9.1	4.1	0.3	–	–	–
British Leyland	300	520	360	90	–	–	–	–	–	–	–
British Technology Group	49	39	37	8	–	–	–	–	–	–	–
Concorde	36	35	13	–2	1	2	–	–	–	–	–
Private Sector Steel Scheme	–	–	10.3	14.8	4.4	2.7	–	–	–	–	–
Steel Castings Rationalisation	–	–	–	7.1	–	–	–	–	–	–	–
Total recoverable (R)	**–**	**200**	**–**	**–**	**–**	**–**	**–**	**–**	**–**	**–**	**–**
Total non-recoverable	**460**	**634**	**452**	**143**	**25**	**15**	**4.1**	**0.3**	**–**	**–**	**–**

Sources: *Annual Reports on the 1982 Industrial Development Act* (London: HMSO); *Government Expenditure Plans* (London: HMSO).

each Task Force were around £500 000 per annum, although this was later increased to about £1.5m, so that much of their work was concerned with the provision of advice and making use of other sources of funds, such as the Enterprise Allowance Scheme. However, they could offer grants of up to £4000 towards the cost of business plan preparation, market research, feasibility studies, training, business start-up and fixed capital costs, and this was usually linked to a bank loan. Demand was strong, so that by May 1991 around £73m had been committed by the Task Forces to more than 2700 projects.

Urban policy was based on spatial targeting, but the gradual shift towards economic projects in the Urban Programme exposed an inherent flaw, as it became clear that this was at best an indirect way of helping disadvantaged inner area residents. Further, even within the designated areas, the nature of the defined problem was uneven, making the link between project benefit and take-up by target resident uncertain and made worse by in-commuting (Robson, 1988). The CATs and Task Forces were an attempt to address these deficiencies, but the basis of the policy rested on the scattering of a large number of small projects across the designated areas. The government praised the work of the CATs in accelerating work and attracting private-sector finance, but now sought an intensification of this approach by extending the Urban Development Corporation model to other inner areas.

Four new Urban Development Corporations (UDCs) were announced in early 1987, covering run-down areas in the Black Country, Teesside, Trafford Park, and Tyne and Wear, and a similar arrangement was made for Cardiff Bay.[16] The designation of these was rushed through prior to the June 1987 election, and so-called mini-UDCs were declared at Bristol, Central Manchester and Leeds in December 1987, and at Sheffield in March 1988. Each UDC was scheduled to run for seven to ten years, but whereas the earlier UDCs were each allocated £150m–£200m, the mini-UDCs were each given only about £50m. The UDCs were mainly concerned with land reclamation and property developments, and focused their efforts on a small number of high-profile 'flag-ship' developments, sometimes involving substantial private-sector investment. The intention was to give private firms the confidence to invest in such areas, usually in commercial property, but sometimes in housing. The experience of the UDCs differed markedly, as reflected in the scale of spending shown in Table 8.5. Taking the year 1989/90, the London Docklands Development Corporation spent £226m, which was associated with around £1200m in private funds; the mini-UDCs spent £34m in total, with £170m from private sources; and the other English UDCs, including the

Table 8.5 Spending by the Urban Development Corporations, 1987–92 (£m, current prices)

UDCs	*1987/8*	*1988/9*	*1989/90*	*1990/1*	*1991/2*
London Docklands	82.8	116.4	225.8	333.0	248.7
Merseyside	20.9	20.5	23.0	24.0	25.4
Other UDCs	21.9	83.2	123.1	136.1	171.0
Mini-UDCs	–	13.5	34.3	60.4	62.0
Total	**125.6**	**233.6**	**406.2**	**553.5**	**507.1**

Notes: Other UDCs comprise those for the Black Country, Teesside, Trafford Park, and Tyne and Wear. Mini-UDCs comprise those for Bristol, Central Manchester, Leeds and Sheffield.
Source: *Hansard*, 24 June 1992, written answers.

one on Merseyside, spent £146m, with nearly £500m in private funds. Around this time, spending on the UDCs overtook that on the Urban Programme and was running at about £400m per annum.

Other changes to urban policy after the 1987 general election included extensions to the Black Country and Merseyside UDC areas, new City Action Teams and the introduction of a City Grant in May 1988.[17] The City Grant replaced three existing schemes: the Urban Development Grant (UDG), which had begun in 1982; the private-sector element of the Derelict Land Grant, which had been extended to the private sector in 1980; and the Urban Regeneration Grant (URG), which had been introduced in 1986 to provide assistance to large-scale projects, but for which only five applications had been received by the time of its closure (Lawless 1988). Unlike the UDG, the URG did not require formal local authority involvement in the application process and this approach was embodied in the new City Grant (Martin, 1990). Applicants for the City Grant had to demonstrate a proof of need, an interim appraisal was promised within four weeks, and a decision within a further ten weeks. A grant ceiling of £200 000 was proposed for the City Grant, but in the event this was waived, and by September 1989, £63.1m had been awarded to eighty-five projects. A further £24.6m was offered to thirty-one projects by the UDCs, which under the scheme had responsibility for those projects falling within their areas (HC 169, 1990).

As spending on urban policy increased (see Table 7.2 on page 137) so it came under close scrutiny in a series of House of Commons reports. The arrangements for the Partnership Areas under the Urban Programme had in some cases been found to have broken down (HC 169, 1990), and the Public Accounts Committee was concerned that a methodology had not been developed for evaluating the public-sector element of the Derelict Land Grant (HC 27, 1989). The Employment Committee recommended that the remit of the London and Merseyside UDCs be altered to include employment objectives (HC 327, 1988), but both the Task Forces and City Action Team initiatives were viewed as being successful. The UDG was thought to offer good value for money, but take-up apparently depended on the enthusiasm with which it was promoted, so that ten local authority areas accounted for half the expenditure on this scheme (HC 169, 1990). In total, £130m was allocated to more 200 UDG projects.

As early as 1986 it was clear that the cost of Enterprise Zones would be substantial. The National Audit Office in April 1985 put the cost of rate relief at £49m, in October 1984 estimated capital allowances at £50m, and public investment in the Zones at £80m (HC 209, 1986), and the government-commissioned study of the Zones later put the net public sector cost at more than £300m by April 1986. This proved expensive, at around £30 000 for each job created, and in 1987 it was announced that further Zones would only be designated in exceptional circumstances (HC 169, 1990).[18] The Zones attracted a substantial amount of development, so that by April 1988 there were 4344 firms trading in the Zones, compared with 1353 at designation; 72 per cent of the land was developed, compared with 27 per cent at designation; and there were 100 000 jobs, compared with 30 000 at designation (Department of the Environment, 1990). However, much of this was diverted from elsewhere, with only 10 500 of the extra jobs deemed to be additional to the national economy, as firms took advantage of the capital allowances which the government admitted were 'over-generous' and which gained in significance after the national capital allowances were phased out in 1984 (HC 169, 1990). Further, the rates holiday raised rents (Roger Tym and Partners, 1984), perhaps substantially, and when the Zone status expired, the government had to make provision under the 1988 Local Government Finance Act to lower rateable values in the former Zones.

RURAL DEVELOPMENT

The Development Commissioners were replaced by the Development Commission in 1984, which not only kept all matters affecting the economic and social development of rural areas under review, but was enpowered to give financial aid to appropriate bodies, acquire land and property and provide premises for use by industrial or commercial undertakings. The Commission focused its activities on Rural Development Areas (RDAs), which replaced the pre-existing Special Investment Areas, and were designated on the basis of factors such as unemployment and population sparsity. Funding of the Commission increased steadily to stand at around £28m in 1987/8, and as well as providing financial assistance to major job-creating projects in the RDAs, it offered 50 per cent grants towards marketing, consultancy and trade exhibitions. In addition, advice was provided by its main agency, the Council for Small Industries in Rural Areas (CoSIRA), which, while being deemed complementary to the Small Firms Service, was nevertheless merged with the Development Commission in 1988 to form the Rural Development Commission. This ran several financial assistance schemes, including low interest loans to encourage commercial developments in the RDAs.

The English Industrial Estates Corporation continued to operate in support of regional policy in England, but increasingly it developed a role outside formal regional policy, leading it to operate as English Estates from the end of 1983 to reflect its broader role. In rural areas it carried out work for the Development Commission, but also became involved in activities such as the redevelopment of the closed Chatham Dockyard in 1983 and providing managed workshops in the inner cities. Changes were made in the financing of English Estates, so that under the 1985 Industrial Development Act it could use income from rents and the sale of assets to fund development programmes, and in 1990 it was required to sell certain of its assets and to put development work out to tender. However, it retained responsibility for providing serviced sites where there were difficulties of land assembly, and for the provision of market information on development opportunities in the Assisted Areas. In 1986/7 less than half of its funds came from government grant in aid, and in 1990/1 its programme amounted to £52.8m, which included provision for the Sunderland special measures and £10.1m for the construction of managed workshops in inner city areas.

LONG-TERM UNEMPLOYMENT

Expenditure on the special employment measures grew in line with unemployment (see Figure 8.1), and by 1985 there were 341 000 people receiving support through these measures – including the Community Programme (174 000 participants), the Young Workers Scheme (58 000), the Enterprise Allowance Scheme (51 000), the Job Release Scheme

Figure 8.1 The rise of the special employment measures, 1975–90

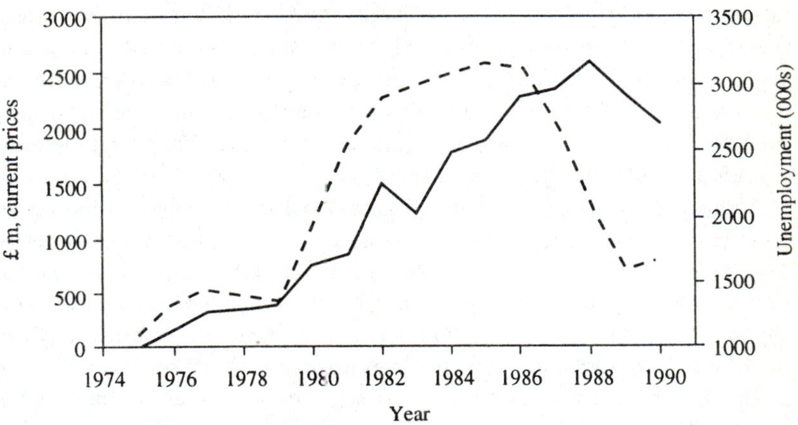

Notes: Expenditure on the special employment measures (left scale) is in gross terms. Unemployment figures (right scale) are averaged quarterly figures. Financial years are represented as calendar years.

Key: Special employment measures ——— Unemployment - - -

Sources: *Economic Trends* (London: HMSO), tables 6.2 and 7.1.

(49 000), Community Industry (8000) and the Job-Splitting Scheme (1000) – and a further 270 000 places were available on the Youth Training Scheme (YTS). However, these were inadequate to deal with the scale of long-term unemployment, which stood at 1.35m by late 1985, and over half a million people had been unemployed for three years or more. Some argued that the schemes were in fact harmful, since they displaced workers from elsewhere and raised taxation, but the view of the House of Commons Employment Committee was that 'they are primarily intended to lower the number of unemployed in the *short-term* in a cost-effective way whilst other policies take effect, and help them to get permanent jobs' (HC 199, 1986, para 6).[19]

The Employment Committee recommended a plan of action to create 750 000 jobs over three years, consisting of £1500m per annum on a building improvement programme to improve the inner cities, £400m a year for the creation of an extra 100 000 jobs in the social services, including the National Health Service, and £1400m a year on a £40-a-week wage subsidy to employers to take on the long-term unemployed.[20] The government formally rejected the proposals in May 1986, arguing that the plan underestimated the cost and would have an adverse effect on the economy, and instead favoured an intensification of the existing measures. In January 1986 the YTS was extended to two years for all 16-year-old school-leavers (one year for 17-year-olds), with at least 20 weeks (13 weeks) off-the-job training. By 1986, nearly two-thirds of school-leavers went on to YTS, and the changes were expected to increase the number of participants to around 450 000 at any one time. The Exchequer cost of YTS was around £1bn per annum, of which about a quarter was provided by the European Social Fund (ESF).

As unemployment peaked, the March 1986 Budget introduced further measures, including a planned expansion of the Enterprise Allowance Scheme from 65 000 to 100 000 entrants per annum, an expansion of the Community Programme from 200 000 to 255 000 places, and an offer of a counselling interview under the Restart programme for each of the 1.4 million long-term unemployed. Since by now the concern was to find employment for those coming off YTS, the Budget also replaced the Young Workers Scheme with a New Workers Scheme. The earlier scheme related to those under the age of 18 years, but now a £15-a-week subsidy was paid to employers in respect of new recruits either aged 18 to 19 and paid less than £55 a week, or 20 years of age and paid less than £65 a week. As before, part of the explanation was that youths had priced themselves out of the market, but the scheme was phased out in 1988. A Jobstart Allowance of £20 a week was also offered in the Budget to long-term unemployed people taking a job with a weekly wage of less than £80. The subsidy was paid directly to the employee and was designed to offset the loss of benefits, but the payment meant that those in receipt of it could earn more than other people in similar jobs (Gregg, 1990). However, the take-up was poor, averaging about 4000 participants a year.

Unemployment fell sharply from the end of 1986 (see Figure 8.1), but expenditure on the special employment measures remained high as policy was reorientated in the context of a tighter labour market to get the long-term unemployed back into work. The framework was Employment Training, which in September 1988 replaced the Community Programme and a number of smaller schemes, and was aimed at those aged 18–25 years who had been unemployed for at least six months, and others who had been unemployed for more than two years and were under the age of 50 years. At an annual cost of around £1500m, Employment Training offered 300 000 places of six months' duration, with some taking follow-on courses in on-the-job training, off-the-job training at colleges, and project-based work similar to that under the old Community Programme. Whereas previous schemes maintained benefits entitlement through the payment of an allowance plus some travel expenses, Employment Training offered

£10–£12 a week plus benefits, and was criticized as a further attempt to drive down wages for the young.

THE 'ENTERPRISE INITIATIVE'

The strong economic growth prompted a further review and restatement of general industrial support, with the results published in the January 1988 White Paper *DTI – Department for Enterprise* (Cm 278, 1988). This styled the Department of Trade and Industry as the 'department for enterprise' and dealt with areas ranging from deregulation, competition and the single European market to innovation, trade, business development, regional policy and the inner cities. Table 8.6 shows that some turnaround in the spending of the Department of Trade and Industry had already occurred within the context of a much reduced budget, and the White Paper sought to reinforce this shift of emphasis, while increasing the DTI budget by some £200m.

In relation to industrial aid, the general stance of the government was that 'companies seeking Government assistance for investment projects should be required to show that they genuinely need grant in order to proceed and that their projects are viable and will produce identifiable and significant benefits' (Cm 278, 1988, para 7.8). Subsidies to large firms had already been reduced substantially, and now the presumption was that these firms could obtain sufficient finance from private sources, so it sought to concentrate resources on improving the competitiveness of small and medium-sized firms through advisory-based schemes and limited

Table 8.6 The pattern of DTI expenditure, 1979–85 (£m, current prices)

Spending area	*1979/80* £m	%	*1985/6* £m	%
Nationalized industries	1 100	53	400	31
Non-selective regional aid	460	22	270	21
Selective aid	390	18	210	17
Assistance for exporters	0	0	30	2
Research, development and innovation	130	7	370	29
Total	**2 080**	100	**1 280**	100

Source: Cm 278 (1988).

capital grant assistance. The General Investment Support for Major Projects, which had superseded the Selective Investment Scheme in 1979, was replaced by a scheme known as Assistance for Exceptional Projects, for which projects had to be genuinely exceptional, resulting in only two offers being made in the four years after introduction.[21] All the same, the European Commission sought to freeze this section 8 assistance as part of a fresh attempt to clamp down on state aid in 1990, but the government resisted this, arguing that the Treaty of Rome allowed the Commission to review systems of aid only, while section 8 was an enabling power and not a provider of aid.

The review of technology-based support sought to move assistance further from near-market research and development to focus 'primarily on the circumstances where research is necessary before commercial applications can be developed, or where the benefits of the research are likely to be widespread, and on technology transfer' (Cm 278, 1988, para. 8.4). With the exception of SMART, support for single company projects was virtually ended, so that the Fibre Optics and Opto-Electronics Scheme and the Microelectronics Industry Support Programme ceased immediately, and the Support for Advanced Manufacturing Technology was also terminated at around this time. Instead, the emphasis continued to be on collaborative ventures between higher education institutes and companies and on technology transfer, with 50 per cent grants available for projects that would not otherwise have gone ahead, which tapered as the market potential became clearer.

Existing collaborative programmes, such as LINK and EUREKA, continued, and were supplemented by an extra £84m for projects that were complementary to ESPRIT II, including both the Advanced Technology Programmes (ATPs), which aimed to encourage pre-competitive research in new technologies, and the General Industrial Collaborative Projects (GICP), which aimed to fund projects and programmes not covered by any of the above. In 1989/90 total project costs were: LINK, £23m; EUREKA, £10m; ATPs, £74m; and GICP, £26m. Technology transfer measures included Regional Technology Centres, the Teaching Company Scheme, through which young academics undertook key projects in companies under supervision, and various training, demonstrator and awareness schemes. To these, the government added small firm innovation grants and some business development measures, which are described below.

The revised Regional Development Grant scheme was scrapped in the review, and replaced by a number of new initiatives 'based on the successful experience of the Business Improvement Scheme' (para. 7.7). From April 1988 the Regional Enterprise Grant (REG) became available in two forms: the Regional Investment Grant (RIG) which offered a 15 per cent grant towards investment in new and secondhand plant and machinery, buildings, purchase of land, site preparation and the purchase of vehicles used solely on site, up to a maximum grant of £15 000; and the Regional Innovation Grant (RIN) which offered a grant of 50 per cent of eligible costs towards projects leading to the development and introduction of new products and processes, up to a maximum grant of £25 000. Under RIN, the project had to be innovative to the applicant, involve a degree of novelty and technical risk, and improve either the company's product range or its efficiency. The grant covered all costs incurred up to the point of commercial exploitation, including capital expenditure.

The Regional Enterprise Grant was available under section 8 of the 1982 Industrial Development Act to firms in the Development Areas with fewer than 25 employees, which could claim at most one RIG and at most one RIN. Most manufacturing and service sector projects were eligible, with the exception of banks and insurance companies, and in the case of RIG, service sector projects had to serve a non-local market. From September 1988 the eligible areas were extended to include certain European Regional Development Fund programme areas for steel and shipbuilding, which included the Intermediate Areas of South Yorkshire, Fife and Plymouth.[22] Applications for REG ran at about 3000 a year, involving around £18m in offered grant, giving an average grant of £6000 (see Table 8.2 on page 159). Significant changes were made in May 1992, when applicants for RIG had to demonstrate a proof of need, while the coverage of RIN was extended to the Intermediate Areas, Inner City Task Force areas, Scottish urban areas, and to the City Challenge areas and EC designated Objective 2 areas described below, so that eventually the REG was to be administered by the Department of the Environment. At this time, firms with up to fifty employees were made eligible and the restriction of one RIN offer was lifted. An evaluation of the scheme found that the aggregate impact of both components of the Regional Enterprise Grant depended heavily on the success of a relatively small number of firms, and that only around half the RIG-supported projects could be classified as additional (Segal Quince Wicksteed, 1992).

The *Enterprise Initiative* greatly expanded the subsidy for private consultancy under the Business Development Consultancy Initiative. This was available in the areas of design, manufacturing and service systems, marketing and product quality from January 1988, and business planning and financial and management information systems from April 1988. With the exception of the Business Improvement Scheme, for which some allocated funds remained unused, the initiative replaced existing advisory assistance under the Business and Technical Advisory Service and the Support for Advanced Manufacturing Technology, of which there had been about 1100 consultancies. The Consultancy Initiative applied to firms with fewer than 500 employees and paid for two days' free consultancy from an 'Enterprise Counsellor' to carry out a Business Review, and, subject to this, offered assistance towards 5–15 days' consultancy in the above areas. The grant rate was 50 per cent, but this increased to two-thirds in the Assisted Areas and Urban Programme areas, reflecting the gradual merging of regional and urban policies. Firms could claim assistance in at most of the above areas, and consultants were usually members of the appropriate professional body, which also took a role in promoting the scheme. One of these was the Production Engineering Research Association, which had operated the Manufacturing Advisory Service since 1977, and another was the Design Council, which had been involved in a similar scheme since 1982.

In 1988/9 the government set aside £50m for the Consultancy Initiatives and planned for 1000 consultancies per month, but 12000 applications had been received after nine months, owing partly to the marketing of the scheme and its promotion by local enterprise agencies. By this time, 9000 business reviews had been completed by the Enterprise Counsellors, of which the marketing initiative proved to be the most popular. A number of amendments were made in June 1989 to improve the operation of the scheme, and by April 1992 more than 100 000 applications had been received and total grant payments stood at £157m in respect of 71 500 approved projects, of which 42 000 had been completed. Of the approved projects, 43 per cent of firms had fewer than 10 employees; 53 per cent were in manufacturing; and 52 per cent were in an Assisted Area or Urban Programme area. The evaluation of the Consultancy Initiatives questioned the relevance of the Business Review to most firms, but reported that it raised awareness of the potential benefits of consultancy (Segal Quince Wicksteed, 1991). The scheme closed in September 1994.

INWARD INVESTMENT

At the time of the 1988 reforms it was anticipated that regional policy spending would remain broadly constant at around £470m in 1990/1, but it subsequently became clear that £115m of this would be on amounts already committed under the old RDG schemes. Of the remainder, £61m was to be spent on the new measures and £284m on Regional Selective Assistance, representing a one-third increase in spending on this scheme.

Grant applications for Regional Selective Assistance (RSA) above £500 000 were dealt with by the Industrial Development Advisory Board in London, and the burden of proof was placed on large firms to demonstrate that they were in need of the assistance. Around this time, the National Audit Office reported that it found RSA project files generally gave narrative on additionality, but that where the grant amount was less than £100 000 and subject to simplified procedures, then proof of need was sometimes not demonstrated (HC 346, 1988).

Other eligibility criteria for RSA were unchanged, so projects had to be viable; had to satisfy efficiency objectives – such as strengthening the regional or national economy; the applicant had to demonstrate an employment link; and the greater part of the project was to be financed from sources outside the public sector. Referring to these conditions, the 1988 White Paper stated that 'internationally mobile investment projects will by their nature frequently meet these criteria' (Cm 278, 1988, para. 7.10), and indeed Community rules meant that the Assisted Areas were the principal areas in which this assistance could be given. Thus, as RSA took a rising share of the budget, so regional policy became increasingly geared to these inward investment projects. In 1986/7 the Invest in Britain Bureau recorded 322 decisions by foreign-owned companies to newly invest or expand in the UK, of which 111 were offered RSA totalling £75m; by value this represented half of RSA offers in that year. Indeed, by value of offer, inward investment took half the section 7 selective assistance in years 1986–90 and most of the section 8 offers for which information is available. The pattern has changed little since then: 43 per cent of UK inward investment projects in 1993/4 received RSA (HC 356, 1995).

The take-up of Regional Selective Assistance reflected the surge in inward investment in the 1980s, attracted to the Assisted Areas by slack labour market conditions and by the preferential assistance (Taylor, 1993). The United States continued to be the main source of inward investment, but much of this was in the form of additions to existing facilities. Japan represented the major source of new investment, and the number of UK-based Japanese manufacturing plants increased from twenty-five in 1983 to fifty at the start of 1987, and to over a hundred by the end of 1989. The major recipient of this investment in employment terms was Wales, partly as a result of the availability of factory space in the wake of the steel closures. However, the most prominent case was the Nissan company, which announced its intention to establish a £200m car assembly plant in Britain in 1981, and acted as an important demonstrator project for other Japanese companies considering inward investment. Regional aid was offered to Nissan amounting to £88m if the plant located in a

Development Area, or £112m if located in a Special Development Area, including RSA at a rate of 11.72 per cent and RDG at either 15 or 22 per cent. In the event it located in a Special Development Area near Sunderland shortly before these areas were withdrawn.[23] Other Japanese car producers announced plans for UK plants in 1989, but these were to be outside the Assisted Areas. In total, £190m in assistance was paid to Japanese-owned companies in the UK between 1979 and 1989.[24]

In Scotland the attraction of overseas investment was made the joint responsibility of the Scottish Development Agency and Scottish Office in 1982, and the investment promotion activities of local authorities and new town development corporations were curtailed with the establishment of Locate in Scotland (Keating and Boyle, 1986). In England the inward investment role was also centralized, and while this avoided competition at the regional level, it was fragmented between government departments. Latent Development Agencies existed in the English regions in the form of Regional Development Organisations (RDOs), but the combined budget of these was less than £600 000 in 1981, and government support was in the form of a matching grant which required the RDOs to obtain half their funds from other sources. The government made it known that if the RDOs could co-ordinate the inward investment function for all the local authorities and new town development corporations in their regions, then it was willing to increase resources to give them parity with the Scottish and Welsh Development Agencies in overseas promotional activities. This was broadly achieved, with the overall level of funds increasing to £4m in 1990/1. Having reduced competition at the subregional level, an English Unit was established in the Department of Trade and Industry to encourage greater co-operation between the RDOs, while the Invest in Britain Bureau remained responsible for promoting the UK overseas and handling enquiries.

REFORM OF THE STRUCTURAL FUNDS

The previous reforms of the European Regional Development Fund failed to assert EC control over regional policy matters, but the introduction of the National Programmes of Community Interest (NPCIs) and Integrated Development Operations Programmes (IDOPs) in 1984 were an important watershed in EC economic development policy. These programmes were jointly-agreed packages of projects designed to tackle identified problems in some area, which not only gave the Commission a role outside the regional policies of member states, but the programmes were also seen as yielding synergy and being more likely to give additionality to EC funds.

A further major reform of the Community's structural policy was made in the run-up to the completion of the Single European Market in 1993, since not only was it thought that this would disproportionately benefit the more prosperous areas, but the accession of Spain and Portugal made disparities in living standards much more pronounced. The Commission mapped out new guidelines in 1987, which were taken up by the Council in 1988 and came into effect from January 1989. These doubled regional aid and brought together the previously separate Structural Funds to focus resources on a common set of objectives that sought to reduce regional and sectoral imbalances.[25] These were the European Regional Development Fund, the European Social Fund and the Guidance Section of the European Agricultural Guidance and Guarantee Fund, each of which had a regional component. Funding for these was increased from ECU 7bn (£4.62bn) in 1987 to ECU 14bn (£9.23bn) in 1993 (1988 prices), and five Objectives were declared to which these would be committed (together with total allocations over 1989–93 at 1989 prices), as follows:

Objective 1: to assist those regions whose development is lagging behind (ECU 38.3bn);
Objective 2: to revitalise regions affected by serious industrial decline (ECU 7.2bn);
Objective 3: to combat long-term unemployment (ECU 7.5bn for Objectives 3 and 4 combined);
Objective 4: to integrate young people into the job market;
Objective 5: (a) to adjust the structure of agriculture (ECU 3.4bn); and (b) to develop rural areas (ECU 2.8bn).

While more than one Fund could contribute to each Objective, the ERDF was to deal principally with Objectives 1 and 2, the ESF with Objectives 3 and 4, and the EAGGF with Objective 5, while loans from the EIB, ECSC, NCI and Euratom could also contribute to any of these Objectives.

Assistance under Objectives 1, 2 and 5(b) was available in designated areas, but a departure was that these areas for intervention were defined by the Community separately from those of the member states (see Armstrong and Taylor, 1993). Further, unlike the UK Assisted Areas, for which the main criterion was unemployment, the EC made use of per capita GDP with the aim of reducing the gap between richer and poorer regions. Four-fifths of ERDF assistance was to be reserved for the least favoured regions under Objective 1, which were defined as regions where GDP was less than 75 per cent of the EC average, mainly comprising the poorest parts of Italy, Greece and Spain and the whole of Portugal and Eire, but later including Merseyside and North West Scotland. Northern Ireland was included for its special circumstances, even though it did not satisfy the criterion, and was to receive around £244m from this source up to 1993. Declining industrial areas eligible under Objective 2 were defined according to a number of economic indicators, and in the UK mainly comprised the Assisted Areas and areas which were adjacent or suffering from decline in vital industrial sectors.[26] The UK was projected to be the major recipient of Objective 2 aid amounting to £941m up to the end of 1991, or 40 per cent of the total allocation. Undeveloped rural areas were singled out for support under Objective 5(b), and in the UK these comprised parts of Devon and Cornwall, including the relevant Assisted Areas, the Highlands and Islands, the Intermediate Areas of Dumfries and Galloway, and rural Wales. These were set to receive 7.5 per cent of total allocated funds, which amounted to around £200m in 1989, and rising to about £600m in 1993.

Supported programmes were implemented by national bodies, so that applicants for funding under any of the five Objectives had to submit a three- to five-year development plan which identified the priorities and work to be undertaken, together with the arrangements for monitoring and evaluation. In response, the Commission produced a Community Support Framework (later known as a Single Programming Document) which set out the priority actions and financial support for each project. Important to the reform was that Community funding should be additional to that of member states, and the Commission expected at least an equivalent increase in national spending commensurate with any increase in spending from the Funds (CEC, 1989). Further, Community funds could not exceed 50 per cent of total project costs (75 per cent in Northern Ireland), with grant aid to firms fixed at 50 per cent in Objective 1 regions and 30 per cent elsewhere. The reform required the EIB to be involved in identifying those projects in the development plan which could be funded by a loan and grant mix, with loans more likely to be specified in the Community Support Framework where an income stream was generated (CEC, 1991a).

The types of programme assisted under the reformed Structural Funds were Integrated Development Operation Programmes (IDOPs), national assistance schemes, global grants administered by intermediaries designated by member states, large-scale projects, studies and technical assistance, and pilot projects, of which the predominant form of programme in the UK were the IDOPs. These involved local authorities and other public and private bodies, and were usually co-ordinated by the relevant government regional office. By the time the reform came into effect there were already 8 NPCIs and 5 IDOPs in Great Britain, and a further six IDOPs were adopted at the end of 1989 (CEC, 1991b).[27] These gave priority to the provision of industrial estates, transport infrastructure, developing new businesses, research and development, training facilities, tourism and environmental schemes. In the case of Northern Ireland, the Objective 1 Community Support Framework focused on the physical and social environment, external transport links, the development of agriculture and tourism, human resource development, and the strengthening industry, covering the aid schemes run by the Industrial Development Board and the Local Enterprise Development Unit (CEC, 1991b).

Funding under Objectives 3 and 4 was horizontal in that it was neither sectorally nor geographically specific, but available in respect of those aged over 25 years of age who had been unemployed for more than twelve months, and job-seekers aged under 25 years. These two Objectives accounted for around one-eighth of total Structural Funds, and in view of the frequent amendments to vocational training and employment policy the Commission drew up one Community Support Framework for these for each member state, extending over a three-year period. In the case of the Community Support Frameworks for the UK Objective 5(b) areas these focused on economic development, infrastructure, tourism and training, and measures were also taken to aid diversification and the address problems of peripherality. Funding amounted to £100m for the Highlands and Islands, £87m for rural Wales, £54m for Devon and Cornwall, and £10m for Dumfries and Galloway.

PROGRAMMES INITIATED BY THE COMMUNITY

The 1984 reform created a distinction between National Programmes of Community Interest and other programmes which were initiated by the EC. At the time of the 1988 reform, four EC programmes had been established, comprising the Special Telecommunications Action for Regional Development (STAR), VALOREN, RENAVAL and RESIDER. The STAR and VALOREN schemes were adopted in 1986 for a period of five years, and sought respectively to improve telecommunications and exploit indigenous energy potential in the most disadvantaged regions. The RENAVAL and RESIDER schemes were introduced in 1988 to run for five years and these served as a bridge between the Business Improvement

Scheme, which was due to terminate in March 1989, and the commencement of the reformed Structural Funds. RENAVAL provided funds for economic development work and support of small and medium-sized businesses in declining shipbuilding areas, which included Tyne and Wear, Middlesbrough, Langbaurgh, Glasgow and Greenock (Mellors and Copperthwaite, 1990). Areas on Merseyside and Plymouth were added later, with £1m in Community funds for Plymouth financing the extension of Regional Enterprise Grants to this area. RESIDER offered grants for environmental improvements, job creation and measures to promote small firms, tourism and innovation in rundown steel areas. In the UK, the extra money was used to support consultancy grants and Regional Enterprise Grants to small firms in Cleveland, South Yorkshire, Humberside, Strathclyde, Clwyd and Gwent.

Under the Structural Fund reform, five new Community Initiatives were announced in 1989, comprising: ENVIREG to tackle certain environmental problems in lagging regions; the Science and Technology for Regional Innovation and Development in Europe (STRIDE) to improve research and development capacity in Objective 1 regions; INTERREG to encourage co-operation between border areas of the EC; REGIS to develop remote regions and islands of the EC; and RECHAR to help diversify areas affected coal mining closures. Others were added to run from 1994, including: KONVER to assist areas affected by decline in defence industries; PESCA and RETEX to diversify fishing and textiles areas; LEADER to promote innovative development in rural areas; ADAPT to retrain those whose jobs are at risk; and URBAN to regenerate urban areas. These were set to take 9 per cent of the Structural Fund budget over 1994–9, and in most cases were directed towards the designated areas, with Objective 1 regions taking nearly two-thirds of this expenditure.

In total RECHAR offered £210m for environmental improvement, vocational training for the unemployed and the promotion of new economic activity, including the construction of industrial workshops, the establishment of common services, and assistance for small firm investment and innovation.[28] The UK was allocated £100m, but the funds were withheld in August 1991 as the argument over additionality came to a head. To control public expenditure, UK central government reduced the capital allocation to local authorities by £1 for every £1 that these authorities received from outside sources, and this not only had implications for the RECHAR money, but also for around half of the £3bn in EC funding agreed up to 1995. Further, the government took account of the assistance from the Structural Funds in fixing its overall spending budgets and this meant that the EC money was effectively spread across programmes and leaked outside the designated programme areas (HL 20, 1991). In addition, Treasury control over local authority finance was such that many authorities did not have sufficient funds to match the 50 per cent contribution from the ERDF, and in 1991/2 the Treasury was forced to increase the capital spending allocation of thirty authorities to enable them to take up the available money (*Economist*, 1991). The issue was resolved in February 1992, when the government agreed to raise local authority spending by the value of the grants, but this still meant that the local authorities had to find the matching funds from other sources. Further, the local authorities could only claim grants in respect of those projects with which they were committed to proceed, rather than those conditional European funding (HC 356, 1995).

Outside the Structural Fund reform, the European Investment Bank continued to offer long-term loans to promote economic development, focusing in the UK on industry, energy and infrastructure projects in the Assisted Areas, Wales, the Scottish Highlands and recognized textiles, steel, shipbuilding or fisheries areas. Projects could also qualify for loans if they improved industrial competitiveness, promoted EC policy in the fields of energy or environmental protection, or helped to develop telecommunications or transport links. Under the latter, loans of £150m and £100m were made for new passenger terminals at Gatwick and Stansted, and a £1bn loan was made for the construction of the Channel Tunnel. In 1987 the capital project loans for small and medium-sized enterprises were extended to all geographical areas, provided the firm had fewer than 500 employees, net fixed assets of less than £50m and the project cost did not exceed £14m, although loans for hotel and tourism projects continued to be available in the Assisted Areas only. EIB loans in the UK amounted to around £385m in 1987, of which a quarter went to private concerns, with total loans to the private sector amounting to £660m in the five years up to 1987. Global loans from the EIB continued to be administered by the clearing banks, of which £24m had been lent to 240 projects by 1989.

THE EUROPEAN COMMISSION AND STATE AIDS

The Commission stepped up its surveillance and control of state aid measures in the run-up to the completion of the internal market, since these were a possible substitute for trade protection (CEC, 1990a). Surveys in 1989 and 1990 attempted to quantify subsidies across the EC, and found that over 1986–8 state aids amounted to around 2.2 per cent of the EC's GDP, ranging from 4.1 per cent in Luxembourg to 1 per cent in Denmark and the UK (CEC, 1990b). Of total EC-wide aid, manufacturing took 41 per cent, transport 30 per cent, the coal industry 16 per cent, and agriculture and fisheries 13 per cent. Further, 36 per cent (32 per cent in the UK) of the aid went in regional aid, 27 (34) per cent in sectoral assistance and 37 (34) per cent towards horizontal objectives such as innovation, research and development, small and medium-sized businesses, trade, exports and general investment (CEC, 1990b). A similar OECD study found that, of the major industrialized countries, only the UK showed a substantial reduction in assistance over the 1980s, with state aid increasing in France, Germany and Italy (Bruce, 1990).

The EC's state aid policy gained some credibility in the 1980s, and a review prepared for the Commission concluded that important steps had been taken in this decade, including greater transparency of aid through EC surveys; the recovery of aid found to violate Treaty Articles; a substantial reduction in aid to the steel sector; a critical review of existing aid schemes; and the elimination of schemes that failed to serve any EC objective (Lehner, Meiklejohn and Reichenbach, 1991). The Commissioner with responsibility for the completion of the single market announced a renewed drive against state aids, to involve a review of existing aid schemes; an improvement in the quality of information on the impact of these schemes; and a limit on the overall volume of aid granted. A number of aid types were identified to which attention was to be turned, including general investment aid schemes; capital injections into publicly-owned enterprises and the acquisition of minority holdings in other companies by public authorities; interventionist industrial policy aids to support national champions; and export aids (Brittan, 1989).

These efforts to curtail assistance were to prove only partly successful, so that while agreement was obtained from Belgium, Holland and Denmark to cease paying state aid under general investment schemes, neither the UK nor Italy would agree to this. Further, while the airline, steel and telecommunications industries came under close scrutiny as the Commission sought to open these up to greater competition in the Single Market, these were state-owned in much of continental Europe and continued to receive substantial state cash injections. This included bail-outs of airlines, such as Iberia, Alitalia and Aer Lingus, with applications pending in the case of Olympic and TAP, a £2.3bn subsidy to the stricken Air France airline in 1994, and support for steel firms including a £70m subsidy for the German steel company Kloeckner and an IR£50m package for Irish Steel. In the case of Irish Steel, the Commissioner for competition policy argued that where there was just one small steel company in a country then these should be looked at with some flexibility, but the enormous subsidy to Air France, which was made under the relatively weak conditions that this should be the last such injection and that it should not be passed on to its domestic arm, opened up inevitable conflicts in state aid policy. At the time of writing, the Commission is considering a UK application for an aid package to Ford for up to £80m to locate its new £400m Jaguar production line in Britain rather than America, and given previous decisions and the large number of jobs involved, the Commission is in a difficult position. Other car manufacturers argue that this would lead to unfair competition, but the UK government's view is that the subsidy is not for production, but to locate employment in an area of high unemployment. However, such a subsidy may lead to other claims, with the Rover Group believed to be asking for up to £100m to locate its new engine plant in Britain.

Despite the apparent relaxing of policy towards companies in difficulty, there was some attempt to tighten the criteria for state aid in the early 1990s. In 1991 the Commission proposed that all publicly-owned manufacturing companies with an annual turnover greater than ECU 250m be required to submit an annual report detailing all state aid received, and in 1992 it tightened the definition of small and medium-sized enterprises eligible for aid. In addition, the ceiling for national investment aid to these companies was set at 15 per cent of investment costs for small firms (less than 50 employees and a turnover of less than ECU 5m) and 7.5 per cent for medium-sized firms (less than 250 employees and a turnover of less than ECU 20m), but these could be increased by 10 or 15 per cent for firms in the regional policy areas. For training, consultancy and technology aid the grant rate could not exceed 50 per cent, and this applied across policy areas. In May 1995 the Commission again announced its intention to tighten up on illegal state aid, insisting on repayment even for procedural infringements such as not notifying the Commission, and for the first time asking for interest to be charged.

THE WITHDRAWAL FROM INDUSTRIAL SUBSIDIES

Figure 8.2 shows that the fall in expenditure on industrial subsidies over the 1980s has been dramatic, from about £5bn in grant equivalent terms in 1979 to a little over £300m in 1990 (1980 prices). The cut-back occurred in each major area of policy, and although the real break in policy came in the 1984 Budget, when the accelerated depreciation allowances and regional capital grants were withdrawn, spending was already in sharp

Figure 8.2 Expenditure on industrial subsidies in the 1980s

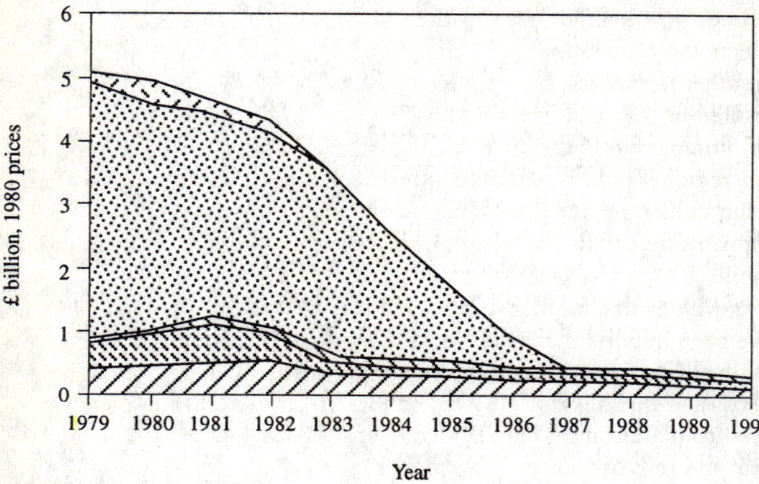

Notes: Figures are in grant equivalents at constant 1980 prices.
Financial years are shown as calendar years.

Key: Regional assistance; Sectoral and firm specific aid; National investment grants; Depreciation allowances; National employment subsidies

Source: Wren (1996b), tables 1, 2 and 3.

decline because of the earlier measures to curb expenditure and the fall in investment as a result of recession and the loss of manufacturing capacity. Along with this general reduction in spending there has also been significant changes in the composition and objectives of industrial assistance.

The withdrawal of the accelerated depreciation allowances and large-scale investment grants has eliminated any stability role for industrial assistance, and the shift away from supporting regions and firms in difficulty has meant that policy has taken on a narrow market failure role aimed at addressing instances of allocative inefficiency. Many of the remaining regional and national measures are now concerned with improving the competitiveness of firms, rather than direct job creation, and this not only includes the various technology and advisory-based schemes, but covers the collaborative research and development programmes carried out at both national and European level, and the measures to promote technology transfer. Further, in a period of high unemployment, the distributive elements of policy have been directed towards helping the adjustment of small areas affected by industrial decline, in a manner akin to the old 'blackspot' approach. This partly reflects the orientation of EC policy which, through its Structural Funds and other initiatives, has provided money for job creation in the wake of closures in the steel, shipbuilding, textiles and defence industries and in coal-mining, but in addition, small area urban policy has taken precedence over regional policy as the main instrument towards the worse-off areas. At the same time, the diversionary component of regional policy has been dropped other than for those projects that are genuinely internationally mobile.

As well as this more restricted and less ambitious role for policy, there have been important changes in its operation. This emphasis on effectiveness has been a dominant and recurrent theme of policy throughout the 1980s, and this has not only led to the effective exclusion of most large firms from assistance, but also led to an emphasis on discretionary assistance, the re-emergence of grant and cost-per-job limits, the systematic monitoring and evaluation of programmes, the introduction of a proof of need condition to virtually area of industrial subsidy policy, and greater targeting and control of assistance through local delivery by government agencies. Further, manufacturing capital investment, which was seen as the key to national and regional economic growth in the 1960s, is no longer the focus for policy, so that assistance has become much more orientated towards the service sector, including commercial property development. In addition, the European Commission has limited the scale and sought to restrict the scope of industrial subsidies, and coupled with privatization and European sponsored rationalization of older industries the claims on industrial subsidies have also been reduced, indicating that demand as well as supply factors have been important in determining the pattern of expenditure shown in Figure 8.2.

RECENT DEVELOPMENTS

The trends established in industrial assistance in the late 1980s have been broadly maintained in the early 1990s, and in this concluding section we may briefly review some of these developments. In this period there have been further reductions in subsidy, increased efforts to improve effectiveness, and a continued prominent role played by the European Commission in defining the scope for national aid. The professed stance of the government has been to intervene to help industry, but in effect it has disengaged from intervention and strongly resisted the use of subsidy, except as a last resort. This has meant that in contrast to nearly all previous post-war recessions, assistance was not expanded in the recession of the early 1990s, and the constraints posed by the large budget deficit and restrictions imposed by the Commission probably had little bearing on this. Instead, in the wake of the continued run-down of some traditional industries, policy has focused on helping the adjustment of the affected areas through a mixture of economic development measures, part-funded by the European Union (EU), and through an extension of the technology measures.

The 1988 policy changes largely terminated assistance for the introduction of new technology, but this has since been partly reversed by new measures to encourage innovation in small and medium-sized business. In 1991, the Support for Products Under Research (SPUR) was introduced to exploit innovative processes and products, and with an allocation of £32m it was scheduled to run for three years, providing grants at a rate of 30 per cent. Further schemes in 1991 were £11m for the Manufacturing, Planning and Implementation Studies Scheme for advanced manufacturing systems acting as a showcase for other small firms, and £5m for the Small and Medium-sized Enterprises Technical Advisory Service (SMETAS) for providing technical advice through regional technology centres and similar bodies. In addition, the SMART scheme has continued to provide competitive awards to small firms developing innovative technology with commercial potential, and the allocation for this was increased by a further £60m in 1992. Following a poor take-up, the LINK initiative (which was launched in 1986, but of the approved budget of £160m only £7m had been spent by August 1990) was made more accessible to small and medium-sized businesses and single company projects, and after a further review in May 1993 responsibility for the scheme was transferred to the new Office of Science and Technology (Cm 2250, 1993).

Despite these new measures for smaller firms, considerable industrial support has continued to go towards collaborative ventures. The major new UK initiative in this area has been the Joint Framework for support in Information Technology (JFIT), which, like the Alvey Programme, is joint funded by the Department of Trade and Industry and the Science and Engineering Research Council. This offers 50 per cent funding for industry/academic collaborative research; funding was set at £34m in 1990 but later increased. Various European collaborative technology programmes have also continued in the form of BRITE/EURAM, EUREKA and STRIDE. Under BRITE/EURAM, 163 European-wide research and development projects were chosen in early 1990, which sought to rejuvenate traditional industries by applying new technologies and advanced materials, and proposals have been sought for a second stage. Under STRIDE, which initially operated in Objective 1 regions, Northern Ireland has received £18m for various research and development measures, and in 1992 areas in Great Britain experiencing industrial decline were allocated £11.5m.

Modifications have been made to urban and regional policies, cumulating in the effective merging of these policies under the Single Regeneration Budget from 1994. Along with various training, housing and crime initiatives, the budget for these are now jointly determined and administered by ten new Government Offices for the regions, bringing together the functions of the Department of Trade and Industry, Environment, Employment (Training, Enterprise and Education) and Transport. The intention is for a more integrated approach to be taken towards regeneration, with policy tailored towards local circumstance. In a similar way to European regional policy, UK policy is now area-based in its operation, rather than project- or firm-based, and it is also competitive, with local authorities and the Training and Enterprise Councils (TECs) expected to take a lead in putting forward bids for funds in partnership with business and the voluntary sector. The Single Regeneration Budget can be used to fund schemes in any part of England, but Regional Selective Assistance continues to be administered outside this framework. A national regeneration agency was formed in 1994, known as English Partnerships, bringing together English Estates, the City Grant and the Derelict Land Grant. The agency is expected to raise finance through the sale of land of the former English Estates and from its unified grant schemes, with its budget determined under the Single Regeneration Budget. The agency's role is to lever private sector and matching European funds to certain areas to encourage the reclamation and reuse of derelict land and buildings.

Prior to the Single Regeneration Budget, changes were made to urban and regional policies. In 1991 it was announced that the Urban Programme was to be made partly competitive, and known as City Challenge, fifteen Urban Programme authorities were initially invited to make bids for £350m in funds over five years. All 57 Urban Programme authorities were invited to apply for £750m in funds for twenty programmes under a second round. However, in the same way that the monetary crises of the mid-1970s became a turning-point in regional policy, so the sterling crisis of September 1992 proved to be the same for urban policy. In November 1992, it was announced that future rounds of City Challenge were suspended and that the Urban Programme would be wound down, with expenditure falling to £156m in 1993/4 and to £91m in 1994/5 from previously planned levels of £232m and £238m. Other changes have included the establishment of some Inner City Task Forces in City Challenge areas and the availability of the Small Firm Loan Guarantee Scheme on favourable terms in these areas. In May 1992 responsibility for the Inner City Task Forces was transferred to the Department of the Environment, putting the whole of urban policy under the control of this department, and later the Regional Enterprise Grants were transferred under the Single Regeneration Budget.

Regional policy came under scrutiny after each of the previous three general elections, and a futher review of the Assisted Areas map was announced in June 1992. Parts of the south of England were severely affected by the recession, and representations were made from these areas, not least so that they might gain access to the European Union Structural Funds. At December 1992 the national unemployment rate at was 10.5 per cent, but non-Assisted Area travel-to-work-areas such as Thanet, Clacton and Skegness had unemployment rates of 16, 16.7 and 17 per cent respectively, while Assisted Areas such as Accrington/Rossendale and Darlington had rates of 8.1 and 9.7 per cent, and this situation had come about partly because the Assisted Areas map had been unchanged since 1984. The revised map became effective from August 1993, and while the overall coverage remained roughly constant at 35 per cent of the working population, it signalled a return to local employment policy with parts of travel-to-work areas designated for assistance, including splits between Development and Intermediate Areas and between Intermediate and Non-Assisted Areas. Every region now contains an Assisted Area, with substantial parts of South East England designated for aid, including London (see Figure A.4 in the Appendix, p. 218), suggesting that the problem is once again perceived as sub-regional. Areas affected by the run-down in the coal and defence industries were designated, including Alfreton and Ashfield in Nottinghamshire, Barrow-in-Furness in Cumbria, and the area around the Rosyth naval dockyard in Scotland, while the main loser was Wales. The government has announced that this new map will be reviewed in 1996.

9 Conclusions

THE PATTERN OF EXPENDITURE

In this book we have traced government interventions in industry since the turn of the century, focusing on the use of industrial subsidies for purposes which may be described according to the allocative, stability and distributional functions of government. As we have seen, these interventions initially involved very little real subsidy and were small in scale, so that the pre-war measures in the Special Areas consisted of some make-work schemes, physical measures and loans at commercial rates, but by the outbreak of war less than £2m had been disbursed in assistance from Treasury-backed funds. It is therefore only in the past fifty years that industry has been subsidized to any great extent, confirming that the use of industrial subsidies is truly a modern phenomenon.

Of course, substantial assistance was extended to agriculture in the Depression and expanded in the years leading up to the Second World War, but important to understanding the widespread adoption of industrial assistance was undoubtedly the gradual acceptance of Keynesian ideas. These ideas gained ground at precisely the time when the government exercised substantial wartime control over the economy and was actively engaged in considering ways in which to avoid the instability that had followed the First World War. In the pause provided by the war, and despite initial Treasury scepticism, plans were laid for an active fiscal policy to moderate demand, tax incentives to encourage investment, and an industrial transference programme to bolster the areas vulnerable to unemployment.

Accelerated depreciation allowances in the form of initial allowances were announced in 1945 to compensate firms for the effect of inflation on existing capital allowances. These were assessed on a historic cost basis, but thought insufficient to replace capital at post-war prices. Once introduced, the tax allowances became an important means by which the government sought to fine-tune the level of economic activity, and as such formed the first large-scale industrial assistance measure outside the agricultural sector. However, while they were a readily available means by which the government could give a boost to investment, they were rarely used to deflate the economy in the up-swing of the cycle, and rather than having the effect of moderating demand they became progressively more generous as the government sought to stimulate investment. At first, the rates on initial allowances were increased, but since these led to a subsequent reduction in the writing-down allowance, they were later replaced by investment allowances. Both types of allowance then ran side by side, and finally, the tax allowances were replaced by nationally available investment grants, with higher rates of grant available in the Assisted Areas. These grants were seen as an improvement over allowances, which were slow and uncertain in their effect, only benefited firms earning profits, and were available towards some investment in non-productive assets such as office furniture. By such means, the principle of large-scale direct subsidies to industry became firmly established.

To gauge the scale and composition of industrial subsidies, we can refer to the figures for grant equivalent expenditure over the post-war period, shown in Figure 9.1. These have been referred to previously, and details of

Figure 9.1 Expenditure on UK industrial subsidies, 1946–90

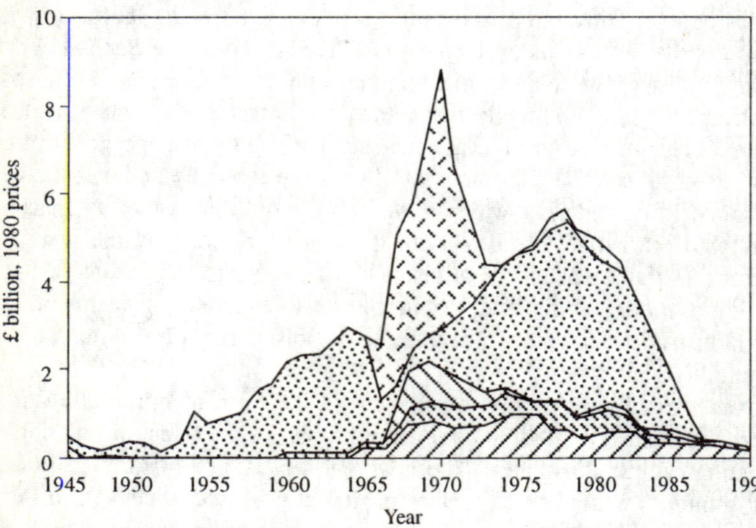

Notes: Expenditure is in grant equivalents at constant 1980 prices. Financial years are shown as calendar years.

Key: Regional assistance; Sectoral and firm-specific aid; National investment grants; Depreciation allowances; National employment subsidies

Source: Wren (1996b), tables 1, 2 and 3.

this expenditure by sub-period have already been given in Figures 4.1 (p. 71), 6.1 (p. 123) and 8.2 (p. 198). Assumptions underlying these grant equivalent estimates are given in Wren (1996b). Broadly speaking, the subsidy element of each incentive is calculated as its present value to a firm in investment under the assumption that it uses a discounted cash flow method of appraisal. These grant equivalent subsidy rates are then applied to actual spending on each measure, to give grant equivalent expenditure at constant 1980 prices. In so doing, we take as the discount rate the long-term rate on external borrowing and assume that firms have static expectations and are able to take advantage of the subsidy at the earliest possible opportunity, so that subsidies are calculated at their maximum value. In addition, we allow for a payment lag between the date of offer and the receipt of assistance.

According to this method and our definition of an industrial subsidy set out in the introduction, we are able to identify £125.1bn in grant equivalent expenditure on industrial subsidies over the period 1946–90, and it is this which is shown in Figure 9.1. It is apparent that the bulk of this industrial assistance has been in the form of tax allowances (£71.3bn or 57 per cent) and that a further £25.5bn has been in the form of employment subsidies, mainly comprising the refund on the Selective Employment Tax. Nationally available investment grants at £5.6bn have accounted for only a very small share of the total subsidy, while regional assistance at £13.3bn, and that on firm and sectoral interventions (including support for civil aviation and shipbuilding) at £9.4bn, are also relatively small.

Figure 9.1 shows clearly the different phases of policy, including the gradual increase in subsidy expenditure from the early 1950s, as the tax allowances became progressively more generous. Investment allowances on plant, machinery and buildings were reintroduced in 1959, and when the rates on these were increased in the early 1960s expenditure rose steeply, until first recession and then the switch to grants led to a sharp fall in spending. The period of the mid-1960s is noteworthy for the number of structural shifts in policy. We see the switch from tax allowances to the nationally available investment grants, but also the growth in regional, sectoral and firm-based assistance as a strong distributive component was added to industrial subsidy policy, which hitherto had been primarily concerned with stability objectives, at least in intention. The Selective Employment Tax refund favoured industries with a relatively high export content, and along with investment grants, this sought a fundamental increase in the level of national economic activity, partly to be achieved by the relaxation of the balance of payments constraint. This meant that grant equivalent expenditure on industrial subsidies peaked in the late-1960s at about 5.4 per cent of GDP, indicating the extent to which these subsidies were an important feature of economic policy.

If the spending on the Selective Employment Tax refund and Selective Employment Premium are taken out of Figure 9.1 (shown as national employment subsidies from 1966 to 1974 in this figure), then a different pattern emerges. In particular, there is a sharp fall in expenditure in 1966/7, but then a steady build-up to a peak in 1978/9 and an approximate fourfold increase in spending over this period, indicating that other than this one very large measure, the heyday of industrial assistance did genuinely occur in the late 1970s. However, as we made clear in the introduction, we include these employment schemes in our definition of an industrial subsidy.

The policy reversals of the early 1970s are clearly evident from Figure 9.1. First, we see the dramatic reduction in total subsidy expenditure associated with the gradual withdrawal of the Selective Employment Tax announced in the 1971 Budget. Second, we observe the dwindling of spending on the nationally available investment grants following their abolition in 1970, and third, we see the substantial increase in expenditure on the tax allowances after these had been reinstated for plant and machinery in 1970 and extended nationwide in 1972 in the form of free depreciation. The rate of increase in expenditure on these tax measures is far greater than that in the late 1950s and early 1960s than is perhaps immediately apparent from Figure 9.1, since total spending on the other measures was in decline from 1970. Indeed, taking the national investment grants, regional assistance and the sectoral and firm aid together, we see that expenditure on these fell from £2.2bn in 1969/70, to £1.6bn in 1974/5, and to £1.2bn in 1978/9, so that decline in the trend was established well before the arrival of the first Conservative government of the 1980s. The 1979/80 recession meant that spending under the accelerated depreciation allowances was also in decline before these were phased out in the 1984 Budget.

Figure 9.1 shows the sharp reduction in total expenditure on industrial subsidies from the late 1970s, so that by the late 1980s, overall spending had returned to the level of the immediate post-war period. The 1980s saw the stripping away of the stabilization and distribution functions of industrial subsidies as the role of government was more narrowly defined. Indeed, other than the depreciation allowances, the pattern of assistance is similar to that of the early 1960s, with industrial support consisting primarily of that for shipbuilding and civil aviation, while regional assistance is really a local employment policy in which effectiveness is an important concern. Regional selective assistance continues to operate, but it is used chiefly to attract new inward investment projects to the UK. Industrial subsidies are now much more orientated to correcting instances of allocative inefficiency, so that the new avenues for assistance consist of limited technology and small firm support, plus support for various collaborative ventures. In addition, there are measures excluded from our spending figures, including urban economic schemes and programmes funded under the European Union Structural Funds.

EXPLAINING SUBSIDY EXPENDITURE

To gain further insight into the underlying motivation for industrial subsidies we can report the results of a time-series analysis of the grant equivalent expenditure figures undertaken by Wren (1996b). This disaggregates industrial subsidy expenditure according to its availability, comprising national assistance (the national investment grants, employment subsidies and depreciation allowances shown in Figure 9.1), regional assistance and sectoral/firm-specific assistance. It attempts to explain the long- and short-run determinants of each of these components in terms of the national levels of GDP and unemployment; our discussion having shown that the level of economic activity and high rates of national unemployment (which tend to widen regional disparities) have been important in accounting for the pattern of industrial subsidy expenditure over time. The estimated coefficients from the regression analysis are reported in Table 9.1, and allow for structural breaks in the estimated relationships related to both economic and political events.

At a broad level, Table 9.1 shows a positive relationship between the underlying long-run or equilibrium level of expenditure on national and on sectoral/firm assistance and the level of economic activity, as reflected by the positive coefficients on the output term (GDP) and the negative coefficients on unemployment (UN), but that the converse follows for regional assistance. This reflects the different nature of these components, so that demand factors have been more important in determining the level of national aid, which has usually been available at fixed rates, while regional aid has distributional aims and its supply has been inversely related to the level of economic activity. A number of more detailed points can be observed from the long-run relationships shown in Table 9.1, which help quantify some of the effects described in this book.

First, national assistance has run at about 5 per cent of output, but the increase in this over the 1966–70 electoral period was unsustainable, leading to a further shift in this relationship over 1971–4. Second, the

Table 9.1 Long- and short-run determinants of industrial assistance

	Long-run		*Short-run*			
(a) **National assistance**	UN_{-1}	GDP_{-1}	ΔNAT_{-1}	ΔUN_{-1}	ΔUN_{-2}	ΔGDP_{-1}
1949–65	–2.6	0.05	0.27	0.86	1.12	–
1966–70	–0.1	0.2	2.70	0.86	1.12	–0.77
1971–4	–25.3	–0.2	0.27	0.86	1.12	–
1975–90	–2.6	0.05		Unchanged		
(b) **Regional assistance**	UN_{-1}	GDP_{-1}		ΔREG_{-1}	ΔNAT_{-1}	ΔSEC_{-1}
1962–5	0.47	0.01		0.18	0.04	0.35
1966–70	0.47	–0.01		Unchanged		
1971–6	0.47	0.01		Unchanged		
1977–90	–	–0.01		Unchanged		
(c) **Sectoral/firm assistance**	UN_{-1}	GDP_{-1}		ΔUN_{-1}	ΔGDP_{-1}	ΔGDP_{-2}
1949–65	–	0.004		–	–	–
1966–9	–0.22	0.004		0.73	0.01	0.03
1970–4	Unchanged			0.73	0.03	0.03
1975–9	Unchanged			0.73	0.04	0.03
1980–90	Unchanged			0.73	0.01	0.03

Notes: The figures reported here are based on regression estimates in Wren (1996b) using annual data, where the dependent variables are ΔNAT, ΔREG and ΔSEC for parts (a), (b) and (c) respectively and the long-run terms were entered in error correction form. The equations pass standard tests and only significant parameter estimates are shown (constant terms are not shown). Financial years are represented by calendar years, so that 1946 indicates 1946/7, etc.

UN = UK unemployment, annual averages, thousands. *Source*: *Employment Gazette* (London: HMSO).
GDP = UK gross domestic product, factor cost, £m,1980 prices. *Source*: *National Income and Expenditure* (London: HMSO).
NAT = National industrial assistance, £m, 1980 prices
REG = Regional industrial assistance, £m, 1980 prices
SEC = Sectoral/firm-specific industrial assistance, £m, 1980 prices
Δ is the first-difference operator ($\Delta X_t = X_t - X_{t-1}$)
Source: Wren (1996b), table 5.

reduction in national assistance from the mid-1970s is accounted for by the rise in unemployment from this time. As an explanation, this may appear odd, but a causal link exists if the rise in unemployment can be seen as promoting disillusionment with the workings of industrial subsidies and to their withdrawal. Third, the long-run equation for regional assistance exhibits a structural break from 1976, and this is related to the conditions on the IMF stand-by loan, which led to the withdrawal of the Regional Employment Premium and the cutting of regional aid from this time. Fourth, while regional assistance is generally negatively related to output, the positive coefficients on this term over 1962–5 and 1971–6 reflect the commencement and recommencement of regional policy in these periods when spending was increasing with demand as the policy built up. Finally, there is a structural break in the sectoral/firm assistance relationship from 1966 coinciding with the introduction of a distributional element into this component of assistance, and in particular the commencement of assistance to shipbuilding.

The regression analysis also allows us to identify the short-run determinants of assistance, which may be interpreted as determining fluctuations in expenditure around the long-run trend. As a general point, these short-run coefficients are much more stable than the long-run terms, indicating that while economic and political events have led to shifts in the underlying structural relationships, the use of industrial assistance as a short-run response to events has been much more constant, both across time and across governments. Again, there are a number of detailed points.

In relation to the national and sectoral/firm interventions, the results in Table 9.1 show that an increase in unemployment of a thousand people has led to an increase in national subsidy of around £2m over two years and a further £750 000 increase in the sectoral/firm assistance. The unemployment term lagged two years in the national assistance equation indicates the longer period over which the tax allowances take effect, while the positive coefficient on the output term in the sectoral/firm assistance equation reflects the mixed nature of this component of assistance, which includes the assistance to the civil aviation industry. The unemployment and output terms are insignificant in the regional assistance equation, but Table 9.1 shows that fluctuations in regional subsidy are positively related to changes in the previous year's levels of national and sectoral/firm assistance, indicating that expansions of spatially-based assistance have been preceded by these other forms of assistance. This can be read from our discussion, and suggests a natural order for intervention, whereby national, sectoral and firm-specific assistance is used to support industry in recession, and regional aid is used subsequently to address the resulting higher unemployment in some areas. The coefficients suggest that a rise in unemployment of a thousand people over the course of the economic cycle has led to an extra £300 000 in regional assistance over two years.

LESSONS FROM THE UK EXPERIENCE

Throughout our discussion we have tried to give motivation for the large number of changes that have been described in the composition and scale of industrial subsidies. For this we have relied on sources including policy statements, contemporary accounts, academic writing and various parliamentary publications. However, our focus has not been explicitly evaluative in nature, so that while we have tried to indicate the relative success or failure of particular measures and have reported the results of some assessments, we have not sought to summarize the large body of work examining the effects of the different instruments of policy. Nevertheless, we may ask what have been the lessons from the UK experience of industrial subsidies?

The post-war UK economic record suggests that industrial subsidies were an almost unmitigated failure, since not only were they unable to foster economic growth and to avert the repeated balance of payments crises, they were even inadequate in the more modest task of holding down unemployment. Indeed, some have gone so far as to argue that they were part of the problem, in that they diverted resources from more productive uses and so exacerbated the problems they sought to address (Burton, 1979). The pattern of expenditure shown in Figure 9.1 also suggests that this experience was wholly unsuccessful, so that a casual reading of this would tell us that industrial subsidies were tried, found not to work and then discarded. Of course, these views are simplistic, since we can only guess at what would otherwise have happened, and a proper examination must inevitably be more sophisticated than this.

Previous commentators who have surveyed this experience have been highly critical, but have tended to focus on the administration of policy, particularly the apparent imprecision over policy objectives. Denton's (1976) appraisal is fairly typical, 'Industrial policy in the United Kingdom since 1960 can only be characterised as incoherent. The basic objectives have not been clear, trade-offs between competing objectives have not been calculated in advance, the relevance of intermediate to final objectives has been obscure, and the efficiency of the methods employed have been uncertain' (p. 150). Similarly, the House of Commons Expenditure Committee (HC 651, 1972) thought selective assistance gave 'a convincing picture of the confusion of objectives and the shortcomings of control that have too often characterised the actions of Government' (para. 261). This focus on objectives may to some extent reflect the lack of hard information on the effects of these measures, and the difficulties involved in obtaining this information, but it is nevertheless the case that policy objectives have appeared confused both in intent and in the perceived effects of policy.

Evasiveness over policy objectives can frustrate evaluation, but equally it can give discretion in administration, and may genuinely reflect the difficulty in articulating the way in which policy operates, which may best be assessed *ex post* through evaluation. Earlier, we highlighted a distinction between *incentives* and *profitability supports*, and there clearly exists an important difference between those measures designed to strengthen firms through new investment, restructuring or even rationalization, possibly leading to long-term employment creation, and those measures seeking to support firms in crisis and in declining markets, and which are concerned with short-term employment retention. The success of the profitability supports depends on the subsidy being temporary rather than permanent, so that measures must be taken to improve the competitiveness of the subsidized firms. It is the failure of the government to distinguish clearly between these different objectives, and to restructure ailing companies effectively, that has done so much to undermine the case for industrial subsidies.

Sometimes the apparent confusion and failure of assistance has resulted from policy being overtaken by events, so that the attempt to restructure the shipbuilding industry was wrecked by high inflation, and in the face of rising unemployment the government was drawn into providing profitability supports. The prolonged decline of other traditional industries, such as iron and steel, textiles and cotton, has also thwarted restructuring attempts, with policies which initially sought to improve efficiency again becoming long-term profitability supports in which there was a failure to carry out the necessary restructuring, giving rise to the apparent confusion over policy. Where one-off attempts have been made to strengthen industries through the various sectoral schemes in the late 1970s then these were overwhelmed by the events of the early 1980s. More recently, restructuring has been forced on some industries through privatization and other means, but adjustment has been sharp in some cases.

This apparent confusion over objectives has also undermined general aid schemes, which were not sectorally specific in intention. However, what is remarkable about these general aid schemes is that throughout much of the period over which they were most intensively applied, little was in fact known about their effects, so their application was in some sense an act of faith. Moreover, it was only the dire economic conditions of the late 1970s which seemed to provide convincing evidence as to their lack of effectiveness. Some measures, such as the loans and grants under the Local Employment Acts, had very strong grant-per-job limits imposed on them, but with the general expansion of assistance in the mid-1960s and the devolution of responsibility away from the Treasury, the concern with effectiveness was largely forgotten. In the case of regional aid, this point was made by the House of Commons Expenditure Committee (HC 651, 1972) just prior to the expansion of this policy. In a much quoted passage, the Committee argued that 'far too little information is available to Government on the effectiveness of regional incentives. Large sums are being spent with inadequate knowledge of how far they are contributing towards the desired objectives or whether the money could be better spent on alternative means of reaching them' (para. 265).

Some elements of subsidy, such as tax measures and national investment grants, have still not been fully evaluated, but we can at least indicate some of the deficiencies of these general aid schemes by focusing on an area of policy that has perhaps been subject to the most scrutiny – that of regional policy assistance. In Table 9.2 we reproduce estimates for the cost and employment effect of this policy over its most intensive period of operation, 1966–76, disaggregated between capital-intensive and other industries. These figures were derived by Moore, Rhodes and Tyler (1986) by applying the shift-share standardization technique to aggregate regional level data, and formed the basis for the estimates of effectiveness given in the 1983 White Paper, *Regional Industrial Development*.

The figures in Table 9.2 indicate that regional policy operated with a considerable degree of inefficiency, in that a very much larger employment effect could have been obtained simply by directing assistance away from the capital-intensive industries. The problem was that while policy

Table 9.2 Costs and employment effect of regional policy

Industry	*Regional assistance (£)*	*Employment created*	*Expenditure per job (£)*
Capital-intensive	4 293m	6 000	715 500
Labour-intensive	5 735m	231 000	25 000
All industries	10 028m	237 000	42 500

Notes: Regional assistance expenditure is for the period 1966–76 at 1982 prices. The jobs shown are those estimated to have been created by policy over this period and existing at 1976. Capital-intensive industries comprise coal and petroleum, chemicals, metal manufacture and the mechanical engineering sectors. Labour-intensive industries comprise all other manufacturing sectors.
Source: Moore, Rhodes and Tyler (1986), table 6.2.

appeared to be creating jobs in many parts of the economy, in the larger capital-intensive industries it was in fact financing restructuring and massive job-shedding, so that again there was confusion over objectives, or at least about the way in which policy was operating. The problem was severe and perhaps should have been detected much earlier than it was, but it was to undermine a policy which was judged on its ability to create jobs. In the Northern region, for example, half of published regional assistance went to just three companies over the 1970s, of which two of these, ICI and British Steel, were mainly located on Teesside. ICI shed around 10 000 jobs on Teesside between 1975 and 1984, and British Steel lost three-quarters of its national workforce over a similar period.

Other work in this area, but at the firm level, indicates further sources of inefficiency. The figures in Table 9.3 show the average number of jobs created associated with each £1m of assistance under the respective schemes over time. This suggests that assistance to small firms is much more effective than that given to large firms, perhaps because it relaxes tighter capital market conditions in these firms, and that jobs can be lost to policy at very high rates over time, particularly in the case of large firms where, in fact, most regional assistance has gone. Further, Regional Selective Assistance appears to be more effective in these respects than the Regional Development Grant Scheme. Taking these studies together, these results suggest that where job creation is the primary objective of policy, then a larger employment effect can be obtained through greater

Table 9.3 Job effect of regional policy instruments

Scheme/firm	*First year*	*Second year*	*Third year*	*Fifth year*
RDG and RSA: large firms	17	47	101	4
RDG: small firms	44	127	147	82
RSA: small firms	119	682	1 189	279

Notes: The table gives the average net cumulative job effect at different times for each £1m of assistance received over 1975–81 for the different groups (1985 prices). Thus, on average, each £1m of RSA to small firms created 119 jobs after one year, 682 jobs after two years, and so on. RDG = Regional Development Grant; RSA = Regional Selective Assistance. The schemes shown in the table also include a small number of payments under some other schemes. Small firms are those establishments with less than 200 employees at 1975. Large firms have at least this number of employees at this time.
Source: Wren (1994), table 7.

selectivity: not only can assistance be directed away from those firms likely to give a poor employment effect, such as large capital-intensive establishments, but by negotiating the assistance it can be ensured that projects lead to job creation and not job destruction.

The approach taken by the European Commission in its interpretation of the Treaty of Rome Articles has strongly favoured incentives over profitability supports, as it has sought to render obsolete those measures considered incompatible with free trade. This has manifested itself in reviews of state aid programmes and the clawing-back of assistance, but also in policies to rationalize capacity, particularly in coal, steel and shipbuilding, rather than accommodating gradual adjustment. As such, its economic development policy resembles something of a palliative as it seeks alleviate adjustment in *areas* affected by closures, while its various collaborative programmes may only serve to foster further rationalization through merger. While this approach may be weakening, and the Commission seems more willing to support companies in difficulty, it is nevertheless reminiscent of UK policy in the inter-war years, and is mirrored by the current UK policy which is strongly focused on competitiveness and against industrial intervention. While the elimination of the large-scale automatic blanket subsidies and greater selectivity may be welcome, there does seem to be greater scope for intervention through selective measures, particularly to ease adjustment in *firms* accompanied by restructuring measures, rather than existing economic development measures targeted on areas affected by decline. While critics argue that the government cannot 'pick winners', it can at least show greater willingness to 'help losers'.

Appendix
The Assisted Areas

Figure A.1 The pre-war Special Areas

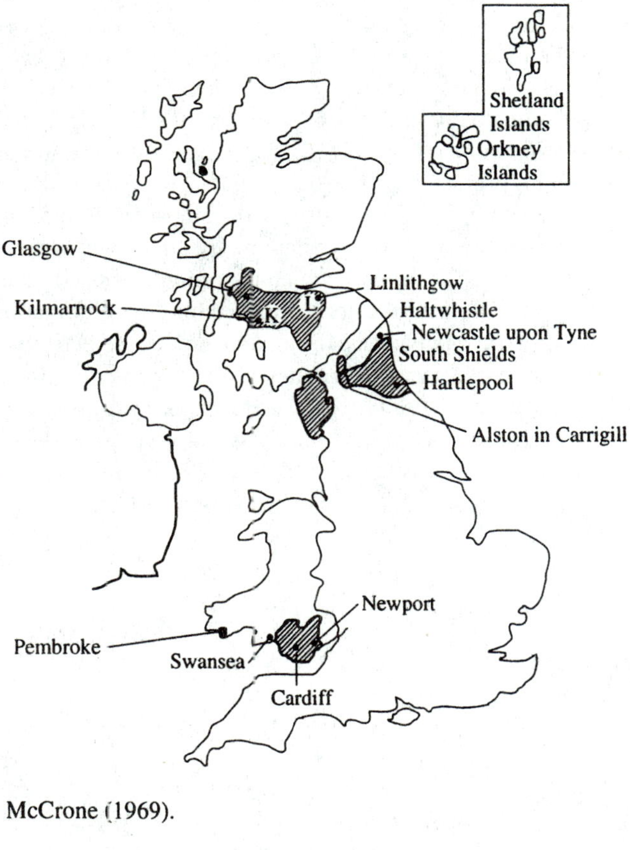

Source: McCrone (1969).

Figure A.2 Assisted Areas, 1966

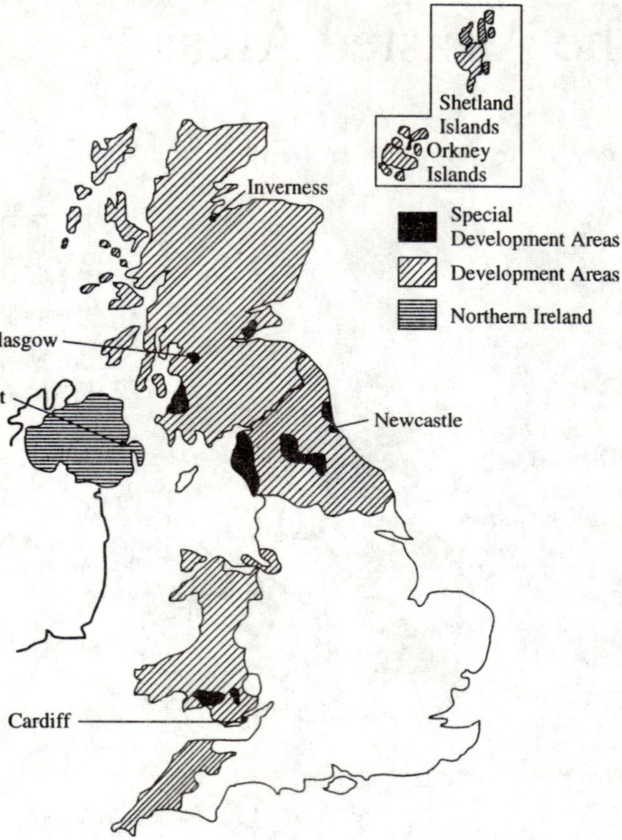

Source: McCrone (1969).

Figure A.3 Assisted Areas, August 1982

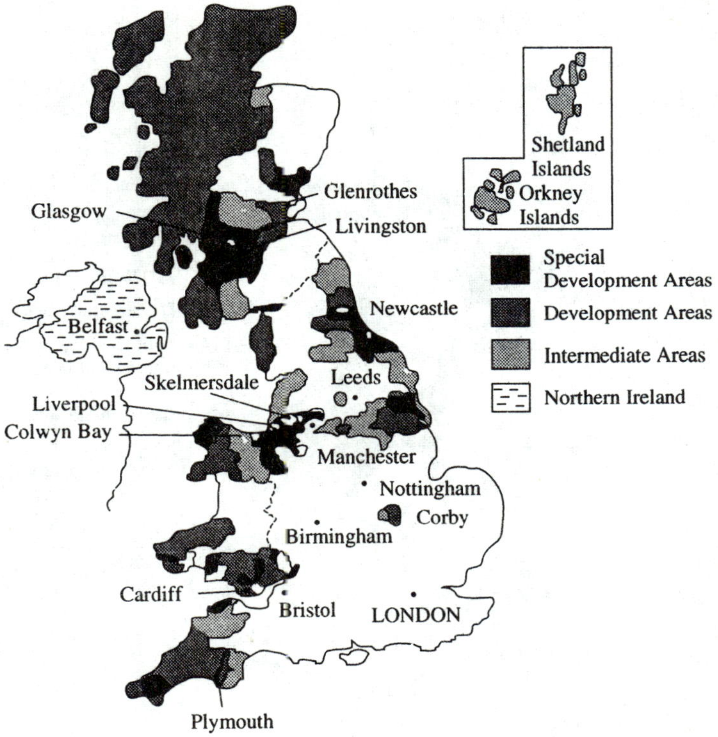

Source: *Annual Report on the 1972 Industry Act* (London: HMSO).

Figure A.4 Assisted Areas, August 1993

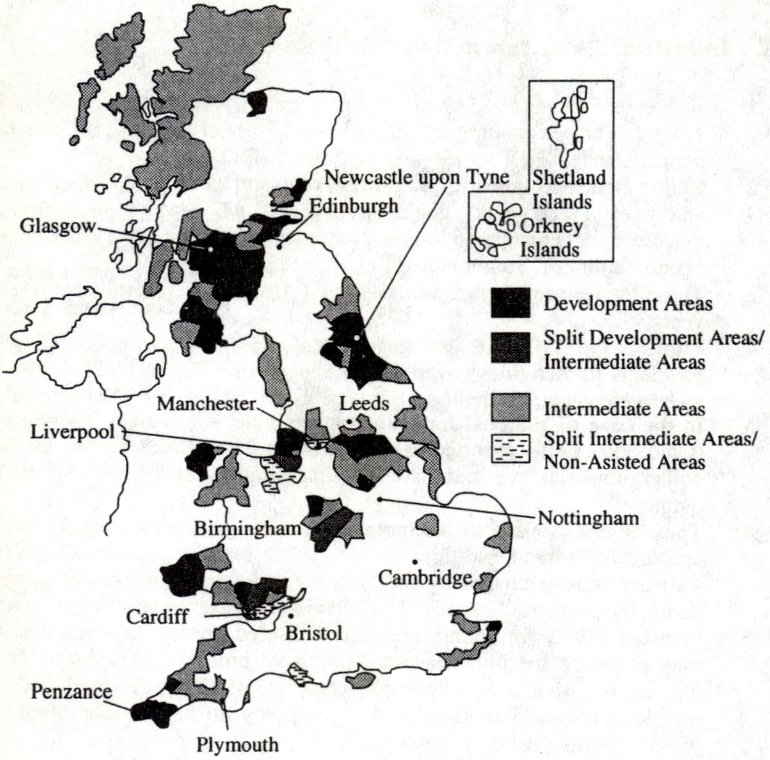

Source: Department of Trade and Industry, Victoria Street, London.
Note: In London, the Lea Valley, Park Royal and the London end of the East Thames Corridor were declared Intermediate Areas.

Notes

2 Industrial Assistance in Pre-War Britain

1. Between 1873 and 1913, the annual growth in UK real GDP is estimated at 1.8 per cent per annum, compared with 4.5 per cent in the USA and 2.8 per cent (in real NDP) in Germany (Floud, 1981, table 1.2).
2. Cotton alone accounted for 24 per cent of export earnings, followed by iron and steel (11 per cent), coal (10 per cent), woollens (6 per cent), and machinery, chemicals and ships combined accounted for 11 per cent of export earnings (Drummond, 1981).
3. These figures are taken from the *Annual Abstract of Statistics* for relevant years.
4. Prior to the 1909 Act the government did make some one-off grant payments for activities covered by the legislation (see HC 278, 1909), but these were generally small-scale and *ad hoc*.
5. In the case of the coal industry, for example, the Sankey Commission (Cmd 359, 1919) reported that there were 2500 mines owned by 1400 colliery undertakings, and that 700 of these mines produced 85 per cent of output.
6. These figures relate to unemployment among insured workers, which account for around two-thirds of the labour force over the period. These statistics were published by the Ministry of Labour, and provide a breakdown by industrial sector. Comparison of these figures with those in Feinstein (1972) for both insured and uninsured workers indicates that they may overstate the inter-war unemployment problem, particularly in the Depression, when a peak unemployment rate of 17 per cent obtained. The high level of unemployment in 1921 was partly attributable to a stoppage in the coal-mining industry in that year.
7. In the immediate post-war period, the government made a number of payments to industry to compensate for the cancellation of military contracts, and for government control of railways, canals and coastal transport, amounting to £49m.
8. Derating was first introduced in 1896, when agricultural land was relieved of half of the rates falling on it; this was extended to three-quarters in 1923. The rate of relief against industrial property rates under the 1929 Act was cut by half in 1958 and scrapped in the mid-1960s.
9. The idea of industrial rationalization had been introduced from Germany in 1924 and gained in popularity to the extent that monopolistic practices and trade restrictions were often actively encouraged by the government as a means of achieving greater international competitiveness (Pollard, 1992).
10. Quoted in Peden, 1984, p. 167.
11. In 1936, unemployment of insured workers was 29.4 per cent in Wales, 22.7 per cent in Northern Ireland, 18.7 per cent in Scotland, and 16.8 per cent in North East England.
12. New factory openings in Special Areas as a percentage of total Great Britain openings increased substantially from 2.2 per cent in 1936 to 17.1 per cent

in 1938. However, the level of openings in 1938 was quite small, at sixty-three, and a number of these were foreign firms which had escaped from the Continent (McCrone, 1969, p. 96).

13. Feinstein (1972, table 4.3) notes a payment of £63.7m to agriculture in 1920/1 in respect of produce sold at a loss.

3 The Legislative Basis for Industrial Intervention (1940–63)

1. In fact, the White Paper was put together hurriedly to pre-empt the publication in 1944 of William Beveridge's *Full Employment in a Free Society*, which promised to be far more forceful in its advocation of a full employment policy. Furthermore, the Treasury was sceptical about deficit financed spending as a temporary counter-cyclical measure, arguing for the traditional rules of public finance to prevent the government running permanent deficits (Booth, 1983).
2. Established in 1937, the Commission's terms of reference were essentially to examine the causes, direction and disadvantages arising from the concentration of industry and industrial development in large towns and particular areas. The majority report recommended that the government should establish a Board with powers to refuse consent for new development in London and the Home Counties, while a minority report recommended a new ministry to take over the functions of the Special Area Commissioners continuously to review the industrial and social environment, and for a three-tier designation of area covering Great Britain to control development (Odber, 1965). Neither report was accepted by the government, although the idea of restricting industrial development in some areas was later put into practice, and the minority report anticipated events in the early 1960s.
3. Controls and other measures meant that the government share of GNP doubled over the course of the war to stand at 38 per cent in 1946, and it remained at this much higher level thereafter, standing at 35 per cent in 1951 (Dow, 1960).
4. Prior to nationalization, electricity and gas supplies were already a mixture of municipal and private ownership, and civil aviation had been partly nationalized in 1939 with the creation of the British Overseas Airways Corporation (BOAC). Only the more important steel firms were taken into public ownership.
5. Wartime powers were retained under the 1946 Borrowing (Control and Guarantees) Act, which made Treasury sanction necessary for all new borrowings or share issues for sums over £50 000.
6. These measures had been recommended by a number of wartime reports, including the Barlow Report (Cmd 6153, 1940), the Control of Land Use (Cmd 9537, 1944) and the Committee on Land Utilisation in Rural Areas (Cmd 6378, 1942).
7. The number of government approvals for new factories and extensions of at least 5000 square feet were as follows: January 1945–June 1948: Development Areas, 1055; other areas, 1995. July 1948–June 1951: Development Areas, 1035; other areas, 5258 (Fogarty, 1952, table 5). By

value, the reduction in the Development Areas' share of approved expenditure was from 54 per cent over 1945–48 to 21 per cent over 1948–51.

8. Initial allowances were also allowed on mining works (at 10 per cent) and on the construction of ships (at 20 per cent), and in one form or another these were maintained up to 1966 when investment grants became available.
9. These figures are given in HC 142 (1962) and Cmnd 2738 (1965). This includes some indirect assistance to industry through the Board of Trade, and so does not perfectly match the figures given in Table 3.4.
10. Figures for 1920–38 are calculated from Feinstein (1972), table 17. Industrial output increased by 3.7 per cent per annum in 1948–60, compared with 3.1 per cent in the inter-war years and 1.6 per cent during 1877–1913 (Pollard, 1992).
11. The government continued to construct factory buildings in the Development Areas after 1947, but as an economy measure during the Suez crisis, building became limited in June 1956 to 'cases of special importance or emergency'. Informal means of dissuading expansion in Greater London and Birmingham also continued after 1951, but this seems to have been generally ineffective (Henderson, 1962, pp. 338–42).
12. Other sectors experiencing significant net job losses over this period were construction and miscellaneous services (45 000 jobs each), while net job losses in iron and steel, mechanical engineering and shipbuilding combined amounted to 37 000.
13. In one of its few regional policy interventions in the mid-1950s, the government declared North-East Lancashire a Development Area in 1953, but a further 80 000 jobs were lost in textiles in Lancashire between 1954–8.
14. The criticisms at the time were that it was unfair to single out a particular company for assistance, that the assistance was too generous, and that the days of the large ocean-going liner was over. The eventual successor, the *Queen Elizabeth II*, was launched in 1967 and at 58 000 tons was smaller than the 1959 proposal for a 75 000-ton vessel.
15. Payments were made under the 1960 Local Employment Act. Of £51m offered under this legislation by 31 March 1961, £36m was offered to the motor industry, of which £16m was in building grants and £20m in general purpose loans and grants (HC 291, 1961).
16. In the first three years of the Act, 90 applications for lodging allowances and 189 applications for household removal expenses were authorized (HC 300, 1963). As regards general grants, £5.2m was paid out in the first three years to between forty and fifty firms. Applications for these were on average scaled down by over two-thirds (Odber, 1965).
17. The gross cost per job in Scotland was £1440 compared with £600 in England, which was attributed to the more capital-intensive nature of firms establishing in Scotland, and because larger subsidies were necessary to encourage moves further north. In the case of the motor industry, expansion projects noted above the usual cost per job limits were waived, but again the details were not disclosed (HC 229, 1963).
18. The table shows related assistance, including assistance towards the cost of horticultural buildings and equipment, assistance to fisherman for the purchase of boats, engines and nets, and for fuel conversion, and that

administered by the Forestry Commission to private owners of woodland to encourage planting and improved management.

4 The Expansion of Industrial Assistance (1960s)

1. In giving evidence to Estimates Committee in March 1963, a senior Treasury civil servant said that a year earlier he believed spending under the 1960 Local Employment Act would soon disappear or at least decline (HC 229, 1963, questions 1536–37).
2. The effective rate of return on these factories was about 2.5 per cent, something like half the rate at which the government could borrow funds (Wilson, 1967).
3. As a share of the world total, British manufactured exports fell from 21.4 per cent over 1951–3, to 16.5 per cent over 1959–61, and were set to fall further to 10.9 per cent over 1969–71 (Pollard, 1992).
4. In its first report (HC 252, 1968), the Industrial Reorganization Corporation said that it lent 'on terms which differed from those normally acceptable to existing institutions', which in practice were at interest rates 1 per cent to 1.5 per cent above that paid by the IRC to the National Loans Fund. The IRC did make a commitment to assist in government regional policy as far as possible, but in practice most schemes did not make any mention of regional effects as a motive (Mottershead, 1978).
5. Unemployment was not the prime motivation for the designation of these Development Areas, since unemployment had fallen from 2.6 per cent in 1963 to 1.6 per cent in 1966 (Table 4.1), and across the Development Areas averaged 2.3 per cent in 1966 as against 3.0 per cent in the old Development Districts (McCrone, 1969).
6. The assumptions are those set out in Wren (1996b), and are similar to those adopted by Wilson (1967).
7. *Hansard*, 13 July 1978, written answers.
8. The 1967 Agriculture Act consolidated much of the previous legislation, and increased the loan guarantee funds of the Agricultural Mortgage Corporation and Scottish Agricultural Securities Corporation to £12m and £2m respectively.

5 The Retrenchment and Reinvigoration of Industrial Subsidies (1970–4)

1. *Hansard*, 4 November 1970.
2. Since November 1962, the annual reducing balance writing-down allowance on plant and machinery had been at rates of between 15 and 25 per cent depending on the expected life of the asset, but in October 1970 this was standardized at 25 per cent. The straight-line annual writing-down allowance on industrial buildings was fixed at 4 per cent in 1962.
3. Firms in the Assisted Areas could carry back trading losses attributable to free depreciation and set them against profits from the three preceding years.
4. At the October 1970 Conservative Party Conference, the Secretary of State for Trade and Industry said 'to abandon great sectors of our productive com-

munity at their moment of maximum weakness would be folly, but I will not bolster up or bale out companies where I can see no end to the process of propping them up'. However, some industries such as aircraft production were 'going through a period of world-wide disarray and need a helping hand' (quoted in Hogwood, 1979, pp. 145–6).

5. The right to carry back trading losses attributable to free depreciation and to set them against profits in the three preceding years was also extended to all firms.
6. Concern over the level of shipbuilding assistance led the OECD to set up a working party with the aim of progressively reducing direct and indirect subsidies to shipbuilding, and a resolution to this effect was passed in 1972. Mobile offshore installations were not covered by this understanding, but these could receive credit guarantees from the ECGD on the usual terms.
7. In fact, BOTAC had been renamed the Ministry of Technology Advisory Committee (MOTAC) in October 1969 when Mintech took over the responsibility for administering the Local Employment Acts, and renamed again as the Local Employment Act Financial Advisory Committee (LEAFAC) a year later, when responsibility was transferred to the Department of Trade and Industry.

6 The Heyday of Industrial Assistance (Late 1970s)

1. Consumer subsidies were paid on bread, butter, cheese, flour, milk and tea under section 1 of the 1974 Price Act, to help hold down prices. In February 1976, the subsidies were estimated to reduce the Retail Price Index by 1.3 points, but the butter subsidy alone came to £87.7m in 1975/6 (Cmnd 6393, 1976).
2. In fact, the August 1974 White Paper had been produced only after considerable debate within the government and had reputedly gone through twenty-five drafts (Parr, 1979). Further debate and controversy ensued, and it was not until November 1975 that the proposals were given effect, by which time a further set of proposals had been produced in the November 1975 White Paper *An Approach to Industrial Strategy* (Cmnd 6315, 1975).
3. Further areas were designated as Assisted Areas in August 1974, and the expenditure limits on RSA were raised by £100m in February 1975 and again in January 1976 to stand at £350m (see Bowers, 1991).
4. In opposition, the Labour Party envisaged that the NEB should have the powers to compulsory purchase and take over twenty to twenty-five of the largest manufacturing companies (Labour Party, 1973a).
5. The other transferred companies were Ferranti, Brown Boveri Kent and Dunford & Elliott (sold April 1978). Not all the government's shareholdings were transferred to NEB, and some later cases were dealt with under section 8 (Parr, 1979).
6. Meriden was one of several attempts to establish workers' co-operatives during the tenure of Tony Benn and Eric Heffer at the Department of Industry. Other cases of finance for workers' co-operatives were Scottish News Enterprises and Kirby Manufacturing and Engineering Ltd.
7. At this time, expenditure on the Machine Tool Industry Scheme amounted to £22.9m, and £13.9m on the Clothing Industry Scheme.

8. Gregg (1990) defines special employment measures as all direct interventions in the labour market with varied aims and means, but with the common theme of reducing the claimant count of unemployment.
9. In the case of the aircraft industry, British Aerospace was formed in April 1977, by bringing into public ownership the former British Aircraft Corporation, Hawker Siddeley and Scottish Aviation.
10. The IDC and ODP location controls had been relaxed in 1970 when the Conservatives took office, and were relaxed further in July 1972, by which time the IDC limit stood at 10 000 sq ft in the South East and 15 000 sq ft elsewhere. Shortly after a programme to disperse government offices from London, IDCs were tightened in September 1974 to 5000 sq ft in the South East, 10 000 sq ft for other non-Assisted Areas and 15 000 sq ft in Intermediate Areas, but then in the face of rising unemployment in the South East, IDCs were again relaxed in early 1975 to stand at 15 000 sq ft in IAs and 10 000 sq ft outside the Assisted Areas (McCallum, 1979).
11. Robson (1988) notes that the designated inner areas were defined on the basis of eight indicators of well-being: unemployment; overcrowded households; households lacking exclusive use of amenities; pensioners living alone; single-parent families; population in households with heads born in the New Commonwealth or Pakistan; population change; and mortality rates.
12. The London Docklands Partnership was dissolved in 1981, when the London Docklands Development Corporation was formed. This gave rise to a further Programme Authority and four Other Designated Districts, and the Hackney/Islington Partnership Authority was also separated into two. Further changes were made in February 1983, after which there existed seven Partnerships, twenty-three Programme Authorities and sixteen Other Designated Districts.
13. Calculated from Armstrong (1988), table 7.2 by applying population figures to per capita spending.
14. The relevant legislation in Scotland was the 1964 Local Government (Development and Finance) Act.
15. The relevant legislation in Scotland was section 83 of the 1973 Local Government (Scotland) Act. The 1972 Local Government Act stipulated that after reorganization, local legislation in force at the time should apply only in those areas to which it previously related. This led to a hotch-potch of powers in many new administrative areas (Rogers and Smith, 1977).
16. *Hansard*, 14 May 1982, written answers. In Northern Ireland similar arrangements existed under the 1977 Research and Development Grant Scheme, but the assistance was more generous in that the grant rate was 50 per cent on the first £50 000 of eligible expenditure in any twelve-month period and 40 per cent after that, up to an overall ceiling of £250 000 per project.

7 Change and Continuity in Industrial Assistance (Early 1980s)

1. The minimum value requirements for RDG were also increased from £100 to £500 for individual items of plant and machinery, and from £1000 to

£5000 for buildings. A further measure that cut back simultaneously on subsidy and increased the differential in favour of the Assisted Areas was that the Small Firm Employment Subsidy was limited to firms in the Development and Special Development Areas only.

2. *Hansard*, 3 February 1981, written answers.
3. As further evidence it was later revealed that at least £91.7m had been paid in Regional Development Grant towards the Sullom Voe oil terminal by the end of September 1983 (*Hansard*, 6 December 1983, written answers), and of course much of this would have gone ahead without regional aid.
4. The 1981 Industry Act raised the financial limits of the Scottish and Welsh Development Agencies by £200m each, to £700m and £450m respectively.
5. A full list of the NEB's holdings at this date is given in *Hansard*, 19 February 1980, written answers.
6. At 31 January 1980, the 50 per cent stake in Ferranti had an historic cost of £6.9m.
7. At this time Rolls-Royce aero-engines company was still in the public sector.
8. ICL was formed with assistance under the 1968 Industrial Expansion Act to help build up a significant British presence in the computer industry. Between Septembers 1972 and 1976 £40m was provided in government support, including share capital, to help develop the 2900 Series computer system. This assistance was to be recovered by taking the profits from the firm for years 1977/8 to 1983/4 above an annual 7.5 per cent return on the company's turnover, but less than 25 per cent. However, technical difficulties meant that by 1978 it had become apparent that no repayment would be made in either 1977/8 or 1978/9 (HC 623, 1978), and in the light of cost-cutting and agreements on collaborative ventures the government eventually extended the guarantees. An explanation of this was that the government itself was highly dependent on ICL, with computer equipment valued at some £300m spread across twenty government departments.
9. Also, the Community Industry (CI) scheme, which had commenced in 1972 to provide job opportunities for disadvantaged individuals, continued throughout this period.
10. In opposition, the Chancellor said the Enterprise Zones would act as 'test market areas or laboratories in which to enable fresh policies to prime the pump of prosperity, and to establish their potential for doing so elsewhere' (quoted in Talbot, 1983). There were seventeen Enterprise Zones in England, three each in Scotland and Wales and two in Northern Ireland. In both rounds the government announced more Zones than originally intended; in the first round because of the poor economic climate (it had originally anticipated setting up around half a dozen Zones) and in the second round because of the good response to invitations (HC 209, 1986).
11. The allocation to Partnership Authorities (excluding the London Docklands Partnership) increased from £82m in 1980/1 to £127m in 1985/6, and the allocation to Programme Authorities increased from £50m to £97m over the same period, together representing a real increase of 30 per cent in Urban Programme spending.
12. Scotland and Wales had separate schemes, administered by the respective Development Agencies.

13. Written response of the Industry Secretary on 18 February 1981, quoted in *British Business*, 27 February 1981.
14. The Flexible Manufacturing Scheme was open to firms in mechanical, instrument and electrical engineering, shipbuilding, marine engineering, vehicles and metal goods.
15. Quoted in *British Business*, 7 October 1983.
16. *Hansard*, 2 December 1981, written answers.
17. The 1982 Industrial Development Act consolidated the legislation under the 1972 Local Employment Act, Parts I and II of the 1972 Industry Act, the 1975 Industry Act and some parts of the 1980 and 1981 Industry Acts.
18. The merger of the NEB with the NRDC was prompted by the resignation of the NEB chairman in December 1980 to be replaced by the chairman of the NRDC. However, the merging of these two agencies would have occurred in any case and was promoted by the establishment of a £2m NRDC fund in September 1980 to invest in innovative new and small businesses. At the time of the merger, the NRDC was sponsoring 699 projects, of which 379 were concerned with the licensing of publicly-supported inventions and the remainder involved private firms. The NRDC was meant to be self-financing and in most years it made a surplus, so that in the year ended 31 March 1981 it received revenue of £21.9m and invested £12.5m.
19. The assistance to De Lorean comprised £17.8m in Northern Ireland Development Agency share capital, £18.7m in capital grants, £9.8m in employment grants, loans of £20.7m for buildings and working capital, and a loan guarantee of £10m.
20. *Hansard*, 12 July 1984, written answers. In early 1981, the government also announced that £3550m in loans to the British Steel Corporation were to be written off (Burton, 1983).
21. As well as physical measures, the WDA financed innovations where a demonstrable prototype existed, and in 1983 extended this to include loans of between £2000 and £20 000 for the development of such prototypes. Around this time it introduced loans for new enterprises with a variable interest rate related to turnover or profits.
22. This was acknowledged by the Secretary of State for Trade and Industry, who noted that 'expected ERDF contributions are taken into account by the government in determining the appropriate overall levels of the public expenditure programme concerned' (*Hansard*, 13 March 1984, written answers). The government could claim ERDF money in respect of RSA, but generally not RDG.
23. The New Community Instrument was made up of the proceeds from the borrowing operations by the Commission on the capital markets.
24. In 1982 alone this included £38.7m for the WEEP subscheme of the Youth Opportunities Programme (YOP).

8 The Recasting of Industrial Support (1983–Present)

1. Public expenditure as a proportion of GDP rose from 43.25 per cent in 1979/80 to 47.75 per cent in 1982/3 (Tomlinson, 1990, table 11.2).
2. *Hansard*, 13 March 1984.

3. The government believed that the extension of the map to cover more than 35 per cent of the working population would have led to difficulties with the European Commission (*Hansard*, 6 May 1986, written answers).
4. The Permanent Secretary to the DTI told the Public Accounts Committee in March 1988 that the DTI's monitoring of fraud was 'not as effective as it might be'. One solution considered was for accountants carrying out an audit to provide certified proof of jobs created, but this was opposed by the Accountancy Bodies (HC 346, 1988).
5. The Alvey Report estimated that the £300m trade deficit in information technology would grow to £1000m by 1990. The report argued that 'Government support and a high ratio of Government funding are seen as necessary conditions for this collaboration. In spite of the mounting awareness of the need to collaborate, there are basic issues of commercial interest, exploitation and industrial property rights which will inhibit firms from freely sharing with their competitors work which they have funded themselves' (Department of Industry, 1982, para 3.11).
6. After the first MISP scheme had closed (projects had to be completed by the 31 March 1985) the MISP 2 scheme was renamed 'Investment Support for Microelectronics'.
7. This included general research and development projects on standard Support for Innovation terms, development and investment projects under MISP 2 and the Fibre Optics and Opto-Electronics Scheme, and application, development and installation projects under the FMS including robotics. The Alvey Programme and non-Support for Innovation aid for civil aviation, aero-engine and space technology were exempted.
8. The quote is from *British Business*, 29 March 1985. In a memorandum to the House of Lords Select Committee on Science and Technology in November 1986, the Department of Trade and Industry anticipated that assistance for single firm projects would fall from 70 per cent of its support for science and technology to 36 per cent over 1984/5–1988/9, while spending on collaborative projects would increase from 10 to 23 per cent, and non-project-based spending, including advisory and awareness schemes, would increase from 20 to 41 per cent (HL 20, 1986).
9. This change was made in November 1984. An earlier change, in May 1984, increased the number of weekly places on the scheme from 600 to 1000. Applicants for the Enterprise Allowance Scheme had to be in receipt of either unemployment or supplementary benefit, but in Scotland similar assistance was extended to all persons by a scheme known as Effy (Enterprise Fund for Youth). This was established by the Scottish Development Agency and administered by local enterprise trusts, providing £3000 loans for 16–25-year-olds to start new small firms.
10. In Scotland and Northern Ireland the scheme was referred to under a number of separate headings, including Better Business Services, Better Technical Services, Innovation Support Services and Special Promotion Services. England received the lion's share of the allocation at £66m, with £16m going to Northern Ireland, £10.4m to Scotland and £8.7m to Wales (Moreton, 1984).
11. The Steel Closure Areas existing at 1983 comprised Garnock Valley (which contained the former Glengarnock steelworks) and Clyde Valley in

Scotland; Derwentside, Hartlepool, Scunthorpe and Corby in England; and Deeside (Shotton), Newport, Blaenau Gwent, Port Talbot and Cardiff in Wales. The Steel Closure Areas were later referred to as 'opportunity areas'.

12. Receipts from privatization came to £11.9bn by April 1987 and £33.7bn by April 1991 (Cm 1920, 1992). A chronology of privatizations is given in Sloman (1991).
13. *Hansard*, 8 April 1986, written answers.
14. *Hansard*, 14 November 1988, written answers.
15. The aim of the Inner City Task Forces was to 'stimulate enterprise and provide a stronger base for the local economy [and to] give special attention to the problems of young people from ethnic minorities where they are particularly disadvantaged' (*Hansard*, 6 February 1986, written answers). Later this was put more bluntly as 'providing more jobs for local people' by identifying and removing impediments to recruitment, by improving their employability through training and by encouraging enterprise through training, financial and managerial assistance (*Hansard*, 25 January 1988, written answers).
16. The government considered establishing a UDC in Birmingham in 1986, but this was opposed by the City Council. With private sector developers, the Council later established an urban development agency, known as Birmingham Heartlands Ltd, which covered 2000 acres of east Birmingham. This was declared an Urban Development Corporation in 1992.
17. Further private sector initiatives prompted by central government were the establishment of a CBI Inner Cities Task Force in Tyne and Wear and Birmingham in 1987, and British Urban Development in 1988 by eleven large property and construction concerns to identify development opportunities in urban areas.
18. In fact, the figure of £30 000 for each new permanent job created in the Enterprise Zones was far worse than it looked, since it is not directly comparable with the estimate of £35 000 obtained for each regional policy job over the 1970s (Cmnd 9111, 1983), which was calculated on a different basis.
19. Concern was raised because the Community Programme was considered to displace voluntary activity and the Enterprise Allowance Scheme was thought to have a high rate of job substitution, even though the Department of Employment estimated that up to half of supported businesses would have begun anyway.
20. The Employment Committee came to this conclusion even though it took evidence to the effect that some of these measures were a relatively expensive means of providing new jobs. The year two costs of cutting unemployment per person were put at: special employment measures, £2650; public services, £15 000; public investment, £26 000; income tax cuts, £47 000; and cuts in National Insurance contributions, £60 000 (Davies and Metcalf, 1985; HC 487ii, 1985).
21. The Support for Major Projects provided general selective investment support, and offers under this amounted to £69.5m in respect of 186 projects, including £9.5m to British Aerospace to purchase Rover shares as part of the £44m 'sweetener'.

22. These were the steel areas under the RESIDER scheme and shipbuilding areas covered by RENAVAL (see below). In the case of the Plymouth RENAVAL area, the government agreed to pay REG from January 1991.
23. Details are given in the written answers of *Hansard*, 1 and 17 February, and 26 March, 1984.
24. *Hansard*, 9 March 1990, written answers.
25. The increased resources were viewed as quid pro quo by some of the poorer countries for allowing the richer countries access to their markets from 1993 (HL 82, 1988).
26. The eligible areas in England comprised the whole of Tyne and Wear, County Durham, Cleveland, South Yorkshire, Greater Manchester, Merseyside and the West Midlands, and parts of Northumberland, Humberside, Nottinghamshire, Lancashire and West Yorkshire. In Scotland the areas comprised parts of Tayside, Lothian, and Dumfries and Galloway; and in Wales they comprised Mid-Glamorgan, West Glamorgan, and parts of Gwent and Clwyd (*Hansard*, 14 March 1989).
27. At the time of the reform the NPCIs were the Highlands and Islands, Newton Aycliffe/Bishop Auckland, West Lothian, Tayside, Mid Glamorgan, Dyfed/Gwynedd/Powys, Plymouth and the Cornwall Assisted Areas. The IDOPs were Strathclyde, Birmingham, South Yorkshire and Humberside, Bradford and Shildon.
28. To be considered for RECHAR funds an area had to show that 1000 jobs had been lost in a coal-mining undertaking since 1984.

Bibliography of Parliamentary Papers

Cd 4896 (1896) *Final Report from the Royal Commission on the Depression in Trade and Industry* (London: HMSO).

Cmd 359 (1919) *Report of the Royal Committee on the Coal Industry* (Sankey Committee) (London: HMSO).

Cmd 1811 (1923) *Report of the Committee on Government Financial Assistance to Civil Air (Cross-Channel) Transport Companies* (Hambling Committee) (London: HMSO).

Cmd 2600 (1925) *Report of the Royal Commission on the Coal Industry* (Samuel Commission) (London: HMSO).

Cmd 2581 (1926) *Agricultural Policy* (London: HMSO).

Cmd 3897 (1931) *Committee on Trade and Industry* (Macmillan Committee) (London: HMSO).

Cmd 4354 (1933) *Final Report of the Unemployment Grants Committee* (London: HMSO).

Cmd 4728 (1933) *Reports of Investigations into the Industrial Conditions in Certain Depressed Areas* (London: HMSO).

Cmd 6153 (1940) *Royal Commission on the Distribution of Industrial Population* (Barlow Report) (London: HMSO).

Cmd 6527 (1944) *Employment Policy* (London: HMSO).

Cmnd 827 (1959) *Report of the Committee of the Working of the Monetary System* (Radcliffe Report) (London: HMSO).

Cmnd 1965 (1963) *Estimates 1963/4: Memorandum by the Financial Secretary to the Treasury* (London: HMSO).

Cmnd 2738 (1965) *The Development of Agriculture* (London: HMSO).

Cmnd 2764 (1965) *National Plan*, Department of Economic Affairs (London: HMSO).

Cmnd 2853 (1965) *Report of the Committee of Inquiry into the Aircraft Industry* (Plowden Report) (London: HMSO).

Cmnd 2874 (1966) *Investment Incentives* (London: HMSO).

Cmnd 2937 (1966) *Shipbuilding Inquiry Committee* (Geddes Report) (London: HMSO).

Cmnd 3310 (1967) *The Development Areas: Regional Employment Premium* (London: HMSO).

Cmnd 3998 (1969) *The Intermediate Areas* (Hunt Committee), Department of Economic Affairs (London: HMSO).

Cmnd 4337 (1970) *Committee of Inquiry into Shipping* (Rochdale Report) (London: HMSO).

Cmnd 4516 (1970) *Industrial Incentives*, Department of Trade and Industry (London: HMSO).

Cmnd 4942 (1972) *Industrial and Regional Development*, Department of Trade and Industry (London: HMSO).

Cmnd 5710 (1974) *The Regeneration of British Industry*, Department of Industry (London: HMSO).
Cmnd 6315 (1975) *An Approach to Industrial Strategy*, Department of Industry (London: HMSO).
Cmnd 6393 (1976) *Public Expenditure to 1979–80* (London: HMSO).
Cmnd 6845 (1977) *Policy for the Inner Cities* (London: HMSO).
Cmnd 9111 (1983) *Regional Industrial Development*, Department of Trade and Industry (London: HMSO).
Cm 278 (1988) *DTI – The Department for Enterprise*, Department of Trade and Industry (London: HMSO).
Cm 1920 (1992) *Public Expenditure Analysis to 1994–95* (London: HMSO).
Cm 2207 (1993) *Department of the Environment: Annual Report 1993* (London: HMSO).
Cm 2250 (1993) *Realising our Potential: A Strategy for Science, Engineering and Technology* (London: HMSO)

HC 278 (1909) *Memorandum on Existing Powers as to Making Grants for Various Purposes*, Session 1909 (London: HMSO).
HC 139 (1955) *Development Areas*, Select Committee on Estimates, Second Report, Session 1955/6 (London: HMSO).
HC 291 (1961) *First Annual Report on the 1960 Local Employment Act*, Board of Trade, Session 1961/2 (London: HMSO).
HC 142 (1962) *Civil Estimates and Estimates for Revenue Departments*, Memorandum by the Financial Secretary to the Treasury, Session 1961/2 (London: HMSO).
HC 191 (1962) *Assistance to the Cotton Industry*, Estimates Committee, Fourth Report, Session 1961/2 (London: HMSO).
HC 229 (1963) *Administration of the Local Employment Act, 1960*, Estimates Committee, Seventh Report, Session 1962/3 (London: HMSO).
HC 300 (1963) *Third Annual Report on the 1960 Local Employment Act*, Board of Trade, Session 1963/4 (London: HMSO).
HC 252 (1968) *First Report and Accounts*, Industrial Reorganisation Corporation, Session 1967/8 (London: HMSO).
HC 329 (1969) *Annual Report on the 1966 Industrial Development Act*, Board of Trade, Session 1968/9 (London: HMSO).
HC 297 (1970) *Third Report*, Committee of Public Accounts, Session 1969/70 (London: HMSO).
HC 651 (1972) *Public Money in the Private Sector*, Expenditure Committee, Trade and Industry Sub-Committee, Sixth Report, Session 1971/2 (London: HMSO).
HC 1365 (1972) *Annual Report and Accounts*, Shipbuilding Industry Board, Session 1971/2 (London: HMSO).
HC 1 (1973) *Regional Development Incentives: Minutes of Evidence*, Expenditure Committee, Session 1972/3 (London: HMSO).
HC 85 (1973) *Regional Development Incentives*, Expenditure Committee, Second Report, Session 1973/4 (London: HMSO).
HC 342 (1975) *British Leyland: The Next Decade*, Report by Sir Don Ryder's Inquiry Team, Session 1974/5 (London: HMSO).
HC 536 (1977) *Committee of Public Accounts Tenth Report*, Session 1976/7 (London: HMSO).

HC 623 (1978) *Committee of Public Accounts Tenth Report*, Session 1977/8 (London: HMSO).

HC 185 (1979) *Accounts of the Development Fund*, Session 1978/9 (London: HMSO).

HC 500 (1982) *Government Support for Trade and Industry in Northern Ireland*, Industry and Trade Committee, Seventh Report, Session 1981/2 (London: HMSO).

HC 378 (1984) *Regional Industrial Incentives*, Committee of Public Accounts, Twenty-first Report, Session 1983/4 (London: HMSO).

HC 487i (1985) *Special Employment Measures: Memorandum Submitted by the Department of Employment and Manpower Services Commission*, Employment Committee, Session 1984/5 (London: HMSO).

HC 487ii (1985) *Special Employment Measures: Minutes of Evidence*, Employment Committee, Session 1984/5 (London: HMSO).

HC 513 (1985) *Department of the Environment: Urban Programme*, National Audit Office, Report of the Comptroller and Auditor General, Session 1984/5 (London: HMSO).

HC 81 (1986) *Department of the Environment: Urban Programme*, Committee of Public Accounts, Tenth Report, Session 1985/6 (London: HMSO).

HC 199 (1986) *Special Employment Measures and the Long-term Unemployed*, Employment Committee, First Report, Session 1985/6 (London: HMSO).

HC 209 (1986) *Department of the Environment, Scottish Office and Welsh Office: Enterprise Zones,* National Audit Office, Report of the Comptroller and Auditor General, Session 1985/6 (London: HMSO).

HC 223 (1986) *Financial Assistance to the Lear Fan Aircraft Project*, Committee of Public Accounts, Thirty-first Report, Session 1985/6 (London: HMSO).

HC 327 (1988) *The Employment Effects of Urban Development Corporations*, Employment Committee, Third Report, Session 1987/8 (London: HMSO).

HC 346 (1988) *Department of Trade and Industry, Scottish Office and Welsh Office: Arrangements for Regional Industrial Incentives*, National Audit Office, Report by the Comptroller and Auditor General, Session 1987/8 (London: HMSO).

HC 27 (1989) *Derelict Land Grant*, Committee of Public Accounts, Seventeenth Report, Session 1988/9 (London: HMSO).

HC 169 (1990) *Regenerating the Inner Cities*, National Audit Office, Report of the Comptroller and Auditor General, Session 1989/90 (London: HMSO).

HC 356 (1995) *Regional Policy*, Trade and Industry Committee, Fourth Report, Session 1994/5 (London: HMSO).

HL 20 (1986) *Civil Research and Development*, Memorandum Submitted by the Department of Trade and Industry, Select Committee on Science and Technology, First Report, Session 1986/7 (London: HMSO).

HL 82 (1988) *Reform of the Structural Funds*, Select Committee on the European Communities, Fourteenth Report, Session 1987/8 (London: HMSO).

HL 20 (1991) *EEC Regional Development Policy*, Select Committee on the European Communities, Fourth Report, Session 1991/2 (London: HMSO).

General Bibliography

ACARD (1979) *Technological Change: Threats and Opportunities for the UK*, Advisory Council for Applied Research and Development (London: HMSO).

ACARD (1980) *Computer Aided Design and Manufacture*, Advisory Council for Applied Research and Development (London: HMSO).

Allsopp, C. (1991) 'Macroeconomic Policy: Design and Performance', in M. Artis and D. Cobham (eds), *Labour's Economic Policies* (Manchester University Press).

Armstrong, H. (1988) 'A Comparison of Industrial Development Initiatives of Metropolitan and Non-Metropolitan District Councils in England and Wales', Discussion Paper, Department of Economics, University of Lancaster, March.

Armstrong, H. (1989) 'Community Regional Policy', in J. Lodge (ed.), *The European Community and the Challenge of the Future* (London: Pinter).

Armstrong, H. and J. Taylor (1993) *Regional Economics and Policy* (Oxford: Philip Allan).

Bailey, R. (1968) *Managing the British Economy: A Guide to Economic Planning in Britain since 1962* (London: Hutchinson).

Begg, H. M., C. M. Lythe, R. Sorley and D. R. MacDonald (1975) 'Annual Expenditure on Special Regional Assistance to Industry, 1960/1–1972/3: A Note', *Economic Journal*, vol. 85, pp. 884–7.

Beveridge, W. (1944) *Full Employment in a Free Society* (London: George Allen & Unwin).

Bird, P. A. and A. P. Thirlwall (1967) 'The Incentive to Invest in the New Development Areas', *District Bank Review*, June.

Black, W., N. Cuthbert and J. B. Simpson (1967) 'Investment Incentives and the 1965 Finance Act', *Scottish Journal of Political Economy*, vol. 14, no. 1, pp. 12–29.

Blackaby, F. T. (1978) 'Narrative, 1960–74', in F. T. Blackaby (ed.), *British Economic Policy 1960–74*, National Institute of Economic and Social Research (Cambridge University Press).

Booth, A. (1983) 'The "Keynesian Revolution" in Economic Policy-Making', *Economic History Review*, vol. 36, pp. 103–23.

Booz-Allen (1973) *British Shipbuilding, 1972*, Booz-Allen and Hamilton International BV (London: HMSO).

Bowen, A. (1991) 'Labour Market Policies' in M. Artis and D. Cobham (eds), *Labour's Economic Policies* (Manchester University Press).

Bowers, J. (1991) 'Regional Policy', in M. Artis and D. Cobham (eds), *Labour's Economic Policies* (Manchester University Press).

Brittan, L. (1989) 'A Bonfire of Subsidies? A Review of State Aids in the European Community', Seminar on Competition Policy, London, 10 March 1989.

Britton, D. K. (1952) 'Agriculture', in G. D. N. Worswick and P. H. Ady (eds), *The British Economy, 1945–1950* (Oxford: Clarendon Press).

Broadway, F. (1976) *Upper Clyde Shipbuilders: A Study of Government Intervention in Industry* (London: Centre for Policy Studies).

Bruce, N. (1990) 'Measuring Industrial Subsidies: Some Conceptual Issues', *OECD Working Paper no. 75*, Economics and Statistics Department (Paris: OECD).

Bruce-Gardyne, J. (1978) *Meriden, Odyssey of a Lame Duck: A Study of Government Intervention in the Motor Cycle Industry* (London: Centre for Policy Studies).

Buck, N., I. Gordon and K. Young (1986) *The London Employment Problem* (London: Clarendon Press).

Burton, J. (1979) *The Job Support Machine: A Critique of the Subsidy Morass* (London: Centre for Policy Studies).

Burton, J. (1983) *Picking Losers ...? The Political Economy of Industrial Policy*, Hobart Paper 99 (London: Institute of Economic Affairs).

Buswell, R. J. (1983) 'Urban and Regional Policy: Assistance from Central Government to the Northern Region' in R. J. Buswell (ed.), *The North in the Eighties: Regional Policies for a Decade of Development* (Newcastle: Regional Studies Association, Northern Branch).

Cairncross, A. (1981) 'The Post-war Years, 1945–77', in R. C. Floud and D. N. McCloskey (eds), *The Economic History of Britain since 1700* (Cambridge University Press).

Cameron, G. C. (1979) 'The National Industrial Strategy and Regional Policy', in D. Maclennan and J. B. Parr (eds), *Regional Policy: Past Experience and New Directions*, Glasgow Social and Economic Research Studies 6 (Oxford: Martin Robertson).

CEC (Commission of the European Communities) (1971) 'Régimes Généraux d'Aides à Finalité Régionale', *Journal Officiel des Communautés Europeenes*, vol. 14 (Brussels: CEC) pp. 1–13. An English translation can be found in HC 327 (1973) p. 138–57.

CEC (Commission of the European Communities) (1975) *General Regional Aid Systems*, COM(75), 77 (Brussels: CEC).

CEC (Commission of the European Communities) (1976) *Fifth Report on Competition* (Brussels: CEC)

CEC (Commission of the European Communities) (1977) *Guidelines for Community Regional Policy*, COM(77), 195 (Brussels: CEC).

CEC (Commission of the European Communities) (1989) *Guide to the Reform of the Community's Structural Funds* (Brussels: CEC).

CEC (Commission of the European Communities) (1990a) *Industrial Policy in an Open and Competitive Environment: Guidelines for a Community Approach*, COM(90), 556 (Brussels: CEC).

CEC (Commission of the European Communities) (1990b) *Second Survey on State Aids in the European Community* (Luxembourg: Office for Official Publications of the European Community).

CEC (Commission of the European Communities) (1991a) *Annual Report on the Implementation of the Reform of the Structural Funds 1989* (Brussels: CEC).

CEC (Commission of the European Communities) (1991b) *The ERDF in 1991*, Directorate-General for Regional Policy (Brussels: CEC).

Chandler, J. and P. Lawless (1985) *Local Authorities and the Creation of Employment* (Aldershot: Gower).

Chapman, J. H. (1978) 'Department of Industry's Accelerated Projects Scheme and Selective Investment Scheme', *National Westminster Bank Quarterly Review*, May, pp. 27–37.

CIPFA (1985) *Employment and Industrial Development: Local Authority Initiatives*, The Chartered Institute of Public Finance and Accountancy (Luton: Inprint).

Curzon Price, V. (1990) 'Competition and Industrial Policies with Emphasis on Industrial Policy', in A. M. El-Agraa (ed.), *Economics of the European Community* (Hemel Hempstead: Philip Allan).

Davies, G. and D. Metcalf (1985) 'Generating Jobs: The Cost-Effectiveness of Tax Cuts, Public Expenditure and Special Employment Measures in Cutting Unemployment', *The Economic Analyst* (London: Simon and Coates).

Davies, W. and E. Butler (1986) *The Freeport Experiment* (London: Adam Smith Institute).

Deakin, B. and C. Pratten (1981) *Effects of the Temporary Employment Subsidy*, Department of Applied Economics, University of Cambridge, Occasional Paper 53 (Cambridge University Press).

Deloitte, Haskins and Sells (1984) *Local Enterprise Agencies* (London: Greenaway Harrison Ltd).

Denton, G. (1976) 'Financial Assistance to British Industry', in W. M. Corden and G. Fels (eds), *Public Assistance to Industry* (Boulder, Colo.: Westview Press).

Department of Economic Affairs (1967) *The Development Areas: A Proposal for a Regional Employment Premium*, Memorandum by the DEA and Treasury, 5 April 1967.

Department of Employment (1978) 'Small Firms Employment Subsidy: An Evaluation of its Effectiveness', *Department of Employment Gazette*, May, pp. 549–54.

Department of Employment (1979) 'The Development of Special Employment Measures', *Department of Employment Gazette*, November, pp. 1122–5.

Department of the Environment (1980) *Review of Local Authority Assistance to Industry and Commerce*, Report of the Joint Group of Officials of Local Authority Associations and Government Departments (Burns Report) (London: DoE).

Department of the Environment (1981) *Enterprise Zones*, April (London: DoE).

Department of the Environment (1983) *Urban Development Grant: Guidance Notes* (London: DoE).

Department of the Environment (1987a) *An Evaluation of the Enterprise Zone Experiment*, Inner Cities Research Programme (London: HMSO).

Department of the Environment (1987b) *The Derelict Land Programme, 1986/7* (London: DoE).

Department of the Environment (1990) *Enterprise Zone Information, 1987–1988* (London: DoE).

Department of the Environment (1995) *Second Interim Evaluation of Enterprise Zones* (London: HMSO).

Department of Industry (1980) 'European Investment Bank: Saving on Borrowing', *British Business*, 7 November 1980 (London: DoI).

Department of Industry (1981) 'Regions: Government Handouts not the Whole Answer – Sir Keith Joseph', *British Business*, 15 May 1981 (London: DoI).

Department of Industry (1982) *A Programme for Advanced Information Technology: The Report of the Alvey Committee* (London: HMSO).

Department of Trade and Industry (1986a) *Industry's Early Reaction to the New Regional Development Grant* (London: HMSO).

Department of Trade and Industry (1986b) 'ERDF: How it Works', *British Business*, 28 February 1986 (London: DTI).

Department of Trade and Industry (1991) *Evaluation of the Alvey Programme for Advanced Information Technology* (London: HMSO).

Dow, J. C. R. (1960) 'Fiscal Policy and Monetary Policy as Instruments of Economic Control', *Westminster Bank Review*, August.

Dow, J. C. R. (1970) *The Management of the British Economy, 1945–60* (Cambridge University Press).

Drummond, I. (1981) 'Britain and the World Economy, 1900–45', in R. C. Floud and D. N. McCloskey (eds), *The Economic History of Britain since 1700* (Cambridge University Press).

Economist, The (1991) 'Regional Policy: Uncollected Cash', *The Economist*, 27 April 1991.

Feinstein, C. H. (1972) *National Income, Expenditure and Output of the United Kingdom, 1855–1965* (Cambridge University Press).

Field, G. M. and P. V. Hills (1976) 'The Administration of Industrial Subsidies', in A. Whiting (ed.), *The Economics of Industrial Subsidies* (London: HMSO).

Fleming, M. C. (1980) 'Industrial Policy', in P. Maunder (ed.), *The British Economy in the 1970s* (London: Heinemann).

Floud, R. C. (1981) 'Britain 1860–1914: A Survey', in R. C. Floud and D. N. McCloskey (eds), *The Economic History of Britain since 1700* (Cambridge University Press).

Fogarty, M. P. (1952) 'The Location of Industry', in G. D. N. Worswick and P. H. Ady (eds), *The British Economy, 1945–1950* (Oxford: Clarendon Press).

Fothergill, S. and G. Gudgin (1982) *Unequal Growth: Urban and Regional Employment Change in the UK* (London: Heinemann).

Gardner, N. K. A. (1976) 'Economics of Launching Aid', in A. Whiting (ed.), *The Economics of Industrial Subsidies* (London: HMSO).

Gibbs, R. and S. Aldridge (1985) 'Economic Assessment of the Electronic Components Industry Scheme', *Government Economic Service Working Paper no. 82* (London: Department of Trade and Industry).

Grant, R. M. (1982) 'Government Cannot Pick Winners', *Journal of Economic Affairs*, vol. 3, pp. 29–32.

Grant, W. (1982) *The Political Economy of Industrial Policy* (London: Butterworth).

Grant, W. and S. Wilks (1983) 'Continuity and Change in Industrial Support', *Public Money*, vol. 3, no. 3, pp. 63–7.

Gregg, P. (1990) 'The Evolution of Special Employment Measures', *National Institute Economic Review*, May, pp. 49–58.

Grove, J. W. (1962) *Government and Industry in Britain* (London: Longman).

Harris, R. I. D. (1991) *Regional Economic Policy in Northern Ireland, 1945–1988* (Aldershot: Avebury).

Hartley, K. (1965) 'The Mergers in the UK Aircraft Industry, 1957–60', *Journal of the Royal Aeronautical Industry*, vol. 69, pp. 846–52.

Hartley, K. (1974) *A Market for Aircraft*, Hobart Paper 57 (London: Institute of Economic Affairs).

Haughton, G. and P. Roberts (1990) 'Government Urban Economic Policy, 1979–89: Problems and Potential', in M. Campbell (ed.), *Local Economic Policy* (London: Cassell).

Hayward, K. (1989) *The British Aircraft Industry* (Manchester University Press).

Henderson, P. D. (1962) 'Government and Industry', in G. D. N. Worswick and P. H. Ady (eds), *The British Economy in the Nineteen-Fifties* (Oxford: Clarendon Press).

Herron, F. (1986) 'The Textile Machinery Industry Scheme', *Government Economic Service Working Paper no. 84* (London: Department of Trade and Industry).

Hicks, U. K. (1938) *The Finance of British Government, 1920–36* (Oxford University Press).

Hindley, B. and R. Richardson (1983) 'United Kingdom: Pulling the Dragon's Teeth – the National Enterprise Board' in B. Hindley (ed.), *State Investment Companies in Western Europe* (London: Macmillan).

Hogwood, B. W. (1979) *Government and Shipbuilding: The Politics of Industrial Change* (Farnborough: Saxon House).

Howson, S. (1981) 'Slump and Unemployment', in R. C. Floud and D. N. McCloskey (eds), *The Economic History of Britain since 1700* (Cambridge University Press).

Howson, S. and D. Winch (1977) *The Economic Advisory Council, 1930–39* (Cambridge University Press).

Hutton, J. P. and K. Hartley (1966) 'The Selective Employment Tax and the Labour Market', *British Journal of Industrial Relations*, vol. 6, pp. 289–303.

Jackman, R. (1987) *A Job Guarantee for the Long-Term Unemployed* (London: Employment Institute).

JURUE (1981) *A Review of Local Economic Initiatives in the United Kingdom*, Joint Unit for Research on the Urban Environment (Birmingham: University of Aston).

Kaldor, N. (1970) 'The Case for Regional Policies', *Scottish Journal of Political Economy*, November.

Kay, J. A. and M. A. King (1986) *The British Tax System* (Oxford University Press).

Keating, M. and F. Boyle (1986) *Remaking Urban Scotland: Strategies for Local Economic Development* (Edinburgh University Press).

King, J. (1990) *Regional Selective Assistance 1980–84*, Department of Trade and Industry (London: HMSO).

Kirby, M. and M. Rose (1991) 'Productivity and Competitive Failure: British Government Policy and Industry, 1914–19' in G. Jones and M. Kirby (eds), *Competitiveness and the State: Government and Business in Twentieth-Century Britain* (Manchester University Press).

Labour Party (1973a) *National Enterprise Board: Labour's State Holding Company* (London: Labour Party).

Labour Party (1973b) *Labour's Programme 1973* (London: Labour Party).

Lambert, J. T. (1983) 'Clothing Industry Scheme', *Government Economic Service Working Paper no. 61* (London: Department of Trade and Industry).

Lambert, J. T. (1985) 'Ferrous Foundry Industry Scheme', *Government Economic Service Working Paper no. 77* (London: Department of Trade and Industry).

Lawless, P. (1981) *Britain's Inner Cities: Problems and Policies* (London: Harper & Row).

Lawless, P. (1988) 'British Inner Urban Policy: A Review', *Regional Studies*, vol. 22, no. 6, pp. 531–41.

Lehner, S., R. Meiklejohn and H. Reichenbach (1991) 'Fair Competition in the Internal Market: Community State Aid Policy', *European Economy*, Commission of the European Communities, Brussels, September.

Lindley, R. (1986) 'Labour Demand: Microeconomic Aspects of State Intervention', in P. E. Hart (ed.), *Unemployment and Labour Market Policies* (Aldershot: Gower).

Maclennan, M. C. (1979) 'Regional Policy in a European Framework', in D. Maclennan and J. B. Parr (eds), *Regional Policy: Past Experience and New Directions*, Glasgow Social and Economic Research Studies 6 (Oxford: Martin Robertson).

Martin, S. (1990) 'City Grants, Urban Development Grants and Urban Regeneration Grants', in M. Campbell (ed.), *Local Economic Policy* (London: Cassell).

Maunder, P. (1979) 'Government Intervention in the Economy of the United Kingdom', in P. Maunder (ed.), *Government Intervention in the Developed Economy* (London: Croom Helm).

McCallum, D. (1979) 'The Development of British Regional Policy', in D. Maclennan and J. B. Parr (eds), *Regional Policy: Past Experience and New Directions*, Glasgow Social and Economic Research Studies 6 (Oxford: Martin Robertson).

McCrone, G. (1962) *The Economics of Subsidising Agriculture: A Study of British Policy* (London: George Allen & Unwin).

McCrone, G. (1969) *Regional Policy in Britain* (London: George Allen & Unwin).

Mellors, C. and N. Copperthwaite (1990) *Regional Policy*, Spicers European Policy Reports (London: Routledge).

Metcalf, D. (1982) *Alternatives to Unemployment: Special Employment Measures in Britain*, Report No. 610 (London: Policy Studies Institute).

Mitchell, B. R. and P. Deane (1962) *Abstracts of British Historical Statistics* (Cambridge University Press).

Moore, B, J. Rhodes and P. Tyler (1977) 'The Impact of Regional Policy in the 1970s', *Centre for Environmental Studies Review*, July.

Moore, B, J. Rhodes and P. Tyler (1986) *The Effect of Government Regional Economic Policy* (London: HMSO).

Moreton, A. (1984) 'Small Companies to Benefit from £100m Regional Aid Package', *Financial Times*, 27 November 1984.

Moreton, A. (1986) 'The Faltering of the Freeports', *Financial Times*, 19 August 1986.

Morgan, A. D. (1978) 'Commercial Policy', in F. T. Blackaby (ed.), *British Economic Policy, 1960–74*, National Institute of Economic and Social Research (Cambridge University Press).

Morgan, E. V. (1952) *Studies in British Financial Policy, 1914–25* (London: Macmillan).

Morris, D. J. and D. K. Stout (1985) 'Industrial Policy', in D. Morris (ed.), *The Economic System in the UK* (Oxford University Press).

Mottershead, P. (1978) 'Industrial Policy', in F. T. Blackaby (ed.), *British Economic Policy, 1960–74*, National Institute of Economic and Social Research (Cambridge University Press).

National Economic Research Associates (1990) *An Evaluation of the Loan Guarantee Scheme*, Research Paper no. 74 (London: Department of Employment).

Nevin, E. T. (1990) 'Regional Policy', in A. M. El-Agraa (ed.), *Economics of the European Community* (Hemel Hempstead: Philip Allan).

Odber, A. J. (1965) 'Regional Policy in Great Britain', in *Area Redevelopment Policies in Britain and the Countries of the Common Market* (Washington, DC: US Department of Commerce).

Opie, R. (1972) 'Economic Planning and Growth', in W. Beckerman (ed.), *The Labour Government's Economic Record, 1964–70* (London: Duckworth).

Owen, G. (1988) *British Coal Enterprise: A First Assessment*, Coalfield Communities Campaign Special Report no. 3 (Barnsley: Coalfield Communities Campaign).

Parkinson, M. and R. Evans (1990) 'Urban Development Corporations', in M. Campbell (ed.), *Local Economic Policy* (London: Cassell).

Parr, M. (1979) 'The National Enterprise Board', *National Westminster Bank Quarterly Review*, February, pp. 51–62.

Parsons, W. (1988) *The Political Economy of British Regional Policy* (London: Routledge).

Peacock, A. (1977) 'Giving Economic Advice in Difficult Times', *Three Banks Review*, vol. 113, pp. 3–23.

Peacock, A. (1990) 'Identifying and Applying Norms for Subsidies to Industry', in R. Gerritse (ed.), *Producer Subsidies* (London: Pinter).

Peacock, A. and J. Wiseman (1967). *The Growth of Public Expenditure in the United Kingdom* (London: George Allen & Unwin).

Peden, G. C. (1984) 'The "Treasury View" on Public Works and Employment in the Interwar Period', *The Economic History Review*, vol. 37, no. 2, pp. 167–81.

Peden, G. C. (1985) *British Economic and Social Policy: Lloyd George to Margaret Thatcher* (Oxford: Philip Allan).

Pettigrew, P. and S. Dann (1986) 'Streamlining Regional Industrial Aid?', Policy Review Section, *Regional Studies*, pp. 182–4.

Pitfield, D. (1978) 'The Quest for an Effective Regional Policy, 1934–37', *Regional Studies*, pp. 429–43.

Policy Studies Institute (1985) *Promoting Innovation: Microelectronics Applications Projects* (London: Policy Studies Institute).

Pollard, S. (1992) *The Development of the British Economy, 1914–1980* (London: Edward Arnold).

Pollard, S. and D. W. Crossley (1968) *The Wealth of Britain, 1085–1966* (London: Batsford).

Potter, D. (1985) 'The Non-Ferrous Foundry Industry Scheme', *Government Economic Service Working Paper no. 78* (London: Department of Trade and Industry).

Potter, D. and G. Davies (1983) 'The Textile Machinery Industry Scheme', *Government Economic Service Working Paper no. 60* (London: Department of Trade and Industry).

Prest, A. R. (1976) 'The Economic Rationale of Subsidies to Industry' in A. Whiting (ed.), *The Economics of Industrial Subsidies* (London: HMSO).

Price, R. W. R. (1978) 'Budgetary Policy', in F. T. Blackaby (ed.), *British Economic Policy, 1960–74*, National Institute of Economic and Social Research (Cambridge University Press).

Rajan, A. (1985) *Job Subsidies: Do They Work?* (Brighton, Sussex: Institute of Manpower Studies).

Reddaway, W. B., D. R. Glynn, J. D. Sugden, P. M. Croxford, C. H. Fletcher and J. S. O'Donnell (1973) *Effects of the Selective Employment Tax: Final Report*, Department of Applied Economics, University of Cambridge, Occasional Paper 32 (Cambridge University Press).

Redmond, J. (1980) 'An Indicator of the Effective Exchange Rate of the Pound in the Nineteen-Thirties', *Economic History Review*, vol. 33, pp. 83–91.

Ricketts, M. (1985) 'The Subsidy as a Purely Normative Concept', *Journal of Public Policy*, vol. 5, pp. 401–11.

Robson, B. T. (1988) *Those Inner Cities: Reconciling the Social and Economic Aims of Urban Policy* (Oxford: Clarendon Press).

Roger Tym and Partners (1984) *Monitoring Enterprise Zones: Year Three Report* (London: Roger Tym and Partners).

Rogers, P. and C. Smith (1977) 'The Local Authority's Role in Economic Development: The Tyne and Wear Act 1976', *Regional Studies*, vol. 11.

Rostas, L. (1943) 'Industrial Production, Productivity and Distribution in Britain, Germany and the United States', *Economic Journal*, vol. 53.

Rowley, C. K. (1982) 'Industrial Policy in the Mixed Economy', in E. Roll (ed.), *The Mixed Economy* (London: Macmillan).

Sawyer, M. (1991) 'Industrial Policy', in M. Artis and D. Cobham (eds), *Labour's Economic Policies* (Manchester University Press).

Sayers, R. (1976) *The Bank of England, 1891–1944* (Cambridge University Press).

Scholefield, H. H. and J. R. Franks (1972) 'Investment Incentives and Regional Policy', *National Westminster Bank Quarterly Review*, February, pp. 34–40.

Scottish Council (1961) *Inquiry into the Scottish Economy* 1960–1 (The Toothill Report) Report of a Committee Appointed by the Scottish Council (Development and Industry) Edinburgh.

Segal Quince Wicksteed (1991) *Evaluation of the Consultancy Initiatives: Third Stage* (London: HMSO).

Segal Quince Wicksteed (1992) *Evaluation of Regional Enterprise Grants: Third Stage* (London: HMSO).

Self, P. and H. Storing (1962) *The State and the Farmer* (London: George Allen & Unwin).

Shoup, C. S. (1972) *The Economics of Federal Subsidy Programs* (Washington, DC: Joint Economic Committee).

Shoup, C. S. (1973) 'The Terminology of Subsidies', in *Essays in Honour of G. V. Papi* (Papua: Ceda).

Skuse, A. (1972) *Government Intervention and Industrial Policy* (London: Heinemann).

Sloman, J. (1991) *Economics* (London: Harvester Wheatsheaf).

Smith, M. J. (1990) *The Politics of Agricultural Support in Britain: The Development of the Agricultural Policy Community* (Aldershot: Dartmouth).

Storey, D. J. (1993) 'Should We Abandon Support to Start Up Businesses?', Working Paper no. 11, SME Centre (Coventry: University of Warwick).

Storey, D. J. (1994) *Understanding the Small Business Sector* (London: Routledge).

Talbot, J. (1983) 'Inner City Policy and the Development of the Enterprise Zone Concept', *Research Working Paper 83/1*, School of Economics, Newcastle upon Tyne Polytechnic.

Taylor, J. (1993) 'An Analysis of the Factors Determining the Geographical Distribution of Japanese Manufacturing Investment in the UK, 1984–91', *Urban Studies*, vol. 30, no. 7, pp. 1209–24.

Thirlwall, A. P. (1966) 'The Local Employment Acts 1960 and 1963: A Progress Report', *Yorkshire Bulletin*, vol. 18, no. 1, pp. 49–66.

Thompson, G. (1986) *The Conservatives' Economic Policy* (London: Croom Helm).

Tomlinson, J. (1990) *Public Policy and the Economy since 1900* (Oxford: Clarendon Press).

Townsend, A. R. (1977) 'The Relationship of Inner City Problems to Regional Policy', *Regional Studies*, vol. 11, pp. 225–51.

Venn, J. A. (1933) *The Foundations of Agricultural Economics* (Cambridge University Press).

Ward-Perkins, C. N. (1952) 'Banking Developments', in G. D. N. Worswick and P. H. Ady (eds), *The British Economy, 1945–1950* (Oxford: Clarendon Press).

Whitehead, P. (1985) *Writing on the Wall* (London: Michael Joseph).

Wiles, P. J. D. (1952) 'Pre-war and War-time Controls', in G. D. N. Worswick and P. H. Ady (eds), *The British Economy, 1945–1950* (Oxford: Clarendon Press).

Wilson, T. (1967) 'Finance for Regional Industrial Development', *Three Banks Review*, September.

Wiseman, J. (1977) 'The Economics of Subsidies: Some Taxonomic and Analytical Problems', *Quarterly Economic Journal of the Piraeus School of Industrial Subsidies*, vol. 2, pp. 455–61.

Wolfson, D. J. (1990) 'Towards a Theory of Subsidisation', in R. Gerritse (ed.), *Producer Subsidies* (London: Pinter).

Wren, C. (1994) 'The Build-up and Duration of Subsidy-induced Employment: Evidence from UK Regional Policy', *Journal of Regional Science*, vol. 34, no. 3, pp. 387–410.

Wren, C. (1996a) 'Gross Expenditure on UK Industrial Assistance: A Research Note', *Scottish Journal of Political Economy*, vol. 43, no. 1, pp. 113–26.

Wren, C. (1996b) 'Grant Equivalent Expenditure on Industrial Subsidies in the Post-war United Kingdom', *Oxford Bulletin of Economics and Statistics*, forthcoming.

Wren, C. and J. K. Swales (1991) 'An Economic Analysis of the Revised Regional Development Grant Scheme', *Scottish Journal of Political Economy*, vol. 38, no. 3, pp. 256–72.

Young, S. and A. Lowe (1974) *Intervention in the Mixed Economy* (London: Croom Helm).

Index